ESSENTIALS OF
SLOW COOKING

WILLIAMS-SONOMA

ESSENTIALS OF
SLOW COOKING

DELICIOUS NEW RECIPES FOR SLOW COOKERS AND BRAISERS

GENERAL EDITOR
CHUCK WILLIAMS

PHOTOGRAPHY
BILL BETTENCOURT

RECIPES
MELANIE BARNARD
CHARLES PIERCE

TEXT
DENIS KELLY

Oxmoor
House®

Contents

Slow cooking enables you to achieve a combination of delicious results and easy preparation seldom matched by other cooking methods. Left to cook slowly on their own in seasoned liquid with little or no involvement from the cook beyond a recipe's initial assembly, tough cuts of meat turn meltingly tender, their flavors intermingling with sauces that become complex and concentrated through lengthy simmering. Poultry pieces absorb deep color and savor from the liquids and seasonings that surround them, while reaching a point at which meat falls from the bone at the mere touch of a fork. The tastes of vegetables intensify, and even the toughest greens turn delicate. Beans cook like they were meant to, staying perfectly whole yet becoming velvet-smooth and incomparably rich.

Today's busy cooks fortunately have more varied and convenient ways to achieve slow-cooked perfection than leaving a well-blackened cast-iron casserole nestled in the embers of a farmhouse kitchen hearth. This book explains the essentials of those methods and celebrates the delicious results you can achieve for slowly cooked vegetables, seafood, poultry, pork, beef, and lamb.

On the following pages, you'll find a comprehensive explanation of contemporary slow-cooking techniques, providing all the information you'll need to know to cook food slowly whether in an enclosed Dutch oven or other conventional cooking vessel, or using one of the many widely available countertop electric slow cookers that you can virtually set and forget for the better part of a day, coming home to a ready-to-serve meal. This introductory section also features guidelines for planning meals, as well as how to store leftovers: a valuable benefit that comes from the larger cuts and quantities that are often best suited to slow cooking.

Bearing in mind that your choice of slow-cooking method may well depend on your schedule, your mood, or which equipment you have on hand, whenever it is feasible each of the recipes provides you with a choice of two different cooking methods, clearly indicated with headings in the recipe text: one on the stove top or in the oven, the other in a slow cooker. Either way, you'll easily end up with a meal well worthy of lyrical praise.

Denis Kelly

What is Slow Cooking?

Since prehistoric times, humankind has practiced basic techniques for cooking food slowly to economize on fuel while making ingredients more tender and flavorful. Today's slow-cooking methods and equipment enable modern cooks to achieve optimum results with minimal effort.

Archaeological discoveries tell us that some 27,000 years ago, human beings practiced a rudimentary form of slow cooking. They would dig pits in the earth and line them with glowing embers or fire-heated stones. Then, they wrapped large pieces or whole carcasses from the game they hunted in seaweed or large leaves and placed them in the pit, covering them with more greenery. Left for hours, the meat cooked slowly, gaining in tenderness, while the seaweed or leaves scented the food while its natural moisture content kept the ingredients wrapped within from burning.

Around 12,000 B.C., Japanese cooks had begun to use cooking vessels fashioned from clay to cook foods slowly. Six millennia later, clay pots were also being employed in the Middle East and Europe. The dawning of the Bronze Age in the middle of the fourth millennium B.C. and the widespread use of iron some two thousand years after that saw the development of heavy metal cooking vessels in which food could be covered and left to cook for hours in the embers or suspended over the fire.

Along the way, human ingenuity led to the transformation of the process from mere preparation of food for sustenance into the development of actual recipes that could be enjoyed as a communal experience. Cooks learned the benefits of adding other ingredients to bestow their own particular flavors upon the featured foodstuff, including the use of liquids along with or instead of water. No more profound or simple piece of evidence of that fact exists than the one recorded around the 7th century B.C. in the Old Testament dietary injunction in Deuteronomy against cooking meat in milk.

Regardless of the ingredients, down through the centuries to the present day slow cooking came to be regarded as one of the most reliable ways to derive the maximum quality and pleasure from meats, poultry, seafood, vegetables, or dried beans with the minimal effort. Once ingredients had been combined and strategically placed at a spot just close enough to the fire to keep them gently bubbling, they could be left alone for hours, freeing members of a family or tribe to tend to other tasks.

Today in our global culture, the slow-cooked dishes that can be easily prepared at home are as delightfully varied as the cuisines from which they come. Chinese Red-Cooked Chicken (page 135), a centuries-old preparation in which the poultry's meat acquires a ruddy hue though lengthy simmering in a fragrantly seasoned mixture of soy sauce, broth, and rice wine, stands as an exemplar of slow cooking. So does a classic Italian Chicken Cacciatore (page 127), a "hunter's style" stew redolent of garlic, olive oil, tomatoes, and capers.

In short, slow cooking stands today as a highly respected and a time-honored cooking method shared by cultures around the world. And today's kitchens, cookware, and appliances make it possible to enjoy slow cooking in all its delightfully delicious variety like never before.

SLOW COOKING TODAY

Defining slow cooking as most experienced cooks now understand the meaning can seem as first like an exercise from a course in basic logic. To put it as simply as possible: All slow-cooked foods cook slowly; but not all foods that cook slowly are slow-cooked foods.

Let's begin by eliminating those categories of food that fall in the second half of that statement. Many types of food and cooking methods can take hours. Bread, for example, requires you to wait patiently for yeast-leavened dough to rise before you can shape it into loaves and then slowly bake it in the oven until golden brown. Many jams, jellies, and other preserves simmer ever so gently to reduce them to the right consistency, and spend still more time being sterilized in their canning jars before they can be stored away in

THE SLOW FOOD MOVEMENT

The movement known as Slow Food had its start in Rome in 1986, when Italian writer and cultural activist Carlo Petrini successfully rallied his friends and acquaintances to resist the opening of a fast food franchise near the historic Spanish Steps. Since then, Slow Food has won followers worldwide, and the organization has more than 80,000 members belonging to nearly a thousand chapters in over 100 countries. Petrini, who continues to be reelected each year as the organization's president, quickly expanded the mission of the Slow Food Movement to encompass ecology and sustainability, which Slow Food USA succinctly sums up as "the connection between the plate and the planet."

In that regard, Slow Food devotes itself to appreciating and promoting authentic foods by supporting traditional food producers of every type and in every region of the world. In the words of Slow Food USA, the end result of such simple activities can bring about major social changes: "We seek to catalyze a broad cultural shift away from the destructive effects of an industrial food system and fast life; toward the regenerative cultural, social and economic benefits of a sustainable food system, regional food traditions, the pleasures of the table, and a slower and more harmonious rhythm of life."

With such a mission in mind, many of the slow cooking recipes in this book fall well within the goals of the Slow Food Movement. Choose to prepare slow-cooked meals on a regular basis and enable you to slow down the rhythm of your life while sharing the pleasures of the table with your family and friends.

In this Portuguese favorite, mussel are cooked along with chopped tomatoes, white wine, and crushed red pepper. Perfect for a summer evening.

in the pantry. Stocks, that basic building block of so many great cuisines, simmer slowly on the stove top for hours to coax the essences from their ingredients and reduce the liquid's volume to its optimal concentration.

All of those preparations, and more besides, have come to be prized by food lovers in recent years as part of a patient, quality-oriented, environmentally conscious approach to cooking and eating known as the Slow Food Movement, which also embraces the concept of slow cooking. None of them, however, constitutes true slow cooking as it has come to be understood today and as it is defined within the parameters of this book.

Briefly stated, "slow cooking" nowadays generally refers to cooking large or small pieces of food partially or fully covered with liquid, for a lengthy period of time, over gentle heat, in an enclosed cooking vessel. Slow-cooked recipes are generally main course dishes featuring meat, poultry, seafood, vegetables, or dried legumes, categories that define the scope of this book, although some other books devoted to the topic also include soups and novelty "slow-cooked" recipes for such preparations as cakes, puddings, and fruit desserts.

If that definition sounds suspiciously similar to the basic cooking methods known as stewing and braising, that's because stews and braises constitute the most common categories of slow-cooked dishes. Stewing, put simply, is the gentle simmering of generally small, bite-sized to somewhat larger pieces of food in enough liquid to cover them; braising, by only slight contrast, involves larger pieces of food ranging in size from chops to whole roasts or poultry, usually cooked in enough liquid to come only partway up the side.

Other, similar methods also fall comfortably beneath the umbrella, or lid if you will, of slow cooking as this book defines it. Examples include pot-roasting, typified by Roast Pork with Apricots (page 155), which is nothing more than a sort of braise for a whole roast; clay pot cooking such as Vietnamese Clay Pot Fish (page 100), an Asian form of braising or stewing; and even good old-fashioned soup-making, found in recipes like the Mexican meatball soup called Albondigas (page 197) that is so robust it could easily be classified as a main-course stew. All of these hearty recipes can be served with a number of sides including mashed potatoes or creamy polenta.

All such kinds of preparation, along with good old-fashioned stewing and braising, nowadays may also be classified as "slow cooker" recipes thanks to the rise in popularity of that appliance since it was first introduced to the public in 1971 by the Rival Company. Originally designed as an electric bean cooker with the brand name of Crock-Pot®, the machine quickly caught on for a wide range of recipes that, like beans that were traditionally baked in a Dutch oven, benefited from long, gentle cooking. As other manufacturers followed suit with their own versions of the appliance, slow cooking in its convenient modern form came to be regarded as a cooking category in its own right.

Slow cooking chicken on the bone creates an irresistable tenderness and the chicken is deep in flavor.

Benefits of Slow Cooking

Whether you use a traditional Dutch oven or an electric slow cooker, there are so many ways to enjoy slow-cook meals. Not only will you enjoy the tender and flavorful results, but you'll also benefit from the convenience of preparation, and, in many cases, the economies of slow cooking.

SLOW COOKING PROMOTES TENDERNESS

When gently braised or stewed in a slow cooker or a Dutch oven, tough cuts of meat, as well as more tender ones, become especially soft and juicy. The reasons behind this fact are easy to understand.

Meat is muscle, and the harder a particular muscle works, the tougher and more tightly bundled in connective tissue, or collagen, the protein fibers that make up that muscle become. Gentle heat, like that of slow cooking, gradually relaxes those fibers to turn them more tender, while also melting the collagen to make the meat juicier. The most important aspect of slow cooking is patience.

Vegetables such as cabbage retain their essential flavor during braising and make a perfect side dish.

The same thing happens during slow cooking even to more tender cuts of meat, as well as to more naturally tender poultry and seafood, although those ingredients require less cooking time.

Regardless of the type of protein, tenderness also results from the cooking liquids that intermingle with the fibers of meat, poultry, and seafood as they gradually tenderize.

SLOW COOKING CONCENTRATES FLAVOR

That same intermingling of flavors is also responsible for the intense flavor of slow-cooked food. To understand why this happens, think first of stocks and broths and how the relatively low heat at which they simmer gradually coaxes the flavor from meats, bones, aromatic vegetables, and herbs into a relatively large volume of water; then, that liquid is gradually reduced in volume by continued simmering, concentrating its flavor.

In the making of stocks and broths, however, the flavors of the solids are gradually spent, giving their all to the liquid. Slow-cooked dishes are a different story. Being made with relatively less liquid, they don't draw as much flavor from the food; and since that liquid is itself usually rich and often supplemented by a profusion of seasonings, and the cooking temperature is even lower than that at which stocks normally cook, flavors actually transfer into the main ingredients. As a result, food that has been slow-cooked often possesses a concentrated flavor akin to having

simultaneously cooked and marinated. Meanwhile, over the course of several hours, the liquid also reduces, itself becoming a complex and concentrated blend of savors and textures from the ingredients cooking in it. And that holds true for more than just main courses featuring meat, poultry, or seafood. Consider, for example, the intense yet oh so mellow flavors, marvelous bouquets, and deep gemlike colors of Boston Baked Beans (page 60) or Braised Balsamic Onions (page 41). No wonder the tastes of so many slow-cooked dishes have the power to linger in memory.

SLOW COOKING IS CONVENIENT

Today, many people first venture into slow cooking because they've heard how ideally electric slow cookers suit our busy modern lifestyles. Perhaps they have also tasted a slow-cooked dish in the home of a friend or family member. Regardless of the initial reason, most enthusiasts of the method soon find that slow cooking becomes an indispensable part of their lives, and for good reason.

With a little advance planning and shopping, you can easily assemble a slow-cooked dish in the morning before you leave for work, run errands, or drive the kids to school, setting the built-in timer that's part of every electric slow cooker. Then, your work is largely done. Your slow-cooked main course will be ready to serve when you need it, along with a few simple accompaniments of the sort you'll find suggested in many of the recipes in this book. And, if the recipe calls for a shorter cooking time, most slow cookers will automatically switch to a warming mode that keeps the food at serving temperature until you're ready to serve it.

Even old-fashioned Dutch ovens, an alternative cooking vessel option offered in many of the recipes in this book, largely look after themselves once you've put them in the oven or set them over a low heat on the stove top; and while it wouldn't be wise to leave the house while food is cooking in them, they do free you to spend a weekend afternoon doing other things at home.

SLOW COOKING CAN BE ECONOMICAL

There are two compelling reasons that slow cooking can be among the most economical ways to prepare meals. First, many slow-cooked recipes call for cuts of meat that are less costly than the tender cuts destined for the grill or skillet, such as the pork shoulder that features in recipes like the traditional Mexican and Southwestern stew called Chile Verde (page 175) or the Indian curry Pork Vindaloo (page 183), beef short ribs braised in the style of Italy (page 204) or Asia (page 229), or the boneless chicken thighs cooked teriyaki-style (page 130) or used in Filipino Chicken Adobo (page 118).

Of course, that's not meant to suggest that all slow-cooked recipes suit the budget-conscious. Dishes liked Braised Duck Legs with Port and Figs (page 121) or Brazilian Seafood Stew (page 97) include more expensive ingredients that may suit them for special occasions.

There has also been much discussion through the past several decades about how energy-saving slow cookers can be, requiring as little electricity as a 75-watt light bulb. That fact helped spur a surge in slow cooker popularity during the energy crisis of the 1970s and has often been cited in more recent years when global warming is discussed, despite the fact that a slow cooker running constantly for many hours may in actuality require as much as or even more energy than a meal cooked in minutes on the stove.

Regardless of the cost of ingredients and the possibility of energy savings, however, slow cooking also benefits your budget because of the simple fact that it can yield leftovers, as well as relies on key pantry ingredients that are used sparingly. Flip through the pages of this book and you'll see that, because of the size of the most commonly sold slow cookers and Dutch ovens and the logistics of assembling ingredients in them for optimal cooking, a majority of the recipes yield as many as 6, 8, or 10 servings. That fact may enable you to buy larger, more economically priced packages of some ingredients; and it makes the most of the amount of time you spend in the kitchen, yielding additional meals ready for you to pull from the refrigerator or freezer, thaw, re-heat, and enjoy.

When braising large cuts of meat, always ask the butcher to remove tie the roast to ensure even cooking.

Slow Cooking Equipment

Most kitchens in which meals are cooked on a regular basis are already well equipped for slow cooking. In many cases, you may need only one more piece of equipment: either a countertop electric slow cooker, or the heavy covered casserole commonly known as a Dutch oven.

SLOW COOKERS

Modern slow cookers are designed for absolute convenience. Though manufactured by many different companies in a variety of sizes, shapes, and finishes, all of them work in essentially the same way.

An exterior metal casing, sometimes finished in colored enamel and sometimes gleaming stainless steel or aluminum, includes an electric heating element controlled by a display panel on the front of the casing. That panel enables you to set the desired cooking time in half-hour or shorter increments depending on the model, as well as allowing you to select low-heat (usually equivalent to about 170°F/77°C) or high-heat (280°F/138°C)

cooking temperatures, with the high-heat setting completing cooking in roughly half the time of low-heat; these two options make it easier for you to tailor slow cooking to your schedule, with low-heat ideal for recipes you want to start early in the day before leaving the house, and high-heat helpful especially on weekends when you may want to start a slow-cooked recipe in the afternoon for dinnertime. Many models also have a "warm" setting that holds food at the ideal serving temperature, automatically switching to it when cooking is done. And some also have a quick-start option that brings food to cooking temperature more quickly before switching to the high-heat or low-heat cooking setting.

The actual cooking in a slow cooker takes place in a glazed stoneware container, also referred to as an insert or crock that fits inside the housing. It heats up slowly and holds heat well, making it ideal for lengthy cooking at lower temperatures; but it could break if exposed to the higher temperatures of a stove top or oven. (See sidebar, "Caring for Your Crock.") Some deluxe slow cooker models feature cast-aluminum inserts, which can also be used to brown food and then transferred directly into the casing. A tempered glass lid with a heatproof handle fits atop the slow cooker container to hold in heat and moisture during cooking while allowing you to glimpse the food inside without removing the lid.

Slow cooker sizes range from small models (1½–2 1/2 qt/1.5–2.5 l) to medium (3–4½ qt/3–4.5 l) to large (5–7 qt/5–7 l), a choice

that will depend on the quantities you wish to prepare and the kinds of slow-cooked recipes you'd like to make. There are also two basic shapes: the original round slow cooker and the more recent oval. A large, oval slow cooker is ideal for cooking whole chickens and large cuts of meat.

In selecting your slow cooker, give careful thought to how you are most likely to use the appliance, and how often. Most slow cooker brands today are of good quality (be sure to check ratings and comments from consumer magazines and websites), so it makes sense to choose one that has only those features you are truly likely to use.

All of the recipes in this book were developed and tested using a 7-qt (7-l) oval

Contemporary slow cookers have a glazed stoneware insert that is easy to remove and clean.

CARING FOR YOUR COOKER

The glazed stoneware insert or cooking crock of a slow cooker is made to function perfectly and stand up well under prolonged low-heat cooking conditions. But the material from which it is made is sensitive to extreme temperatures or to sudden changes of temperature, which can cause it to crack or break.

For that reason, do not put the insert over the direct heat of a stovetop. Browning food or bringing cooking liquids to a rapid boil should only be done in a frying pan, Dutch oven, or other cookware meant for the stovetop. Neither should the insert ever be used in the oven, or put into the freezer.

When cleaning the insert, handle it with care to avoid chipping or breakage. Never put cold water into the crock if it is still hot from cooking. Wash with soap and water and a sponge, avoiding abrasives that could scratch the surface.

slow cooker, and will also work well in a 6½-qt (6.5-l) model. You can easily halve or even quarter many of the recipes, without changing the cooking times, if you have a smaller slow cooker.

Be sure to follow the specific recipe, as times and temperatures are key to successful cook successful and safe cooking with your slow cooker. Mst recipes offer both low heat options and high heat options to better help plan your meal. Also, take some time to read through the instruction book that comes with your own slow cooker, to learn the manufacturer's own guidelines for getting the most out of its particular features.

DUTCH OVENS

Most scholars of culinary history attribute the development and naming of the Dutch oven not to the people of Holland but rather to the so-called Pennsylvania Dutch, actually German and Swiss immigrants that first settled in the Pennsylvania colony during the early 18th century. The original Dutch ovens were made of heavy cast iron, which holds heat so well, and head heavy cast-iron lids that covered them securely, making the cooking vessels ideal for long, slow simmering of stews and braises on the stove, in the oven, or, as they were originally used, on a hob in the kitchen fireplace.

Cast-iron Dutch ovens, however, were not a good choice for the wine-based stews and braises like a French-style Summer Coq au Vin (page 144) or an Italian Pot Roast (page 217) that became popular recipe choices for enterprising cooks starting back in the 1960s. Wine's acidity has a tendency to eat away at the "seasoning" of cast iron, the stick-resistant patina that builds up with repeated use and proper care, not only spoiling the surface but also effecting the flavor of the food.

For that reason, in recent years Dutch ovens made of other materials have been developed. Many cooks choose enameled cast iron, which has the same cooking properties as the time-honored material with the added benefit of a stick-resistant enameled surface. Dutch ovens of heavy-duty stainless steel, aluminum-clad stainless steel, and anodized aluminum are also good choices.

Dutch ovens range in size from 4–12 qt (4–12 l). For most of the recipes in this book, a 6-7–qt (6-7–l) Dutch oven is the ideal choice, though you can halve the quantities for a correspondingly smaller Dutch oven should you prefer a yield of fewer servings. Some of the vegetable recipes that yield a lesser volume of side-dish servings, such as Vietnamese Eggplant Curry (page 47) and Celery Root with Chestnuts (page 53) also call for a small Dutch oven, which should be in the range of 2–4 qt (2–4 l) capacity.

Dutch ovens are popular for braising because of their their tight fitting lids and two looped handles.

USING A FRYING PAN OR SAUCEPAN

Other than a slow cooker or a Dutch oven, a large, heavy frying pan or saucepan is usually the only other piece of cookware called for in a slow cooking recipe.

Most often, you'll need a good-sized frying pan when a recipe you plan to prepare in a slow cooker calls for the initial cooking step of browning ingredients. For the best results, use a large-diameter pan with a heavy bottom that conducts heat well. One made of a non-reactive metal such as stainless-steel or anodized aluminum, or enamel-coated cast iron, will give good results. A large, heavy saucepan of the same material is also sometimes useful for browning, particular when you're dealing with a large, heavy, awkward roast that may cause more splattering in a shallow pan. Of course, you can also use a Dutch oven itself for the browning step, even if you plan to transfer the food to a slow cooker to complete the recipe.

Some recipes in this book that involve a smaller volume of food than most slow-cooked dishes, such as the Italian Peperonata (page 33), which actually call for the entire cooking to take place in a covered frying pan or saucepan, rather than a Dutch oven or slow cooker.

As you would when selecting a Dutch oven for slow cooking, look for good-quality, heavy covered frying pans or saucepans made of stainless steel, aluminum-clad stainless steel, anodized aluminum, or enameled cast iron. Choose models that are also ovenproof, so that you can safely transfer the covered cookware from the stove top to the oven when a recipe requires.

Left to right: COPPER PANS; CARVING BOARD AND CARVING TOOLS and ROASTING PAN (left to right): always check the pan size before beginning a recipe.

Oven Mitts and Pot Holders

Although slow cooking happens over relatively low heat, Dutch ovens and slow cookers build up and retain temperatures that can nonetheless quickly cause burns on unshielded hands and wrists, and oven mitts and pot holders made of quilted heat-resistant fabric, leather, or silicone should always be used when handling them. Be sure to select a design that is sufficiently flexible or comfortably fitting to provide you with a secure, non-slip grip on the handles of a Dutch oven or the extended lip that is found on the stoneware crocks of most slow cookers, as well as the lids of both kinds of vessels. The surfaces of such cookware may become slippery during cooking, and a sure grip on them will help you guard against possible breakage or spills.

Metal Tongs

Spring-hinged, long-handled metal tongs are useful for picking up and turning pieces of meat or poultry as you brown them before the actual slow-cooking begins. Their blunt ends will not pierce the food, thus preventing a loss of juices that could interfere with the browning process. Stainless-steel tongs with tips that meet precisely will do the most efficient job and last the longest.

Cooking Spoons

Sturdy long-handled wooden spoons made of hard, fine-grained wood are ideal for stirring aromatic vegetables as they brown, and for stirring and scraping to deglaze pan deposits after browning. Stainless-steel slotted spoons make it possible to remove ingredients from the liquid after cooking, when a recipe requires you to put some finishing touches on that liquid to transform it into a sauce. Stainless-steel solid spoons are useful for stirring in seasonings and other ingredients towards the end of slow cooking, as well as for serving food straight from slow cooker or Dutch oven or transferring it to a serving platter or bowl; and the spoons' shallow bowls are also useful for skimming off fat or oil floating on the top of the cooking liquid before serving.

Kitchen String

Some slow-cooked braise recipes, such as Stuffed Veal Breast (page 215), Braciole (page 251), and Stuffed Leg of Lamb (page 253), call for a large piece of meat to be tied up both to enclose a filling and to give it a more compact, uniform shape for even cooking. For this task, use linen kitchen string, which will hold up well at very high cooking temperatures for a long period of time.

Timer

Electric slow cookers today include built-in timers that eliminate all the guesswork and clock-watching while food cooks. If you opt to cook a recipe in a Dutch oven, however, it's smart to have a timer that will remind you when the moment comes to check a dish for doneness or to perform some other task. Whether you want an up-to-date battery-powered digital model or a more traditional spring-operated dial timer, look for one that has large, legible numbers and easy-to-use controls, as well as an alarm that sounds for at least 30 seconds and is loud enough for you to hear in rooms close by your kitchen.

Instant-Read Thermometer

Most of the recipes in this book cook for such a long time that meat is well-done and fall-apart tender, as stews and braises are meant to be. But for certain recipes featuring large cuts of meat, such as Roast Pork with Apricots (page 153), Pork Tenderloin with Braised Cabbage and Figs (page 188), you may also want to check for doneness with an instant-read meat thermometer, particularly with the relatively shorter cooking times involved if you use a Dutch oven. Instant-read thermometers are available in two basic forms: a traditional dial type, in which a coil of heat-sensitive metal turns a pointer to indicate the temperature on a calibrated dial; and a battery-operated digital thermometer, which yields the fastest reading, presenting the temperature in easy-to-read numerals in its display window.

Carving Boards

Slow-cooked stews and many braises may be easily spooned up in ready-to-serve portions. Some braises of large cuts of meat, however, such as Pork Loin Roast with Root Vegetables (page 163), American Pot Roast (page 226), call for carving into slices. Do this work on a solid, heavy wooden carving board with grooves and a trough around its perimeter to catch juices that would otherwise drip off a standard cutting board. Some carving boards also have rubber feet to prevent slippage.

Carving Knife and Fork

Carving sets, as they are also sometimes called, are most commonly used for serving roasts, with the two-pronged fork holding the meat or whole poultry steady while the long, thin, well-honed blade effortlessly cuts neat slices. The sharpness of a carving knife is particularly critical when carving large pieces of braised meat such as Beef Brisket with Yams and Prunes (page 211) that have a relatively stringer texture that could cause it to tear or disintegrate easily after lengthy cooking. Some cooks find that a sharp serrated blade, like that of a bread knife, does an even better job of cutting through meats that might otherwise stick to an ordinary blade.

Ladles

With their deep hemispherical bowls slightly angled off of long, sturdy handles, ladles are particularly handy for serving slow-cooked recipes with small pieces of food and a relatively generous amount of sauce. Furthermore, smaller ladles are key in skimming most of the fat from the surface of the cooking liquid before serving. You'll find ladles the ideal serving implement for such recipes as New England Halibut Stew (page 89), Duck Ragù (page 140), Posole (page 173), Springtime Veal Stew (page 207), or Texas-Style Beef Chili (page 238).

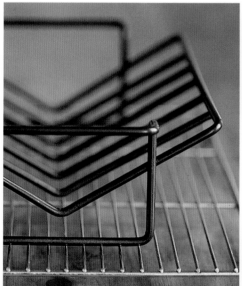  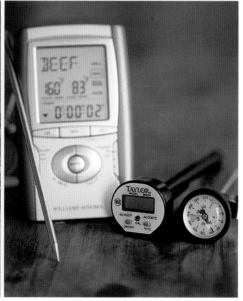

Left to right: ROASTING RACKS; OVEN MITTS and silicone pot holders; THERMOMETERS (right to left): digital probe and instant read

Slow Cooking Basics

Modern slow cooking using an electric slow cooker and traditional slow cooking in a Dutch oven have a great deal in common. Both usually proceed through the same basic stages, with the only differences being cooking time and sometimes the order in which a dish is assembled.

Whenever appropriate, almost every one of the recipes in this book includes two alternative sets of instructions: one using a Dutch oven on the stove top or in the oven, and the other for a countertop electric slow cooker.

Regardless of which method you choose to use, the same basic stages of preparation usually apply: browning ingredients to develop their flavor and color; deglazing pan deposits and then heating the cooking liquid; combining the solids and liquid and cooking them gently, usually for several hours; and the final serving of the dish, which in some cases also involves carving the featured ingredient and perhaps a few finishing touches to complete the cooking liquid's transformation into a sauce.

Trim meat, such as lamb shanks (page 258), of most of the excess fat before browning.

Nevertheless, some distinctions do exist between the two basic processes. The following explanations cover both the commonalities and the differences between them.

PREPARING FOR SLOW COOKING

Before you prepare any slow-cooked dish, read through the recipe thoroughly. Be sure you understand the timing involved, making note of when you'll need to start preparing the recipe in order to use your choice of cooking method and to have the recipe ready at the time you plan to serve it.

Always thaw frozen meats or poultry in the refrigerator, or in your microwave following the manufacturer's instructions, before you start cooking them. Especially if you use a slow cooker, frozen food can lower the temperature inside the stoneware insert to a level that makes unsafe bacterial growth possible. In addition, remove ingredients from the refrigerator 20 to 30 minutes before you start to cook them, especially if the recipe calls for you to brown them first, so they won't drastically reduce the high heat at which browning best occurs.

THE SIMPLEST SLOW-COOKED RECIPES

Some slow-cooked recipes are models of absolutely simple cooking. Dishes like Italian White Beans (page 67), Chicken Adobo (page 120), and Chile Verde (page 177) call for little more than combining all the ingredients in a Dutch oven or slow cooker and turning

on the heat. What such simple, traditional recipes have in common is their combination of distinctively flavored ingredients that, after lengthy gentle cooking, intermingle to especially flavorful effect. Many other slow-cooked recipes, however, call from a little more participation from you at either the beginning or end of cooking, but not much more.

BROWNING

Many slow cooking recipes call for meat, poultry, seafood, and some vegetables such as onions, garlic, and shallots as well as the potatoes and cauliflower in Indian Vegetable Curry (page 38) or the acorn squash in Spicy Squash with Garlic-Yogurt Sauce (page 64), to be browned in oil or fat in a Dutch oven, frying pan, or large, heavy saucepan over medium-high to high heat before the actual slow cooking begins. In most cases, meats should be trimmed of excess fat before browning. Many recipes call for the surface of food to be seasoned first with salt, pepper, herbs, or spices; flour is sometimes also included, both to promote browning and, as slow cooking proceeds, to help thicken the liquid to a sauce consistency.

By caramelizing natural sugars present in food, browning develops a rich surface color and deep flavor that enhance the finished recipe. If you are pressed for time, you could skip this step, but the results, though still delicious, will not look or taste quite as good.

Whenever you brown bite-sized or larger pieces of food, follow the example of experienced home cooks and professionals and resist the temptation to lift them up every few seconds to check how browning is proceeding. Doing so interferes with the browning process and can actually lead to a loss of some moisture and to sticking. When a recipe specifies an approximate browning time per side, wait to check until close to that time; when it gives an overall browning time for, say, an entire roast or other large pieces of meat or poultry, divide up those minutes among the number of times you'll have to turn the meat for all-over browning, and wait until the time is almost up to check and turn.

If you don't use a Dutch oven for browning, a good idea even if you plan to complete the cooking in a slow cooker, you might want to consider browning especially fatty or large pieces of meat in a large, heavy, high-sided saucepan instead of in a frying pan. The saucepan's high sides will help contain splattering, saving you from a possibly messy kitchen cleanup chore afterwards.

When you've finished browning, it's often a good idea to transfer the food to several layers of paper towels to absorb excess surface fat before continuing with the recipe. Most recipes will also instruct you to pour off excess fat from the Dutch oven or pan before you deglaze the pan deposits.

DEGLAZING, REDUCING, AND BOILING

During browning, not only does a flavorful, darkened surface develop on the food, but also some of its juices and small particles form brown deposits that stick to the hot surface of the cookware, sometimes forming what amounts to a glaze. That rich repository of flavor and color is what the step known as deglazing aims to exploit.

Boiling liquid is the best medium for dissolving, or deglazing, those deposits. Whether broth, wine, beer, spirits, juice, or even water, you simply add the liquid to the cooking vessel in which browning was done and bring it rapidly to a boil. Meanwhile, stir

Simple, rustic dishes, such as the Spanish influenced Albondigas, has such bold flavors and are perfect for slow cooking as the intensity of the flavors develop.

and scrape the pan deposits with a wooden spoon, causing them to dislodge and dissolve in the liquid. This is where the richness of the sauce is developed.

Once the pan deposits have been completely deglazed, some recipes, such as Braised Duck Legs with Port and Figs (page 121) or Beer-Braised Pork Roast (page 187) call for the deglazing liquid to be boiled briskly for several minutes until it reduces in volume. This is done to concentrate the flavor and thicken the body of the liquid, as well as to evaporate some of the alcohol content of wines or spirits, eliminating its sometimes-harsh edge. Boiling alcohol brings out the flavor.

Finally, this stage of cooking concludes with adding any other liquid ingredients and bringing the whole mixture to a boil. Doing so jump-starts the slow cooking process, with the browned main ingredient and other solids returning to a cooking medium that's ready to be set to the ideal simmering temperature.

ASSEMBLING AND COOKING

The point at which the cooking liquid reaches a boil is where most sets of recipe instructions in this book diverge between a Dutch oven on the stove top or in the oven, and a countertop slow cooker. Those separate sets of instructions in the recipes are clearly indicated with the capital-letter subheadings "OVEN," "STOVE TOP," and "SLOW COOKER," and the same headings below provide relevant information for each option.

When a Dutch oven is being used, the browned ingredients and other solids are returned to the boiling liquid in that vessel. Generally, smaller items such as vegetables are distributed all around larger pieces of meat or poultry to ensure even cooking.

OVEN: An oven is commonly used when braise-style slow-cooked dishes are prepared in a Dutch oven, because its all-around dry heat provides more even cooking for larger pieces of meat or poultry. A recipe will call for you to preheat the oven, a step you should start around the time you begin to brown ingredients, so the desired cooking temperature will have been reached before you put the Dutch oven into the oven. Before you turn the oven on, be sure to adjust its racks so there is room for the Dutch oven to fit easily in the center of the oven. Once you've put the Dutch oven into the oven, all that remains for you to do is set the timer for the earliest moment in the suggested cooking time range.

STOVE TOP: Stew-style slow-cooked recipes prepared in a Dutch oven, with smaller pieces of solid ingredients immersed in relatively more cooking liquid, generally cook best on the stove top, where the heat source below the cooking vessel can be adjusted to maintain the ideal bare simmer at which such dishes cook most evenly and best. Depending on the recipe and the desired end result, you may be called to cover the Dutch oven completely,

Serve rich pot roast with garlic mashed potatoes and crusty bread.

so minimal cooking liquid evaporates; leave it partially covered, with the lid slightly ajar so that the cooking liquid reduces slightly; or uncovered, allowing the mixture of solids and liquids to reduce and thicken even more. Whichever instruction is given, before you set the timer and go do something else, take a few moments to check inside the Dutch oven and adjust the heat slightly down or up accordingly to keep only a very gentle simmering motion on the surface of the cooking liquid.

SLOW COOKER: Although many people consider using a slow cooker the most convenient option of all, it does call for a few more small steps on your part before the actual slow cooking begins. In general, you will put the main solid ingredients in the slow cooker's stoneware crock first. Because the heat of a slow cooker comes primarily from the bottom, and that heat is even lower than a stove top burner set at very low heat, items that take longer to cook, such as meat and potatoes, should go on the bottom of the crock, and all solids should be arranged as evenly as possible to ensure even cooking. Once the solids are in place, then transfer the crock to the slow cooker base. Finally, add the boiling cooking liquid, taking care not to spill any on the slow cooker base. In general, you'll get the best results when the slow cooker is no more than halfway to two thirds full. Then, cover the slow cooker, choose the high-heat or low-heat setting (see more under "Timing," below), set the corresponding cooking time, and walk away. Your work is largely done. When a recipe calls for you to add other ingredients to the slow cooker partway through or towards the end of the cooking time, handle the lid carefully, using an oven mitt or pot holder and opening it away from you to avoid possible steam; and, to avoid interfering with

cooking by lowering the temperature inside the stoneware crock, leave the slow cooker uncovered as briefly as possible, avoiding removing the lid just to get a better view of how your food is coming along.

TIMING

For the purposes of this book, the term "slow" actually covers a span of times. Fennel with Olives and Orange Zest (page 34), slow-cooked in a Dutch oven, take just half an hour or so to reach tenderness, while Mexican pork Carnitas (page xx) take 10 hours on the low-heat setting in a slow cooker. Cooking times depend, of course, on the inherent tenderness of the ingredients you're cooking, their size, and whether you use a Dutch oven or a slow cooker.

The cooking times in this book's recipes are always approximate, expressed either as a time range or as a specific time qualified by the word "about." There's a good reason why.

No two seemingly identical ingredients you buy are necessarily absolutely identical or will respond to cooking in the same way. One 3 pound (1.5 kg) pork roast, for example, might be tougher than another of the same weight and require a little more time to reach absolute tenderness. One package of dried white beans might have dried longer than another batch, thus requiring more time to soften. Cookware, too, may differ, with one manufacturer's Dutch oven or slow cooker stoneware crock holding heat better than another's, resulting in slightly shorter or longer cooking times.

In short, any recipe involves a certain amount of judgment from you, the cook. That is why, along with times, each recipe in this book offers a sensory cue, such as "until the meat is very tender" or "until the sauce is thick" or even an internal temperature gauged with an instant-read thermometer (page 17) to help you determine doneness.

The length of cooking time in general, however, relates directly to whether you choose to use a slow cooker on the low-heat setting, a slow cooker on the high-heat setting, or a Dutch oven.

Your choice of a low-heat or high-heat setting on a slow cooker depends largely on your own schedule. If you want to start the slow cooker earlier in the day and have the food ready in the evening, then the low-heat setting is ideal. And, cooking food at the gentlest simmer, it generally results in the most tender texture and most concentrated flavor. High heat, which takes about half the time of low heat, also works fine if you get a later start on cooking, and the dish will still be excellent. A Dutch oven, which cooks food at a slightly higher temperature than a slow cooker's high-heat setting, will generally complete the job in slightly less time still. But the all-around heat provided by its heavy bottom, sides, and lid still yield very tender, flavorful results.

LAST-MINUTE ADDITIONS

Many slow-cooked or braised recipes gain even more character from ingredients that are added towards the end of the cooking process, such as the garam masala spice mixture that contributes heady fragrance to Indian Chickpea Curry (page 61) or the sweet dates and crunchy toasted almonds that are folded along with a drizzle of honey into Moroccan Lamb Tagine with Dates and Almonds (page 249). Such flourishes take little extra time to prepare, and whenever they are called for, a recipe will explain precisely when and how to add them to the Dutch oven or slow cooker.

In the case of many slow cooking and braising recipes that feature seafood, such as

Shrimp (prawns) are a popular and common shellfish to use because they cook quickly and evenly. Always add at the end of cooking and cook until opaque throughout.

Cod with Tomatoes and Chickpeas (page 80). Indian Fish Curry (page 88), or Vietnamese Clay Pot Fish (page 100), the fish or shellfish itself is the main last-minute addition.

The bulk of the slow cooking time is devoted to preparing an intensely flavorful sauce, to which the quick-cooking seafood is usually added for the last half-hour or so, more than enough time to bring it to flakey tenderness while imbuing it with the sauce's flavors. Some recipes also include last-minute additions

of ingredients that complete the sauce: a broth-and-cornstarch slurry in Chinese Red-Cooked Chicken (page 133), the butter-flour mixture known in classic French cooking as beurre manié in Chicken with Tomatoes and Olives, a dollop of Dijon mustard in Roast Pork with Apricots (page 153), a generous dose of cream in Springtime Veal Stew (page 207). These and other touches take virtually no time or effort at all, yet dramatically enhance the pleasures offered by the finished dish.

SKIMMING FAT AND FINISHING THE SAUCE

Many slow-cooked dishes such as are ready to serve just as they are, straight from the slow cooker or Dutch oven, at the end of the cooking time. Others, however, call for a few extra simple steps to bring them to perfection.

During slow cooking, recipes that feature fatty meats, such as Beer-Braised Pork Roast (page 187), or Braised Lamb Shanks (page 254), will melt from the meat much of that fat, which floats in glistening pools on the surface of the cooking liquid. A large, shallow spoon or ladle is the ideal tool for skimming that fat away before the dish is served. If you'd like to eliminate the last final traces of fat, try draping some paper towels across the surface to soak them up.

Rendered fat is also easy to remove when you make a slow-cooked dish in advance and store it in the refrigerator for reheating the next day, or when you save leftovers in the refrigerator Cool temperatures will cause the fat to solidify on the surface, ready to be lifted away in chunks or scraped away with a spoon.

GARNISHING

Today, smart cooks everywhere have moved beyond the notion that garnishes are superfluous things: the sprig of parsley that gets tossed away, the cherry tomato or carrot curl that might be absent-mindedly popped into the mouth but adds nothing to the appreciation of the featured food.

A good garnish contributes to food what the right piece of jewelry does to an outfit: With its own distinct yet subtle personality, it enhances everything it accompanies, becoming that final element that helps to make the whole of the dish seem far greater than the sum of its parts.

That's why many of the recipes in this book include garnishes added at serving time: the minced fresh thyme leaves that complete New England Halibut Stew (page 89), the green onions that spark up the mellow savor of Teriyaki Chicken Thighs (page 130), the garlic-parsley-citrus gremolata that adds a final explosion of fragrance to classic Osso Buco (page 212).

STORING AND REHEATING LEFTOVERS

One of the biggest bonuses slow cooking offers is the prospect of leftovers: delicious stews and braises that taste even better when reheated. Follow these few simple guidelines to help you get the most pleasure possible from your slow-cooked leftovers.

From the slow cooker or the Dutch oven, transfer the food to shallow sealable food storage containers suitable for refrigerator or freezer use. Transfer to the refrigerator to cool. Use refrigerated leftovers within 3 or 4 days.

Alternatively, transfer the containers of food to the freezer after they've cooled. Before putting them in the freezer, clearly label the containers with their contents and the preparation date using an indelible marking pen: Write either directly on the lid of disposable containers, or on a piece of freezer-proof tape for reusable containers. Plan to use the leftovers within 2 to 3 months.

Never use a slow cooker to reheat leftovers. Instead, transfer to a covered saucepan and warm over medium-low heat until the solids are fully heated through.

Freah, flat-leafed (Italian) parsely is a bright green herb, also used as a spice. It is very popular in flavoring Middle Eastern, European, Mediterranean, and American cooking.

FOOD SAFETY

Most savvy cooks today already understand the basics of safe kitchen practices that aim to avoid illness from food-borne bacteria. They work with clean hands; use separate cutting boards and knives for animal proteins and produce; keep perishable ingredients properly refrigerated; and always wash up with lots of hot, soapy water.

Slow cooking, however, adds the need for another sort of awareness in food safety: cooking temperature.

Food-borne bacteria thrive in the temperature range of 40°F–140°F (4°–57°C). Between 140°F (57°C) and 165°F (74°C), their growth is dramatically slowed; above that range, the bacteria die.

Both the low-heat and high-heat settings on most modern slow cookers cook at temperatures high enough to kill off bacteria. But the stoneware inserts of slow cookers heat up slowly, taking several hours to reach optimum cooking temperatures. And adding cold ingredients can further slow the heating process and lead to the possibility of bacterial growth.

For that reason, it's wise to follow a few basic guidelines that help ensure your slow-cooked meals will be safe. The following guidelines are also worth bearing in mind when using a Dutch oven.

■ Make sure your slow cooker's stoneware insert is absolutely clean before you start preparing a recipe. If in doubt, wash it thoroughly with hot soapy water and rinse well.

■ Thaw frozen foods, especially main ingredients, before adding them to the slow cooker. Never thaw by running under warm or luke warm water. Always thaw in the refrigerator overnight.

■ Brown large cuts of meat before adding them to a slow cooker, a step that not only promotes color and flavor but also gives the meat a jump-start on reaching a safe cooking temperature.

■ Never fill the stoneware insert more than halfway to two thirds full, the maximum volume of ingredients slow cookers are designed to bring to safe temperatures within specified cooking times.

■ Do not remove the cover from the slow cooker or Dutch oven unless the recipe tells you to do so, to avoid loss of heat.

■ In case of power failure, be prepared to follow a different plan, judging by how long the electricity is off.

When cutting large cuts of meat into serving sized pieces be sure to keep them uniform for even cooking.

Composing a Slow-Cooked Menu

Slow cooking frees you to plan simple or elaborate menus with ease and flair. By letting one slow-cooked dish star, perhaps adding others made ahead or in another cooking vessel, and supplementing the menu with simple recipes or store-bought items to make planning a breeze.

There are no hard and fast rules for building a meal around a slow-cooked recipe. Sometimes, the very convenience of slow cooking may inspire you to take even more dramatic shortcuts to complete the menu: adding coleslaw from the deli, for example, to top off sandwiches of Pulled Pork (page 176) on fresh bakery rolls and complementing the down-home meal with your favorite potato chips and a craft-brewed beer; or having a casual dinner of the Italian-style San Francisco seafood stew Cioppino (page 99) ladled into big bowls and served with crusty bread and a simple salad.

Other occasions may call for a little more cooking, but not much more. Boiled egg noodles tossed with butter admirably complete Hungarian Beef Goulash (page 230). Steamed long-grain rice and maybe some rapidly stir-fried sugar-snap peas with a touch of sesame oil ably complete a slow-cooked dish like Asian Braised Short Ribs (page 229).

Sometimes, however, the ease of slow cooking, and the fact that many slow-cooked dishes can be made up to several days ahead and only improve with reheating, may inspire you to aim for greater menu-planning heights for a special-occasion weekend meal. In such cases, consider a meal featuring multiple slow-cooked dishes, some prepared in advance and others cooked simultaneously, one in a slow cooker and one in a Dutch oven, to offer your guests a themed banquet or buffet filled with many complementary dishes.

SLOW COOKED MENUS

AMERICAN HARVEST CELEBRATION

Orange-Braised Ham

•

Celery Root with Chestnuts

•

Brussels Sprouts with Bacon

HEARTY ITALIAN AUTUMN DINNER

Sicilian-Style Braised Artichokes

•

Escarole with Cannellini Beans

•

Italian Braised Short Ribs

•

Polenta

FRENCH LIGHT WARM-WEATHER SUPPER

Leeks with Herbed Vinaigrette

•

Summer Coq au Vin

•

Buttered Noodles

Garlic Croutons

INDIAN FEAST

Chicken Korma

•

Pork Vindaloo

•

Indian Vegetable Curry

•

Steamed Basmati Rice

FIESTA LATINA

Guacamole and Chips

•

Chicken Mole

Cochinita Pibil

•

Warm corn and flour tortillas

•

Mexican-style rice and refried beans

Salsa

PAN ASIAN CUISINE

Vietnamese Clay Pot Fish

•

Teriyaki Chicken Thighs

•

Steamed Jasmine Rice

TROPICAL BUFFET

Brazilian Seafood Stew

•

Caribbean Pork Stew with Plantains

•

Cuban Black Beans

•

Steamed White Rice

DOWN-HOME BARBECUE LUNCH

Pulled Pork

•

Coleslaw

•

Potato Chips

SEASONAL FRUITS AND VEGETABLES

Always choose fresh fruits and vegetables in season for the best flavor and value. Here is a chart to help get you thinking seasonally.

SEASON	FRUITS	VEGETABLES
Spring	cherries, limes, oranges, rhubarb	asparagus, celery, fava (broad) beans, peas, potatoes
Summer	apricots, dates, figs, nectarines, plantains, rhubarb	bell peppers (capsicums), corn, cucumbers, eggplants (aubergines), peas, shallots, summer squashes, tomatoes
Fall	apples, figs, grapes, dates, pomegranates, rhubarb	artichokes, bell peppers (capsicums), celery, corn, cucumbers, eggplants (aubergines), parsnips, shallots, tomatoes, turnips
Winter	dates, apples, oranges, pears, pomegranates, quinces, tangerines	Brussels sprouts, cauliflower, celery, celery root, parsnips, spinach, sweet potatoes, turnips
Year-round	bananas, lemons, oranges	avocados, beets, broccoli, carrots, chard, fennel, garlic, green (spring) onions, herbs, leeks, mushrooms, onions, potatoes, radishes, scallions

Slow Cooking Pantry Essentials

A well-stocked pantry well help make it all the easier for you to prepare slow-cooked dishes with minimal extra shopping. Take note of the staples featured in your favorite recipes, and make sure you always have them on hand, ready to help you get a fast start on your slow cooking.

GRAINS, PASTAS AND LEGUMES

Black beans, dried

Cannellini beans, dried

Chickpeas (garbanzo beans), dried

Egg noodles, dried

Great Northern beans, dried

Navy beans, dried

Rice, long-grain

Rice, jasmine

DRIED HERBS, SPICES AND SEASONINGS

Allspice, ground

Bay leaves

Black peppercorns

Brown mustard seeds

Cardamom, ground

Caraway seeds

Cayenne pepper

Chile powder, medium-hot

Cinnamon

Cloves

Coriander

Cumin, ground

Curry powder

Fennel seeds

Ginger, ground

Mustard, dry

Nutmeg

Oregano, dried

Red pepper flakes

Saffron threads

Salt

Salt, sea, coarse

Star anise, whole

Sugar

Paprika, hot & sweet

Thyme, dried

Turmeric, ground

BAKING STAPLES

Active dry yeast

All-purpose (plain) flour

Almonds

Baking powder

Brown sugar

Chocolate, semisweet (plain) and milk

Cornstarch (cornflour)

Cocoa powder, Dutch process

Confectioners' (icing) sugar

Hazelnuts (filberts)

Pistachio nuts

Raisins

Vanilla bean and pure extract

OILS, VINEGARS, SYRUPS, AND CONDIMENTS

Apple cider vinegar

Balsamic vinegar

Canola oil

Dijon mustard

Extra-virgin olive oil

Honey

Hot pepper sauce (such as Tabasco)

Red wine vinegar

Rice vinegar

Sesame oil, Asian

Soy sauce

Vegetable oil

White wine vinegar

Worcestershire sauce

CANNED GOODS

Anchovy fillets, oil-packed

Beef broth

Chicken broth

Tomato paste

Tomato sauce

Tomatoes, crushed plum (Roma)

Tomatoes, diced plum (Roma)

Tomatoes, whole plum (Roma)

Vegetable broth

WINE, BEER, AND SPIRITS

Ale

Apple cider

Beer, dark

Beer, lager-style

Brandy

Marsala

Port, ruby

Red wine, dry

Sherry, dry

White wine, dry

MISCELLANEOUS

Baking powder

Bread crumbs, dried

Capers

Cornstarch

Flour, all-purpose (plain)

Olives*

Pine nuts*

Staples marked with an asterisk should be purchased in small quantities and replaced often.

Vegetables

About Vegetables

Vegetables of all kinds, from tough, starchy roots to tender greens lend themselves to slow cooking. As the vegetables simmer the flavor deepens and the texture is transformed. Dried beans and legumes are especially delicious when simmered with aromatic vegetables in a savory broth.

Vegetables have been an essential part of the human diet from the beginning. They add variety, flavor, color, and important nutrients to our diet and most can be cooked by long and slow simmering or slow roasting. The type of vegetable determines when it should be added to a dish or how long it should cook.

Tough, fibrous, or starchy vegetables such as carrots, potatoes, turnips, parsnips, yams, sweet potatoes, or artichokes are best cooked long and slow until tender. This is why all of these tougher vegetables take so well to stewing and braising. Pay attention to recommended cooking times in our recipes, however, as some vegetables will fall apart if cooked too long.

Our Braised Potatoes with Caramelized Onions (page 45) calls for browning potatoes and caramelizing onions and then slow cooking them in broth in the oven or crockpot. When braising potatoes, use a firm variety such as Yukon gold which won't fall apart after long cooking. Artichokes are another fibrous vegetable that takes wonderfully to long, slow cooking. Sicilian-Style Braised Artichokes (page 59) steams artichokes stuffed with bread crumbs, grated cheese, garlic and other savory ingredients. The artichokes take on a luscious, tender texture and the flavorful stuffing adds an extra dimension of flavor.

Dried beans of all types need long and slow cooking for best results. Classic bean dishes such as Boston Baked Beans (page 60), cooked long and slow with bacon and maple syrup, make a memorable main course for a winter meal. Cuban Black Beans (page 48) simmered with garlic, peppers, and ham hocks offer a hearty accompaniment to Chile Verde (page 177) or Caribbean Pork Stew (page 166).

Cabbage and its relatives are all delicious when braised with bacon or pancetta (see Brussels Sprouts with Bacon, page 70 and Savoy Cabbage with Pancetta, page 37) or slow cooked with onions and apples (see Red Cabbage with Apples, page 52). These earthy dishes are a fine match with our Pork Roast with Apricots (page 155) or Braised Pork Chops with Turnips and Greens (page 186).

Tender greens are often eaten raw in salads, but can also be braised or steamed to provide color, nourishment, and flavor in many long-cooked dishes. Tangy greens such as escarole, chard, collard greens, mustard, turnip greens, spinach, and kale are especially delicious.

Indian cookery offers a style of cooking that gives vegetables added spice and exciting flavors. Spicy Squash with Garlic-Yogurt Sauce (page 64) is our version of an Afghan dish that presents pumpkin in a startling and delicious way and Indian Vegetable Curry (page 38) can stand alone as flavorful vegetarian main course or as an accompaniment to Chicken Korma (page 118) or Pork Vindaloo (page 185).

Savory and pungent bulbs such as onions, leeks, shallots, and garlic, all part of the lily family, can add depth of flavor and liveliness to slow cooked food. They are also delicious when braised (see Leeks with Herbed Vinaigrette, page 73 or Braised Balsamic Onions, page 41). Peppers provide exciting flavors that wake up the taste bud in many braised dishes and are very tasty when cooked on their own (see Pepperonata, page 33).

Other aromatic vegetables can add intense aromas, textures, and flavors to slow-cooked foods. Mushrooms (Mushroom Ragù with Polenta, page 46), celery (Celery Root with Chesnuts, page 55), and fennel (Fennel with Olives and Orange Zest, page 34) are a few examples.

USING VEGETABLES IN SLOW COOKING

Using vegetables in slow cooking will depend on the type of vegetable and the role it plays in the dish. Aromatics such as onions or garlic are best browned in the sauté pan or Dutch oven before the liquid is added. This will caramelize the sugars for a rich, sweet taste and adds color and flavor to the finished dish.

Tougher fibrous vegetables can be put into the Dutch oven or slow cooker right at the beginning of cooking and will add plenty of flavor to the stew or braise while staying whole and getting tender with time in the pot. Individual recipes will vary, but generally the tougher the raw vegetable is, the longer it has to cook.

When adding greens to a dish, take care not to over cook them. Most greens are best added towards the end of the recipe although some, for example, Southern Collard Greens (page 42) traditionally cook the greens longer.

Wheat products like pasta, couscous, and farro, whole grain rice, and cornmeal preparations such as polenta or cornbread are all best made separately and then incorporated into the finished dish. There are, however, some recipes that call for adding these to the dish while slow-cooking. Dumplings (see Chicken and Dumplings, page 113) are an example.

Peperonata

This relish made from sweet and smoky roasted peppers resembles ratatouille. Try serving it on toasted crostini. Preheat an oven to 350°F (180°C). Cut a baguette on the diagonal into $^1/_2$-inch (12-mm) slices. Arrange on a baking sheet, brush the tops lighly with olive oil, and bake until golden. A tablespoon of chopped thyme, rosemary, or summer savory can be substituted for the basil. Peperonata can be made up to a week in advance and stored in the refrigerator in an airtight container.

Preheat a broiler (grill) and set the rack about 6 inches (15 cm) from the heat source. Place the peppers on a baking sheet and broil, turning frequently, until the skins are blackened and blistered, about 10 minutes. Transfer the peppers to a paper bag, tightly close the bag, and set aside for 10–12 minutes.

Using a paring knife, peel and scrape away the blackened skin from each pepper. Working over a bowl to catch the juices, remove the stems, seeds, and ribs. Slice the peppers into strips $^1/_2$ inch (12 mm) wide. Strain the juices and set aside

In a large frying pan over medium-high heat, warm the olive oil. Add the onion and sauté until softened but not browned, 3–5 minutes. Add the garlic and cook for 1 minute. Stir in the tomatoes and reserved pepper juices and sauté until some of the liquid has evaporated and the mixture has thickened slightly, 7–10 minutes.

STOVE TOP: Transfer the peppers to a saucepan over low heat. Add the tomato mixture, stir in the basil, and season with salt and pepper. Cover and cook until the peppers are softened and the tomatoes have released all their liquid, about 20 minutes. Uncover, raise the heat to medium-high, and cook, stirring often, until thickened, about 7 minutes.

SLOW COOKER: Transfer the peppers to a slow cooker. Add the tomato mixture, stir in the basil, and season with salt and pepper. Cover and cook until the flavors have blended and the peppers are cooked through, 45 minutes on the low-heat setting. Uncover, raise the heat to high, and cook, stirring frequently, until most of the liquid has evaporated and the mixture has thickened, 10–15 minutes.

Serve at once, garnished with basil.

2 red bell peppers (capsicums)

2 yellow bell peppers (capsicums)

2 tablespoons olive oil

1 yellow onion, thinly sliced

1 clove garlic

2 tomatoes, seeded and chopped

1 cup (1 oz/30 g) loosely packed, roughly torn fresh basil, plus more for garnish

Salt and freshly ground pepper

Fennel with Olives and Orange Zest

4 small fennel bulbs, about 1½ lb (750 g) total weight

3 tablespoons unsalted butter

Salt and freshly ground pepper

¼ cup (2 fl oz/60 ml) chicken broth

¼ cup (2 fl oz/60 ml) dry white wine, such as chardonnay

¼ cup (2 fl oz/60 ml) fresh orange juice

2 teaspoons grated orange zest

½ teaspoon fennel seeds

¼ cup (1½ oz/45 g) pitted, oil-cured, small black olives

Working with 1 fennel bulb at a time, cut off the stalks and feathery leaves and discard or reserve for another use. Peel away the tough outer layer of the bulb, then cut lengthwise into medium-sized wedges. If the core seems very tough, trim it, but do not cut it away fully or the wedges will fall apart.

In a Dutch oven over medium heat, melt the butter. Add the fennel and cook, turning often, until golden on all sides, 4–6 minutes. Season with salt and pepper. Add the broth, wine, orange juice and zest, fennel seeds, and olives.

Cover, reduce the heat to low, and cook until the fennel is tender, 30–35 minutes. Taste and, if necessary, adjust the seasonings with salt and pepper. Transfer to a serving bowl and serve at once.

Fennel, native to the Mediterranean, is widely used throughout Italy and France. Slowly cooking the fennel enhances its mild anise flavor, as does the addition of pungent fennel seeds. Olives and oranges, also popular in the Mediterranean kitchen, make ideal flavor accents. This dish can be prepared several hours ahead and served at warm room temperature.

Savoy Cabbage with Pancetta

Historical and botanical evidence indicates that cabbage has been eaten for more than 4,000 years and cultivated for the last 2,500 years. At some point, probably in cold-weather regions where this cruciferous vegetable seems to thrive, someone was boiling cabbage and decided to add a little bacon. It turned out to be a perfect combination. Pancetta, which is generally less fatty than bacon, has a meaty richness that makes it a superb choice for this braised cabbage dish.

Cut the cabbage in half lengthwise and remove the core. Thinly shred the cabbage and set aside.

In a large frying pan over medium-high heat, sauté the pancetta, stirring often, until the fat is rendered, about 5 minutes. Add the onion and sauté until softened, about 3 minutes. Add the garlic and cook for 1 minute.

Add the cabbage, 1 handful at a time, to the pan and sauté, allowing the cabbage to cook down before adding more. Raise the heat to high, pour in the wine, add the caraway seeds, and cook, stirring frequently, until the cabbage has completely wilted, about 5 minutes.

OVEN: Preheat the oven to 350°F (180°F). Transfer the cabbage mixture to a Dutch oven and season with salt and pepper. Cover and cook in the oven, stirring occasionally, until the cabbage is soft and creamy, 30–45 minutes.

SLOW COOKER: Transfer the cabbage mixture to a slow cooker and season with salt and pepper. Cover and cook, stirring occasionally, until the cabbage is soft and creamy, 2 hours on the low-heat setting.

Serve at once.

1 large savoy cabbage, about 3 lb (1.5 kg), bruised or discolored outer leaves removed

6 oz (185 g) pancetta, cut into ¼-inch (6-mm) dice

1 yellow onion, thinly sliced

1 clove garlic, minced

¼ cup (2 fl oz/60 ml) dry white wine such as chardonnay

2 teaspoons caraway seeds

Salt and freshly ground pepper

Indian Vegetable Curry

½ cup (4 fl oz/125 ml)
canola oil

1 lb (500 g) boiling potatoes,
about 1½ inches (4 cm)
in diameter, cut in half

1 head cauliflower, about
1½ lb (750 g), trimmed
and cut into florets

1 large yellow onion, roughly
chopped

1-inch (2.5-cm) piece fresh
ginger, peeled and grated

1-inch (2.5-cm) piece
cinnamon stick

2 teaspoons ground cumin

2 teaspoons ground coriander

2 teaspoons brown mustard
seeds

1 teaspoon ground cardamom

1 teaspoon ground turmeric

½ teaspoon cayenne pepper

1 cup (8 oz/250 g) plain
whole-milk yogurt

Salt

6 oz (185 g) frozen baby peas

In a large frying pan over medium-high heat, warm the canola oil. Working in batches to avoid overcrowding, add the potatoes and cauliflower and sauté until the potatoes are golden brown and the cauliflower florets are speckled with golden brown, 5–7 minutes. Remove from the pan and set aside.

Add the onion to the pan and sauté over medium-high heat until caramel brown, 12–15 minutes. Stir in the ginger, cinnamon, cumin, coriander, mustard seeds, cardamom, turmeric, and cayenne, and sauté until the spices are fragrant and coat the chopped onion, about 1 minute. Add 1 cup (8 fl oz/250 ml) hot water and deglaze the pan, stirring and scraping up the browned bits on the bottom of the pan with a wooden spoon. Stir in the yogurt and 2 teaspoons salt, reduce the heat to medium, and cook until the onion-yogurt mixture starts to simmer, about 5 minutes.

STOVE TOP: Transfer the potatoes and cauliflower to a large Dutch oven. Pour in the onion-yogurt mixture and stir gently to combine. Partially cover and cook over low heat until the vegetables are tender and the sauce is thick, about 20 minutes. Gently stir in the peas and cook for about 10 minutes longer.

SLOW COOKER: Transfer the potatoes and cauliflower to a slow cooker. Pour in the onion-yogurt mixture and stir gently to combine. Cover and cook until the vegetables are tender and the sauce is thick, 1½–2 hours on the high-heat setting or 3–4 hours on the low-heat setting. About 10 minutes before the vegetables are done, gently stir in the peas.

Remove the cinnamon stick and serve at once.

In northern India, this mild style of curry is traditionally cooked slowly in an earthenware pot, yielding tender vegetables bound together by a thick, creamy, fragrant sauce. The result is easily duplicated by a slow cooker or on the stove top in a Dutch oven. The vegetables taste even better reheated a day or two later after being stored in the refrigerator in a covered container. Try serving with Spiced Basmati Rice, (page 262).

Braised Balsamic Onions

Cipolline are flat, thin-skinned Italian onions that measure 2 inches (5 cm) in diameter. They have a sweet, nutty taste that enhances a variety of dishes. Pearl onions or small boiling onions may be substituted. Balsamic vinegar and red wine give these onions a pleasantly tart depth of flavor.

Bring a large pot of salted water to a boil over high heat. Using a paring knife, cut a small X in the stem end of each onion. Add the onions and bring to a boil. Remove from the heat, drain, and rinse under cold running water. Leaving the stem end intact and using a small, sharp knife, trim off the root end of each onion and slip off the skin. Do not cut too deeply into the onions or they will fall apart.

STOVE TOP: In a large saucepan over medium-high heat, melt the butter. Add the onions and toss to coat. Season with salt and pepper. Add the wine, vinegar, and sugar, and pour in 1 cup (8 fl oz/250 ml) water. Cover, reduce the heat to low, and cook, stirring ocassionally, until the onions are tender, about 45 minutes. Uncover, raise the heat to high, bring to a boil, and cook, stirring constantly, until the onions are shiny and glazed, about 5 minutes. Season to taste with salt and pepper.

SLOW COOKER: Combine the onions, butter, red wine, vinegar, and sugar in a slow cooker. Season with salt and pepper. Pour in 1 cup (8 fl oz/250 ml) water. Set the temperature to low and cook for 20 minutes, stirring ocassionally, to coat the onions with the butter. Cover and continue to cook for 2 hours. Uncover, raise the heat to high, and cook until the liquid has reduced and the onions are shiny and glazed, about 1 hour. Season to taste with salt and pepper

Serve at once.

2 lb (1 kg) cipolline onions,

2 tablespoons unsalted butter

Salt and freshly ground pepper

¼ cup (2 fl oz/60 ml) dry red wine such as Côtes du Rhone

¼ cup (2 fl oz/60 ml) balsamic vinegar

1 teaspoon sugar

Southern Collard Greens

2 teaspoons canola oil

¼ lb (125 g) pancetta, finely diced

5–6 lb (2.5–3 kg) collard greens

Freshly ground pepper

½ teaspoon red pepper flakes

Remove coarse stems and center ribs from the collard greens, then rinse and drain the leaves. Dry completely and coarsely chop.

In a small frying pan over medium-high heat, warm the oil. Add the pancetta and cook, stirring often, until browned, about 6 minutes. Transfer to a paper towel–lined plate and set aside.

STOVE TOP: In a large pot, bring 4 quarts (4 l) of water to a boil. Add the greens to the pot, reduce the heat to medium-high, cover partially, and let simmer, stirring occasionally, until very tender, about 45 minutes.

SLOWCOOKER: Transfer the greens to a slow cooker and add 4 quarts (4 l) of water. Cover and cook, stirring occasionally, until the cabbage is soft and creamy, 2 hours on the low-heat setting.

If any liquid remains, drain the greens before transferring them to a serving bowl. Season with pepper and stir in the reserved pancetta and red pepper flakes. Serve warm.

NOTE: Hearty in flavor and high in nutrients, dark greens, also known as cooking greens are perfect for braising. Represented by several different vegetable familes, they range in flavor from lemony sorrel to peppery turnip greens. Feel free to substitue other hearty greens for the collard greens, or use a mixture.

Cooking collard greens slowly over low heat, is the most traditional approach. The result is tender greens with a pork-flavored broth.

Braised Potatoes with Caramelized Onions

Yukon gold potatoes have a sturdy texture and will not fall apart when cooked for a long time. For contrasting color, add strips of red bell pepper (capsicum) to the potatoes and onions. Serve with glazed ham, roast pork, or beef stew.

In a large frying pan over medium-high heat, melt the butter with the olive oil. Working in batches if necessary, arrange the potatoes in a single layer on the bottom of the pan and cook, turning frequently, until browned on all sides, 7–10 minutes. Remove from the pan and set aside.

Add the onions to the pan, sprinkle with the sugar, and season with salt and pepper. Sauté over medium-high heat until lightly caramelized, about 10 minutes.

OVEN: Preheat the oven to 375°F (190°C). Transfer the potatoes to a Dutch oven and season with salt and pepper. Scatter the onions over the potatoes, and pour in the broth. Cover and cook in the oven, gently turning the vegetables occasionally, until the potatoes are tender, 30–40 minutes. Uncover and cook until most of the liquid has evaporated and the potatoes are shiny, about 20 minutes longer. Stir in the thyme. Season to taste with salt and pepper.

SLOW COOKER: Transfer the potatoes to a slow cooker and season with salt and pepper. Scatter the onions over the potatoes and pour in the broth. Cover and cook until the potatoes are very tender, 1 hour on the high-heat setting. Uncover and cook, gently stirring, until most of the liquid has evaporated and the potatoes are shiny, about 30 minutes longer. Stir in the thyme. Season to taste with salt and pepper.

Transfer to a warmed serving bowl and serve at once.

2 tablespoons unsalted butter

2 tablespoons olive oil

6 Yukon gold potatoes, about 2 lb (1 kg) total weight, peeled and cut into 1½-inch (4-cm) cubes

2 yellow onions, thinly sliced

1 teaspoon sugar

Salt and freshly ground pepper

½ cup (4 fl oz/125 ml) chicken broth

1 tablespoon chopped fresh thyme

Mushroom Ragù with Polenta

2 tablespoons olive oil

1 shallot, minced

1 clove garlic, minced

5 lb (2.5 kg) assorted fresh mushrooms, brushed clean, stems removed, and large caps halved

½ cup (4 fl oz/125 ml) Marsala, port, or sherry

1 cup (8 fl oz/250 ml) chicken broth

⅓ cup (3 fl oz/80 ml) heavy (double) cream

Salt and freshly ground pepper

Creamy Polenta (page 261), prepared with Parmesan cheese

In a large frying pan over medium-high heat, warm the olive oil. Add the shallot and sauté until translucent, about 2 minutes. Stir in the garlic and cook for 1 minute. Add the mushrooms and cook, stirring frequently, until they begin to release their liquid, about 5 minutes. Raise the heat to high and cook, stirring constantly, until all but 1 tablespoon of the liquid has evaporated, about 5 minutes. Add the marsala, bring to a boil, and cook, stirring often, for about 2 minutes. Pour in the broth, bring to a boil, and cook until the liquid is reduced by half, about 5 minutes. You should have about 3 cups (24 fl oz/750 ml) mushrooms and liquid.

STOVE TOP: Transfer the mushroom mixture to a Dutch oven and bring to a simmer over low heat. Partially cover and cook, stirring frequently, until the liquid is dark and concentrated, about 20 minutes. Stir in the cream, raise the heat to high, bring to a boil, and cook, stirring often, until the liquid is thick enough to coat the back of a spoon, 7–10 minutes. Season to taste with salt and pepper.

SLOW COOKER: Transfer the mushroom mixture to a slow cooker and set the temperature to low. Cover and cook, stirring once or twice, until the liquid is dark and concentrated, about 45 minutes. Stir in the cream, raise the heat to high, and cook uncovered, stirring frequently, until the liquid is thick enough to coat the back of a spoon, 15–20 minutes. Season to taste with salt and pepper.

Divide the polenta among warmed bowls, top with the mushroom ragù, and serve at once.

It's not unusual to find several mushroom varieties—cremini, oyster, and shiitake—in addition to button mushrooms in most large markets, so choose a combination for this dish. The ragù has an earthy flavor and is as rich and hearty as a beef sauce. Creamy polenta is the perfect accompaniment. If you like, serve the ragù with squares or wedges of Grilled Polenta (page 261).

Cuban Black Beans

1 lb (500 g) dried black beans

2 tablespoons olive oil

1 yellow onion, chopped

1 clove garlic, minced

1 green bell pepper (capsicum), seeded and chopped

1 red bell pepper (capsicum), seeded and chopped

1 yellow pepper (capsicum), seeded and chopped

1 piece smoked ham hock, 6–8 oz (185–250 g)

2 cup (16 fl oz/500 ml) chicken broth

2 teaspoons ground cumin

2 teaspoons chopped fresh oregano

Salt and freshly ground pepper

Pick over the beans, removing any misshapen beans or grit. Rinse under cold running water. Put the beans in a large bowl, add enough cold water to cover by at least 2 inches (5 cm), and let stand at room temperature overnight. Alternatively, for a quick soak, put the beans in a large pot, add enough water to cover by at least 2 inches, bring to a boil, remove from the heat, cover, and let soak for 1 hour. Drain and rinse the beans.

In a large frying pan over medium-high heat, warm the olive oil. Add the onion, garlic, and bell peppers, and sauté until softened but not browned, about 5 minutes.

STOVE TOP: Transfer the beans and the onion mixture to a large Dutch oven. Add the ham hock, pour in the broth, stir in the cumin and oregano, and season with salt and pepper. Add enough water to cover the beans by 1 inch (2.5 cm). Cover and cook over medium heat, stirring occasionally, until the beans are tender yet firm, 1–1 1/2 hours. Remove the ham hock and let cool. Carefully remove as much of the lean meat as possible, discarding all the skin, fat, and bones. Stir the meat into the beans. Season to taste with salt and pepper.

SLOW COOKER: Transfer the beans and the onion mixture to a slow cooker. Add the ham hock, pour in the broth, stir in the cumin and oregano, and season with salt and pepper. Add enough water to cover the beans by 1 inch (2.5 cm). Cover and cook until the beans are tender yet firm, 3 hours on the high-heat setting. Remove the ham hock and let cool. Carefully remove as much of the lean meat as possible, discarding all the skin, fat, and bones. Stir the meat into the beans. Season to taste with salt and pepper.

Transfer to a warmed serving bowl and serve at once.

Black beans, a staple in Cuban cuisine, have an earthiness that almost begs for a touch of acidity, provided here by onions and a trio of colorful bell peppers. Ask the butcher to cut the ham hock in half, if possible, which makes it easier to immerse in the cooking liquid and adds more flavor.

Vietnamese Eggplant Curry

Use either familiar purple globe eggplants or smaller, more slender Asian eggplants for this recipe. Leaving them unpeeled adds flavor and color to the dish, and helps the eggplant pieces retain their shape when cooked. Serve with Steamed Jasmine Rice (page 262).

In a small Dutch oven over medium high heat, warm the peanut oil. Add the eggplant and sauté until just golden, 4–5 minutes. Stir in the garlic and sauté for 30 seconds. Stir in the curry paste and fish sauce, and then the coconut milk, broth, and lime zest. Add the tofu, cover, reduce the heat to low, and simmer until eggplant and tofu are soft but still hold their shape, 20–25 minutes.

Stir in the green onions, cilantro, and lime juice. Season to taste with salt and pepper. Serve at once.

NOTE: Eggplant should be stored in cool, dry places, and used within one or two days of purchase. The flesh of eggplant discolor rather quickly, so cut eggplant just before you are going to make this dish.

3 tablespoons peanut or canola oil

1½ lb (750 g) globe or Asian (slender) eggplants (aubergines), cut into 1-inch (2.5-cm) chunks

2 cloves garlic, minced

1 tablespoon red curry paste

1 tablespoon Thai fish sauce

1 can (13½ oz/420 ml) unsweetened coconut milk

1 cup (8 fl oz/250 ml) vegetable or chicken broth

1 teaspoon grated lime zest

12 oz (375 g) extra-firm tofu, rinsed, patted dry, and cut into ¾-inch (2-cm) chunks

3 green (spring) onions, white and pale green parts, thinly sliced

¼ cup (⅓ oz/10 g) chopped fresh cilantro (fresh coriander)

1 tablespoon fresh lime juice

Salt and freshly ground pepper

Turkish-Style Green Beans

Slowly braised in tomatoes and onion, green beans take on a richness and depth of flavor. Choose the biggest, thickest beans you can find; this is a good way to use end-of-season green beans.

In a small Dutch oven over medium heat, warm the olive oil. Add the onion and sauté until softened, 4–5 minutes. Add the garlic and sauté for 30 seconds. Stir in the cumin, cinnamon, and red pepper flakes. Add the green beans, stir to coat with the spices, and cook, stirring, until the beans are barely tender and just beginning to deepen in color, 3–4 minutes. Stir in the tomatoes, cover, reduce the heat to low, and cook until the beans are very tender, 15–20 minutes.

Stir in the vinegar and season to taste with salt and pepper. Serve at once.

2 tablespoons olive oil

1 yellow onion, chopped

2 cloves garlic, minced

¾ teaspoon ground cumin

¼ teaspoon ground cinnamon

¼ teaspoon red pepper flakes

1½ lb (750 g) green beans, ends trimmed

1 can (14½ oz/455 g) diced plum (Roma) tomatoes

2 teaspoons red wine vinegar

Salt and freshly ground pepper

Red Cabbage with Apples

**1 large red cabbage, about
3 lb (1.5 kg), bruised or
discolored outer leaves
removed**

**6 slices bacon, about 6 oz
(185 g) total weight, chopped**

1 red onion, thinly sliced

**2 Granny Smith apples,
peeled, cored, and cut into
$\frac{1}{2}$-inch (12-mm) cubes**

**$\frac{1}{3}$ cup (3 fl oz/80 ml) red
wine vinegar**

**2 tablespoons firmly packed
light brown sugar**

**2 teaspoons chopped fresh
thyme**

**Salt and freshly ground
pepper**

Cut the cabbage in half lengthwise and remove the core. Cut the cabbage into slices $\frac{1}{2}$ inch (12 mm) thick. Set aside.

In a large frying pan over medium-high heat, sauté the bacon until lightly browned, about 5 minutes. Transfer to a paper towel–lined plate and set aside.

Pour off all but 1 tablespoon of the fat in the pan. Add the onion and sauté over medium-high heat until slightly softened, about 3 minutes. Stir in the apples, vinegar, brown sugar, and thyme, raise the heat to high, and deglaze the pan, stirring and scraping up the browned bits on the bottom of the pan with a wooden spoon.

STOVE TOP: Transfer the apple mixture to a large Dutch oven. Add the cabbage, season with salt and pepper, and stir to combine. Cover and cook over medium-high heat until tender, about 30 minutes. Stir in the reserved bacon.

SLOW COOKER: Transfer the apple mixture to a slow cooker. Add the cabbage, season to taste with salt and pepper, and stir to combine. Cover and cook until tender, 3 hours on the low-heat setting. Stir in the reserved bacon.

Serve at once.

The tartness of green apples marries well with the mellowness of red cabbage. Serve this hearty side dish with pork or game. Toasted caraway seeds, juniper berries, halved seedless grapes, or a handful of chopped fresh flat-leaf (Italian) parsley can be stirred in just before serving.

Celery Root with Chestnuts

Also called celeriac, good-quality celery root should be firm with light brown skin. The simple braising technique in this recipe results in a rich, golden glaze for the vegetables and nuts. This dish can be made up to an hour ahead and kept warm in the oven.

Preheat the oven to 400°F (200°C). Using a small, sharp knife, cut an X on the flat side of each chestnut, cutting through the shell but not into the meat. Place the chestnuts in a single layer on a baking sheet. Roast the chestnuts, stirring them about halfway through the roasting time, until the slits widen a bit, about 20 minutes. Enclose the hot chestnuts in a damp kitchen towel and let steam for about 5 minutes to soften the shells. When the chestnuts are cool enough to handle, peel them, removing both the hard shell and the skin beneath.

In a small Dutch oven over medium heat, melt the butter. Add the onion and chestnuts and sauté just until flecked with gold, 5–8 minutes. Season with salt and pepper, sprinkle with the sugar, and pour in 1 cup (8 fl oz/250 ml) broth and the brandy. Cover, reduce the heat to medium-low, and cook until the onions and chestnuts are barely tender, about 15 minutes.

Stir in the celery root. The liquid should barely cover the vegetables. If necessary, add a little more broth. Cover and continue to cook over medium-low heat, stirring occasionally, until all the vegetables are tender, 15–20 minutes.

Uncover, stir in the cream and marjoram, raise the heat to high, and cook, stirring often, until the liquid is reduced almost to a glaze, 5–10 minutes. Season with salt and pepper. Serve at once.

1 lb (500 g) chestnuts

2 tablespoons unsalted butter

1 yellow onion, chopped

Salt and freshly ground pepper

2 teaspoons sugar

1 cup (8 fl oz/250 ml) chicken broth, plus more if needed

2 tablespoons brandy

1 small celery root (celeriac), about 1 lb (500 g), peeled and cut into 1/2-inch (12-mm) chunks

1/2 cup (4 fl oz/125 ml) heavy (double) cream

2 tablespoons chopped fresh marjoram

Escarole with Cannellini Beans

1 lb (500 g) dried cannellini beans or Great Northern beans

2 cups (16 fl oz/500 ml) chicken or vegetable broth

½ cup (4 fl oz/120 ml) olive oil, plus more for serving

2 yellow onions, quartered

2 carrots, cut into 2-inch (5-cm) pieces

8 cloves garlic, 4 left whole, 4 minced

2 sprigs fresh sage

½ teaspoon red pepper flakes

2 oz (60 g) pancetta or unsmoked bacon, chopped (optional)

2 heads escarole, about 2 lb (1 kg) total weight, cut crosswise into strips 2 inches (5 cm) wide

1 can (14½ oz/455 g) diced plum (Roma) tomatoes, preferably San Marzano, drained

Salt and freshly ground pepper

Juice of 1 lemon

You can serve this traditional Italian combination of mellow white beans and earthy dark greens in a variety of ways: as a salad to start a meal, as a side dish or base for roasted or grilled meats or poultry, or as a sauce for bite-sized al dente pasta. For a vegetarian version, use vegetable broth and omit the optional pancetta.

Pick over the beans, removing any misshapen beans or grit. Rinse under cold running water. Put the beans in a large bowl, add enough cold water to cover by at least 2 inches (5 cm), and let stand at room temperature overnight. Alternatively, for a quick soak, put the beans in a large pot, add enough water to cover by at least 2 inches, bring to a boil, remove from the heat, cover, and let soak for 1 hour. Drain and rinse the beans.

STOVE TOP: In a large Dutch oven, combine the beans, the broth, and ¼ cup (2 fl oz/60 ml) of the olive oil. Add enough cold water to cover the beans by about 1½ inches (4 cm). Add the onions, carrots, whole garlic cloves, and sage. Bring to a boil, reduce the heat to low, partially cover, and simmer gently until the beans are very tender, 1½–2 hours. Remove the onions, garlic cloves, and sage and discard.

SLOW COOKER: In a slow cooker, combine the beans, the broth, and ¼ cup (2 fl oz/60 ml) of the olive oil. Add enough water to cover the beans by about 1½ inches (4 cm). Add the onions, carrots, whole garlic cloves, and sage. Cover and cook until the beans are tender, 4 hours on the high-heat setting or 8 hours on the low-heat setting. Remove the onions, garlic cloves, and sage and discard.

About 30 minutes before the beans are done, in a large frying pan over medium-high heat, warm the remaining 2 tablespoons olive oil. Add the minced garlic, red pepper flakes, and pancetta (if using) and sauté until fragrant, about 30 seconds. Add the escarole and sauté until the leaves begin to wilt, about 1 minute. Add the tomatoes, 1 teaspoon salt, and ½ teaspoon pepper, and cook, stirring occasionally, until the leaves have softened and the mixture is reduced to about one-third, 5–7 minutes.

When the beans are done, add the escarole mixture and stir, breaking up some of the beans with the back of the spoon to thicken the mixture slightly. Stir in the lemon juice. Season to taste with salt and pepper.

Serve at once, passing the remaining olive oil at the table.

Sicilian-Style Braised Artichokes

Artichokes lend themselves to stuffing. Throughout Italy, you'll find them filled with a variety of ingredients such as canned tuna, sausage meat, or a ricotta-herb mixture. Here is a popular Sicilian version using fresh bread crumbs, Romano cheese, anchovies and fresh herbs.

Squeeze the juice from the lemon halves into a bowl of cold water and add the halves to the bowl. Working with 1 artichoke at a time, use a paring knife to cut off the stem end of each and discard. Using a paring knife, cut off the stem of each artichoke and discard. Separate the leaves slightly with your fingers and pull out the purple leaves from the center and enough yellow leaves to expose the fuzzy choke. Scoop out the choke with a melon baller. Place the artichoke in the lemon water.

In a bowl, stir together the bread crumbs, cheese, garlic, oregano, thyme, anchovies, $1/2$ teaspoon salt, and $1/2$ teaspoon pepper. Add 4 tablespoons (2 fl oz/60 ml) of the olive oil and stir to mix well. Remove the artichokes from the lemon water, reserving the water. Spoon the stuffing into the center of the artichokes, dividing it evenly.

Place the stuffed artichokes upright in a Dutch oven just large enough to hold them. Pour the wine around the artichokes and add enough of the lemon water to reach a depth of about 1 inch (2.5 cm). Add the lemon halves to the pot. Drizzle the tops of the artichokes with the remaining 2 tablespoons oil.

Cover and bring to a boil over medium-high heat. Reduce the heat to medium-low and cook until the artichoke leaves are tender and the choke can be pierced with the tip of a knife, 30–40 minutes. Use a slotted spoon to transfer the artichokes to a platter. Serve warm or at room temperature.

1 lemon, halved

4 artichokes

$1/2$ cup (2 oz/60 g) dried bread crumbs

$1/4$ cup (1 oz/30 g) grated Romano cheese

4 large cloves garlic, minced

1 tablespoon chopped fresh oregano

1 tablespoon chopped fresh thyme

4 oil-packed anchovy fillets, mashed, or 1 tablespoon anchovy paste

Salt and freshly ground pepper

6 tablespoons (3 fl oz/90 ml) olive oil

$1/4$ cup (2 fl oz/60 ml) dry white wine such as chardonnay

Boston Baked Beans

1 lb (500 g) dried white beans such as navy or Great Northern

1/2 cup (4 fl oz/125 ml) ketchup

2 tablespoons dark molasses

2 tablespoons Dijon mustard

2 tablespoons apple cider vinegar

2 tablespoons maple syrup

Salt and freshly ground pepper

1/4 lb (125 g) smoked bacon, chopped

Pick over the beans, removing any misshapen beans or grit. Rinse under cold running water. Put the beans in a large bowl, add enough cold water to cover by at least 2 inches (5 cm), and let stand at room temperature overnight. Alternatively, for a quick soak, put the beans in a large pot, add enough water to cover by at least 2 inches, bring to a boil, remove from the heat, cover, and let soak for 1 hour. Drain and rinse the beans.

In a small saucepan over medium heat, combine the ketchup, molasses, mustard, cider vinegar, maple syrup, and 1/2 teaspoon pepper. Bring to a simmer, stirring to blend. Remove from the heat.

OVEN: Preheat the oven to 300°F (150°C). Pour the molasses mixture into a Dutch oven. Add the beans and bacon and stir to combine. Cover and cook in the oven, stirring frequently, until the beans are tender yet firm, about 1 1/2 hours. Uncover and cook, stirring frequently, until most of the liquid has evaporated and the beans are just tender, about 20 minutes longer. Season to taste with salt and pepper.

SLOW COOKER: Pour the molasses mixture into a slow cooker. Add the beans and bacon and stir to combine. Cover and set the temperature to high. When the liquid begins to boil, reduce the temperature to low, and cook, stirring occasionally, until the beans are tender yet firm, about 3 hours. Uncover, raise the heat to high, and cook, stirring frequently, until most of the liquid has evaporated and the beans are just tender, about 30 minutes longer. Season to taste with salt and pepper.

Serve at once.

Native Americans taught New Englanders about this dish, which is now a classic. They are said to have cooked the beans in maple sugar with a piece of bear fat. Today, there are many variations: brown sugar used in place of the molasses, chopped fresh tomatoes in place of the ketchup, or blanched salt pork in place of the bacon. However the beans are flavored, the essential component is to cook them slowly over low heat

Indian Chickpea Curry

Known in India as *chana masala*, this classic stew of chickpeas can be enjoyed as a side dish or accompanied by rice pilaf as a vegetarian main course. Added at the end of cooking, a sprinkling of garam masala, a widely available blend of spices, heightens the curry's flavor and aroma.

Pick over the chickpeas, removing any misshapen beans or grit. Rinse under cold running water. Put the chickpeas in a large bowl, add enough cold water to cover by at least 2 inches (5 cm), and let stand at room temperature overnight. Alternatively, for a quick soak, put the chickpeas in a large pot, add enough water to cover by at least 2 inches, bring to a boil, remove from the heat, cover, and let soak for 1 hour. Drain and rinse the chickpeas.

In a large frying pan over medium-high heat, warm the canola oil. Add the onion, garlic, and ginger and sauté until the mixture just begins to turn golden, about 5 minutes. Add the cinnamon, cayenne, coriander, cumin, mustard seeds, and turmeric and sauté until the spices are fragrant and thoroughly blended with the onion mixture, about 1 minute. Stir in the tomatoes, the sugar, 2 teaspoons salt, and 2 cups (16 fl oz/500 ml) water. Deglaze the pan, stirring and scraping up the browned bits on the bottom of the pan with a wooden spoon. Bring to a boil.

STOVE TOP: Transfer the tomato-spice mixture to a large Dutch oven and stir in the chickpeas. Partially cover and cook over low heat until the chickpeas are very tender, about 3 hours.

SLOW COOKER: Transfer the tomato-spice mixture to a slow cooker and stir in the chickpeas. Cover and cook until the chickpeas are very tender, 4 hours on the high-heat setting or 8 hours on the low-heat setting.

About 15 minutes before the chickpeas are done, sprinkle the garam masala and lime juice evenly over the chickpeas and stir, breaking up some of the chickpeas with the back of the spoon to thicken the mixture slightly. Season to taste with salt. Remove the cinnamon stick and serve at once, garnished with the cilantro.

1 lb (500 g) dried chickpeas (garbanzo beans)

2 tablespoons canola oil

1 yellow onion, finely chopped

2 cloves garlic, minced

1-inch (2.5-cm) piece fresh ginger, peeled and grated

2-inch (5-cm) piece cinnamon stick, broken in half

1 teaspoon cayenne pepper

1 teaspoon ground coriander

1 teaspoon ground cumin

1 teaspoon brown mustard seeds

1 teaspoon ground turmeric

1 can (28 oz/875 g) diced tomatoes

2 teaspoons sugar

Salt

1 tablespoon garam masala

1 tablespoon fresh lime juice

1 cup (1 oz/30 g) chopped fresh cilantro (fresh coriander) leaves

Spicy Squash with Garlic-Yogurt Sauce

¼ cup (2 fl oz/60 ml) canola oil

2½ lb (1.25 kg) Acorn squash, halved lengthwise, seeded, and cut into 1½-inch (4-cm) pieces

1-inch (2.5-cm) piece fresh ginger, peeled and grated

1 teaspoon ground coriander

½ teaspoon ground cinnamon

½ teaspoon red pepper flakes

1 can (14½ oz/455 g) tomato sauce

½ cup (4 oz/125 g) sugar

Salt and freshly ground pepper

For the Garlic-Yogurt Sauce

1½ cups (12 oz/375 g) plain whole-milk yogurt

2 cloves garlic, minced

3 tablespoons chopped fresh mint, plus more for garnish

Salt

In a large frying pan over medium-high heat, warm the canola oil. Working in batches if necessary, add the squash and sauté until evenly browned, about 7 minutes. Transfer to a bowl and set aside. Add the ginger, coriander, cinnamon, and red pepper flakes and sauté until fragrant, about 30 seconds. Stir in the tomato sauce, the sugar, ½ teaspoon salt, and ¼ teaspoon pepper and bring to a boil.

STOVE TOP: Transfer the tomato-sauce mixture to a large Dutch oven. Add the squash and stir to combine with the sauce. Partially cover and simmer gently over low heat until the squash is very tender and the sauce is thick, 30–45 minutes.

SLOW COOKER: Transfer the tomato-sauce mixture to a slow cooker. Add the squash and stir to combine with the sauce. Cover and cook until the squash is very tender and the sauce is thick, 2 hours on the high-heat setting or 4 hours on the low-heat setting.

Meanwhile, make the garlic-yogurt sauce: Line a fine-mesh sieve with a double layer of cheesecloth (muslin), place in a bowl, and spoon the yogurt into the sieve. Refrigerate until the excess liquid has drained from the yogurt, 20–30 minutes. Transfer the yogurt to a bowl. Stir in the garlic, 3 tablespoons chopped mint, and ½ teaspoon salt. Cover and refrigerate until serving.

Spread about two-thirds of the garlic-yogurt sauce on a serving platter. Mound the curry on the sauce and top with the remaining sauce. Garnish with mint and serve at once.

A traditional favorite from Afghanistan, where it is known as *kadu bouranee*, this dish differs from Indian-style curries with its emphatic note of sweetness to balances the spices. Although it is commonly made with pumpkins, acorn squash makes a much more reliable base than the sometimes bland, starchy pumpkins commonly sold for Halloween jack-o'-lanterns. Draining the yogurt results in a thicker, creamier sauce.

Italian White Beans

In Tuscany, slowly simmered, simply seasoned beans are traditionally served as a rustic appetizer or vegetarian luncheon dish. A drizzle of warm, garlic-scented oil provides an ideal finishing touch for each serving. Feel free to vary the herbs to your liking, or garnish with freshly grated Parmesan cheese.

Pick over the beans, removing any misshapen beans or grit. Rinse under cold running water. Put the beans in a large bowl, add enough cold water to cover by at least 2 inches (5 cm), and let stand at room temperature overnight. Alternatively, for a quick soak, put the beans in a large pot, add enough water to cover by at least 2 inches, bring to a boil, remove from the heat, cover, and let soak for 1 hour.

Drain and rinse the beans.

STOVE TOP: In a large Dutch oven, combine the beans, whole garlic cloves, and rosemary. Add enough cold water to cover the beans by 1–2 inches (2.5–5 cm). Bring to a boil, reduce the heat to low, partially cover, and simmer gently until the beans are very tender, 1 1/2–2 hours.

SLOW COOKER: Bring a large saucepan of water to a boil. Transfer the beans to a slow cooker. Bury the whole garlic cloves and rosemary sprig in the beans. Add enough boiling water to cover the beans by 1–2 inches (2.5–5 cm). Cover and cook until the beans are very tender, 4 hours on the high-heat setting or 8 hours on the low-heat setting.

Just before serving, in a small saucepan over medium heat, warm the olive oil. Add the minced garlic and sauté just until fragrant but not browned, about 1 minute.

Drain the beans and transfer to a serving bowl. Discard the rosemary sprig and season generously to taste with salt and pepper.

Spoon the beans onto warmed plates. Drizzle with the hot garlic oil and garnish with the parsley. Serve at once, passing the lemon wedges at the table.

1 lb (500 g) dried cannellini beans or Great Northern beans

9 garlic cloves, 6 left whole, 3 minced

1 sprig fresh rosemary

1/2 cup (4 fl oz/125 ml) olive oil

Salt and freshly ground pepper

3 tablespoons finely chopped fresh flat-leaf (Italian) parsley

2 lemons, each cut into 6 wedges

Maple-Glazed Carrots

1½ pound (750 g) carrots, peeled

2 tablespoons unsalted butter

2 large shallots, finely diced

salt and freshly ground pepper

2½ tablespoons maple syrup

1 cup (8 fl oz/250 ml) chicken broth, plus more if needed

Cut the carrots on the diagonal into even 1-inch (2-cm) slices. The size of carrots may differ, so be sure to cut them all roughly the same size to ensure the cooking times do not differ.

In a large frying pan with a tight-fitting lid, melt 1 tablespoon of the butter. When the butter has melted, add the shallots and cook, stirring often, until coated, about 1 minute.

Add the carrots to the pan and season generously with salt and pepper. Raise the heat to high and stir well to coat the carrots. Drizzle the maple syrup over the carrots and add the chicken broth. The liquid should come about halfway up the sides of the carrots. If necessary, add more broth or water. Bring the liquid to a boil, reduce the heat to medium-high, cover, and cook for 5 minutes.

Uncover and continue to cook until the liquid has reduced by half and the carrots are tender and have developed a thin but shiny glaze, about 4 minutes longer. Transfer to a warmed serving platter and serve at once.

In this modern form of braising, carrots are cooked together using high heat and then the braising liquid is reduced to a light, thin, sweet glaze. Here, the maple syrup complements the natural sweetness of the carrots and contributes to the sheen and coating qualities of the glaze. The shallots add a nice contrast.

Braised Beets with Orange and Clove

Braised beets are rich and sweet and have a smooth and creamy texture. Most recipes call for wrapping the beets individually in aluminum foil and roasting, but here we have braised them in fresh orange juice to bring out their earthiness.

Preheat the oven to 400°F (200°C).

If the beet greens are still attached, trim them, leaving about 1 inch (2.5 cm) of the stem intact; reserve the greens for another use. Using a vegetable peeler, peel the beets. Brush the beets with the olive oil and transfer to a Dutch oven, just large enough to hold them. Add the orange juice, honey, and cloves and cover.

Braise the beets in the oven for 1 hour. Remove from the pan from th eoven, uncover, and season the beets generously with salt and pepper. Return the pan to the oven and continue to braise, until most of the liquid has evaporated and the beets are caramelized and tender throughout when pierced with a knife, about 30 minutes longer.

Let the beets cool slightly in the pan then transfer to a large warmed serving bowl, season to taste with salt and pepper, and serve at once.

$1^1/_2$ lb (750 g) red, golden, or striped beets

1 tablespoon olive oil

Salt and freshly ground pepper

Zest of 1 orange

1 cup (8 fl oz/250 ml) fresh orange juice

2 teaspoons honey

2 whole cloves

Brussels Sprouts with Bacon

4 slices bacon, about 4 oz (125 g) total weight, cut into ¼-inch (6-mm) slices

1 lb (500 g) small brussels sprouts, bases trimmed and outer leaves removed

3 shallots, thinly sliced

½ cup (4 fl oz/125 ml) chicken broth

½ cup (4 fl oz/125 ml) heavy (double) cream

1 teaspoon fresh lemon juice

Salt and freshly ground pepper

In a saucepan over medium heat, sauté the bacon until crisp, about 5 minutes. Transfer to a paper towel–lined plate and set aside. Pour off all but 1 tablespoon of the fat in the pan.

Add the brussels sprouts and shallots, reduce the heat to medium-low, and sauté until the vegetables are coated and barely tinged with gold, 2–3 minutes. Stir in the broth and cream. Cover, reduce the heat to low, and cook until the brussels sprouts are tender, 25–35 minutes.

Uncover, add the lemon juice, and season with salt and pepper. Raise the heat to medium and simmer, uncovered, until the liquid is lightly reduced, 3–4 minutes. Stir in the reserved bacon and serve at once.

Braising brussels sprouts in broth and cream tames their pungency, and the cooking liquid becomes a luscious sauce. Choose small, firm brussels sprouts. If only large sprouts are available, you may halve or quarter them.

Leeks with Herbed Vinaigrette

Leeks are among the mildest and sweetest members of the onion family. Long and gentle braising in the oven yields buttery-smooth, fork-tender results. Leeks pair well with Tuna with Tomato and Olive (page 83).

Preheat the oven to 325°F (165°C).

In a large ovenproof frying pan over medium-low heat, warm 1 tablespoon of the olive oil. Add the leeks in a single layer. Turn to coat in the oil. Season with salt and pepper and sprinkle with 1 teaspoon of the tarragon. Pour the broth and Pernod evenly over the leeks.

Cover, place in the oven, and cook until the leeks are tender, 30–40 minutes. Using tongs, transfer the leeks to a platter. Place the pan with the cooking liquid over high heat, bring to a boil, stirring ocassionally, until the liquid is reduced to about $1/4$ cup (2 fl oz/60 ml), 2–4 minutes.

In a small bowl, whisk together the remaining 3 tablespoons olive oil, the vinegar, mustard, and remaining 1 teaspoon tarragon. Whisk in about half of the reduced cooking liquid. Season to taste with salt and pepper. Whisk in the remaining liquid, if desired.

Serve the leeks warm or at room temperature, drizzled with the vinaigrette.

4 tablespoons (2 fl oz/60 ml) olive oil

6 leeks, about 3 lb (1.5 kg) total weight, white and pale green parts only, halved lengthwise

Salt and freshly ground pepper

2 teaspoons chopped fresh tarragon

$3/4$ cup (6 fl oz/180 ml) chicken broth

1 tablespoon Pernod or other anise liqueur

$1 1/2$ tablespoons white wine vinegar

1 teaspoon Dijon mustard

Seafood

About Fish and Seafood

Cooking fish and seafood in a tangy, slow cooked sauce can result in dishes with great texture and flavor. In most cases, add the fish or seafood towards the end of the cooking process to keep delicate fish and seafood from fallling apart.

From time immemorial humans have been harvesting fish and shellfish from the water. Much fish and seaood, of course, can be eaten raw and there is a pure pleasure in lifting a briny oyster to your mouth and slurping the succulent bivalve into your mouth for a burst of salty, intense flavor. And of course, sushi and sashimi are masterpieces of culinary art. But many delicious fish and seafood dishes involve slow cooking techniques such as steaming, braising, or stewing.

What makes seafood so delicious raw is its delicate, tender character. Nearly every fish or shellfish is a candidate for slow cooking. Tell your fish monger how you will be preparing the fish and he will help in making the best selection from what is available.

Fresh seafood is ideal, but it's not practical to ship some types, especially shrimp and squid, fresh across long distances, so they are routinely frozen. An increasing share of our seafood is also farmed, or aquacultureed. Aquaculture can be as simple as protecting and harvesting a natural clam or oyster bed, or it may involve ponds, net pens, or even tank farms in the desert.

Sometimes the fish is simply seasoned before cooking while other times the recipe depends on the sauce or cooking aromatics to flavor the fish.

USING FISH OR SEAFOOD IN SLOW COOKING

Keep fish or seafood refrigerated until just before you are going to cook it. And use absolutely fresh fish that has been bought the same day as you cook it. Frozen fish can become unappetizing and mushy when cooked; flash frozen seafood, on the other hand, is often excellent and retains its character and flavor when briefly cooked.

And be careful with the level and intensity of flavors in the accompanying sauce. You don't want to get too intense a flavor in the sauce or you will obliterate fish or seafood's delicacy and subtlety. Our recipes have plenty of flavor, but do not overpower the taste and texture of the fish or seafood.

FISH STEAKS AND FILLETS

Smaller pieces of meaty fish—halibut, swordfish, tuna, salmon—in the form of portion-sized steaks or fillets, are perfect candidates for slow cooking and braising. Searing the steaks or fillets on the stove top will nicely brown the exterior and add a layer of rich flavor. Tuna with Tomatoes and Olives (page 83) is a perfect example of this technique. For the best results, please keep in mind that the fillets must be at leaast 1 inch (2.5 cm) thick and that they must be uniform in size and shape so that all of them are ready at the same time. While you shouldn't cook delicate fish and seafood very long, you can achieve a slow-cooked complexity and depth of flavor by simmering the sauce for some time and then adding the fish or seafood towards the end of cooking.

An example of this type of fish cookery can be seen in our recipe for Indian Fish Curry (page 88) where the aromatic sauce is cooked for 2 or 3 hours and the fish added for the last half hour of cooking. Similar methods can be seen in our Vietnamese Clay Pot Fish (page 100) and Jambalaya with Shrimp, Chicken, and Ham (page 79). Care should be taken with any fish or seafood not to cook it too long. When fish is overcooked it dries out and falls apart. Only cook fish until it is opaque, firm to the touch, and beginning to flake.

Smaller pieces of meaty fish—halibut, swordfish, tuna, salmon—in the form of portion-sized steaks or fillets, are perfect candidates for slow cooking and braising. Searing the steaks or fillets on the stove top will nicely brown the exterior and add a layer of rich flavor.

SHELLFISH

The primary concerns—retaining moisture and adding flavor—that govern cooking fish apply to shellfish. Excellent choices for slow cooking are large shrimp (prawns) and mussels. Scallops, clams, and squid are also good choices and can be found in this chapter as well.

A hearty sauce or curry often accompanies slow cooked fish such as Calamari Fra Diavolo (page 87). The sauce, which includes chopped tomatoes and crushed red pepper is cooked alongside the squid, to help tenderize. For the Brazilian Seafood Stew (page 99), the sauce and the vegetables are cooked togetther and the scallops are added towards the end of cooking to prevent over cooking.

The pairing of salmon and miso (page 84) is a familiar and irresistible, and here the salmon is cooked and removed from the pan to allow the rich sauce to thicken. As with all fish and shellfish recipes, the success of this simple dish depends on a good fish monger supplying you with only the finest—and freshest—seafood. When shopping always pay close attention.

Jambalaya with Shrimp, Chicken, and Ham

The derivation of the word *jambalaya* is said to come from Spanish, French, and African cultures. All three lay claim to the origins of this quintessential Creole concoction that combines chicken and seafood with rice and assorted seasonings. Use crawfish in place of the shrimp if you can find them. This recipe can easily be doubled to serve a crowd.

In a large frying pan over medium-high heat, melt the butter with 1 tablespoon of the olive oil. Add the shrimp and cook until opaque, about 3 minutes per side. Remove from the pan and set aside. Add the chicken pieces and sauté until browned, about 5 minutes. Remove from the pan and set aside with the shrimp.

Warm the remaining 2 tablespoons oil in the pan over medium-high heat. Add the onion, bell pepper, and celery, and sauté until softened but not browned, about 5 minutes. Add the garlic and jalapeño and cook for 1 minute.

OVEN: Preheat oven to 350°F (180°C). Transfer the onion mixture to a large Dutch oven. Stir in the tomatoes, rice, broth, and a pinch of salt. Cover and cook in the oven until the rice is tender, about 45 minutes. Add the shrimp, chicken, ham, paprika, thyme, and cayenne. Stir well, cover, and let stand until warmed through, about 5 minutes. Season to taste with salt and black pepper.

SLOW COOKER: Transfer the onion mixture to a slow cooker. Stir in the tomatoes, rice, broth, and a pinch of salt. Cover and cook until the rice is tender, 3 hours on the low-heat setting. Add the shrimp, chicken, ham, paprika, thyme, and cayenne. Stir well, cover, turn off the cooker, and let stand until warmed through, about 5 minutes. Season to taste with salt and black pepper.

Spoon into warmed bowls and serve at once.

2 tablespoons unsalted butter

3 tablespoons olive oil

12 large shrimp (prawns), about 10 oz (315 g) total weight, peeled and deveined

2 skinless, boneless chicken breast halves, 4–6 oz (125–185 g) each, cut into large pieces

1 yellow onion, finely chopped

1 green bell pepper (capsicum), seeded and chopped

2 ribs celery, finely chopped

1 clove garlic, minced

1 jalapeño chile, minced

2 tomatoes, seeded and chopped

1 cup (7 oz/220 g) long-grain rice

2 cups (16 fl oz/500 ml) chicken broth

Salt and freshly ground black pepper

6 oz (185 g) smoked ham, cut into cubes

1 teaspoon sweet paprika

1 tablespoon chopped fresh thyme

Pinch of cayenne pepper, or more to taste

Cod with Tomatoes and Chickpeas

2 cups (14 oz/440 g) dried chickpeas (garbanzo beans)

3 tablespoons olive oil

1 yellow onion, chopped

3 cloves garlic, minced

2 teaspoons grated orange zest

1/2 teaspoon grated lemon zest

1 teaspoon ground cumin

1 teaspoon ground coriander

1/2 teaspoon ground cinnamon

Pinch of ground cloves

1 can (14 1/2 oz/455 g) diced tomatoes

1/2 cup (4 fl oz/125 ml) dry white wine such as sauvignon blanc

1 cup (8 fl oz/250 ml) fish broth or bottled clam juice

2 lb (1 kg) cod fillets, cut into 2-inch (5-cm) pieces

2 teaspoons fresh lemon juice

2 tablespoons chopped fresh flat-leaf (Italian) parsley

Pick over the chickpeas, removing any misshapen beans or grit. Rinse under cold running water. Put the chickpeas in a bowl, add enough cold water to cover by at least 2 inches (5 cm), and let stand at room temperature overnight. Alternatively, for a quick soak, put the chickpeas in a saucepan, add enough water to cover by at least 2 inches, bring to a boil, remove from the heat, cover, and let soak for 1 hour. Drain and rinse the chickpeas.

In a large saucepan, combine the chickpeas with enough cold water to cover by 1–2 inches (2.5–5 cm). Bring to a boil over high heat, reduce the heat to low, partially cover, and simmer gently until the chickpeas are very tender, about 2 hours. Drain and set aside.

In a small Dutch oven over medium heat, warm the olive oil. Add the onion and sauté until just softened, 4–5 minutes. Stir in the garlic and sauté for 30 seconds. Stir in the orange and lemon zests, cumin, coriander, cinnamon, and cloves. Add the tomatoes, wine, broth, and chickpeas. Raise the heat to medium-high and bring to a simmer.

Add the cod to the pot and spoon the liquid over it. Cover, reduce the heat to medium-low, and cook until the fish is opaque throughout, 10–12 minutes. Stir in the lemon juice. Transfer to a warmed serving platter, garnish with the parsley, and serve at once.

Delicate Moroccan flavors marry well with mild codfish in this dish, with chickpeas adding a hearty dimension. If you prefer, substitute 2 cups canned chickpeas for the dried beans. Serve with warm, crusty bread to soak up the fragrant sauce.

Tuna with Tomatoes and Olives

Tuna has enough flavor and texture to stand up to an assertive braising sauce. If you have fresh, ripe summer tomatoes, substitute them for the canned tomatoes and add an extra ¼ cup (2 fl oz/60 ml) wine. Serve with Roasted Potatoes (page 265) and steamed green beans or broccoli.

In a large frying pan over high heat, warm 2 tablespoons of the olive oil. Season the tuna with salt and pepper. Add to the pan and sear over high heat, turning once, just until golden, about 3 minutes. Transfer to a plate and set aside.

Add the remaining 2 tablespoons oil to the pan and reduce the heat to medium-high. Add the onion and sauté until softened, 3–4 minutes. Add the garlic and sauté for 30 seconds. Stir in the tomatoes, wine, red pepper flakes, olives, and capers. Cover and simmer to blend the flavors, for about 5 minutes. Stir in the pine nuts.

Return the tuna to the pan, spooning the sauce over it. Cook the tuna, occasionally spooning the sauce over it, until it is opaque throughout and the sauce is slightly reduced, 7–10 minutes.

Transfer the tuna steaks and sauce to warmed plates and sprinkle with the basil. Serve at once.

4 tablespoons (2 fl oz/60 ml) olive oil

4 tuna steaks, each about 6 oz (185 g) and ¾ inch (2 cm) thick

Salt and freshly ground pepper

1 yellow onion, thinly sliced

3 large cloves garlic, minced

1 can (14½ oz/455 g) diced tomatoes

½ cup (4 fl oz/125 ml) full-bodied red wine such as merlot

⅛ teaspoon red pepper flakes

⅓ cup (2 oz/60 g) pitted small green or black olives, or a combination

1 tablespoon small capers, rinsed and drained

2 tablespoons pine nuts, toasted

2 tablespoons finely shredded fresh basil

Japanese Braised Salmon

3 tablespoons canola oil

½ cup (4 fl oz/125 ml) vegetable broth

⅓ cup (3 fl oz/80 ml) mirin

¼ cup (2 fl oz/60 ml) sake

2 tablespoons white miso

2 tablespoons soy sauce

1 tablespoon chopped fresh ginger

2 green (spring) onions, white and pale green parts, thinly sliced

4 salmon fillets, each about 6 oz (185 g) and 1 inch (2.5 cm) thick

1 tablespoon rice vinegar

8 cups (5 oz/155 g) mixed assertive greens such as frisée, arugula (rocket), and spinach

2 tablespoons chopped fresh cilantro (fresh coriander)

In a large frying pan over low heat, warm 1 tablespoon of the canola oil. Add the broth, mirin, sake, miso, soy sauce, and remaining 2 tablespoons oil and stir to combine. Stir in the ginger and green onions. Add the salmon fillets and turn to coat.

Raise the heat to medium, cover, and cook until the salmon is opaque throughout, 12–15 minutes. Transfer to a plate and cover to keep warm. Measure out 4 tablespoons (2 fl oz/60 ml) of the cooking liquid and set aside. Raise the heat to high and cook the remaining liquid until it measures about ¾ cup (6 fl oz/ 180 ml). Stir in the vinegar.

In a bowl, toss the greens with the reserved cooking liquid. Transfer the greens to a warmed serving platter and top with the salmon. Drizzle with the reduced cooking liquid and sprinkle with the cilantro. Serve at once.

Miso, mirin, and sake are all highly flavored ingredients and need a strong fish such as salmon for balance. Place the fish atop a bed of mixed greens or Steamed Jasmine Rice (page 262). The cooking liquid is used as a vinaigrette for a warm main-course salad.

Calamari Fra Diavolo

Fra diavolo, meaning "brother devil," aptly describes this Italian classic with its peppery red sauce, which originated in the northeastern United States, not in Italy. The sauce can feature meatballs, clams, or even vegetables. Here, squid takes center stage in a cooking method especially well suited to keep the squid tender and moist. Serve over linguine or accompany with crusty bread.

In a small Dutch oven over medium heat, warm the olive oil. Add the onion and sauté until tender and golden, about 5 minutes. Add the garlic and sauté for 30 seconds. Stir in the tomatoes, breaking them up with the back of a spoon. Add the broth, wine, 2 tablespoons of the oregano, and the red pepper flakes. Reduce the heat to medium-low and cook, uncovered, until the sauce is lightly thickened and the flavors have blended, 15–20 minutes.

Add the squid, cover, reduce the heat to low, and cook until very tender, 25–30 minutes. Stir in the remaining 1 tablespoon oregano and the parsley. Season to taste with salt and pepper. Serve at once.

3 tablespoons olive oil

1 yellow onion, chopped

4 cloves garlic, minced

1 can (35 oz/1.1 kg) whole plum (Roma) tomatoes

½ cup (4 fl oz/125 ml) fish broth or bottled clam juice

½ cup (4 fl oz/125 ml) full-bodied red wine such as merlot

3 tablespoons chopped fresh oregano

½ teaspoon red pepper flakes

2½ lb (1.25 kg) cleaned squid, bodies cut into ½-inch (12-mm) rings and tentacles coarsely chopped

⅓ cup (½ oz/15 g) chopped fresh flat-leaf (Italian) parsley

Salt and freshly ground pepper

Indian Fish Curry

⅓ cup (3 fl oz/80 ml) canola oil

1 yellow onion, finely chopped

2 cloves garlic, minced

2 small, fresh, hot green chiles, seeded and minced

1-inch (2.5-cm) piece fresh ginger, peeled and grated

1 tablespoon ground cumin

2 teaspoons ground coriander

2 teaspoons brown mustard seeds

2 teaspoons ground turmeric

2 tomatoes, chopped

1 tablespoon sugar

Salt

2 lb (1 kg) firm, mild white fish fillets such as tilapia, cod, or halibut, cut into 1-inch (2.5-cm) chunks

3 tablespoons chopped fresh cilantro (fresh coriander)

In a large frying pan over medium-high heat, warm the oil. Add the onion and sauté until it starts to turn golden, 5–7 minutes. Stir in the garlic, chiles, ginger, cumin, coriander, mustard seeds, and turmeric and sauté until the spices are fragrant and evenly coat the chopped onion, about 1 minute. Add the tomatoes, sugar, and 1 teaspoon salt and sauté until the tomatoes begin to release their juices. Pour in 1½ cups (12 fl oz/375 ml) water and deglaze the pan, stirring and scraping up the browned bits on the bottom of the pan with a wooden spoon.

STOVE TOP: Transfer the tomato-spice mixture to a large Dutch oven. Partially cover and cook over low heat for about 15 minutes. Uncover and add the fish, stirring gently to coat with the sauce. Partially cover and cook until the fish is opaque throughout and the sauce is thick, about 30 minutes longer. Check the sauce halfway through the cooking time; if it seems to be getting too thick, stir in more water, about ½ cup (4 fl oz/125 ml) at a time. Season to taste with salt.

SLOW COOKER: Transfer the tomato-spice mixture to a slow cooker. Cover and cook for 2 hours on the low-heat setting. Uncover and add the fish, stirring gently to coat with the sauce. Cover and cook until the fish is opaque throughout and the sauce is thick, about 30 minutes longer. Check the sauce halfway through the cooking time; if it seems to be getting too thick, stir in more water, about ½ cup (4 fl oz/125 ml) at a time. Season to taste with salt.

Transfer the curry to warmed bowls and garnish with the cilantro. Serve at once.

Vivid yellow from turmeric and brightly seasoned from a medley of spices, this fish curry is typical of those found in the eastern Indian province of Bengal. The fish itself needs very little time to cook, but slow advance simmering of the sauce helps develop the complex bouquet that flavors the mild seafood so agreeably.

New England Halibut Stew

Reminiscent of New England chowder, this hearty fish stew needs only a green salad and a basket of chowder biscuits or crusty flatbread to make a satisfying supper. For New England authenticity, you could add some clams.

In a Dutch oven over medium-high heat, sauté the bacon until crisp and golden, about 8 minutes. Transfer to a paper-towel lined plate and set aside. Add the onion, celery, carrots, and potatoes to the pot, raise the heat to medium-high, and sauté just until the vegetables are softened and golden, 3–4 minutes. Stir in 2 tablespoons of the thyme. Add the broth, cream, and wine, and bring to a gentle simmer. Stir in the reserved bacon.

Add the fish, cover, and cook until the fish is opaque throughout and the vegetables are tender, 10–12 minutes. Season to taste with salt and pepper. Ladle the stew into warmed bowls and garnish with the remaining 1 tablespoon thyme. Serve at once.

¼ lb (125 g) thick-sliced bacon, chopped

1 yellow onion, chopped

2 ribs celery, chopped

2 carrots, coarsely chopped

¾ lb (375 g) small red potatoes, diced

3 tablespoons chopped fresh thyme

1½ cups (12 fl oz/375 ml) vegetable broth or bottled clam juice

¾ cup (6 fl oz/180 ml) heavy (double) cream

½ cup (4 fl oz/125 ml) dry white wine such as sauvignon blanc

1½ lb (750 g) halibut fillets, cut into 2-inch (5-cm) pieces

Salt and freshly ground pepper

Portuguese Mussels

¼ cup (2 fl oz/60 ml) olive oil

½ lb (250 g) chourico, linguica, or other spicy cooked sausage, cut into ¼-inch (6 mm) sliced

1 yellow onion, chopped

1 green bell pepper (capsicum), seeded and chopped

4 cloves garlic, minced

2 teaspoons hot paprika

2 tablespoons chopped fresh marjoram

1 can (28 oz/875 g) whole plum (Roma) tomatoes

1 cup (8 fl oz/250 ml) dry white wine such as sauvignon blanc

Pinch of red pepper flakes

¼–½ teaspoon hot pepper sauce such as Tabasco

Salt and freshly ground pepper

2 lb (1 kg) mussels, scrubbed and debearded

2 tablespoons chopped fresh cilantro (fresh coriander)

2 tablespoons chopped fresh flat-leaf (Italian) parsley

In a large heavy-bottomed saucepan or Dutch oven over medium-high heat, warm the olive oil. Add the sausage, onion, and bell pepper, and cook, stirring often, until the vegetables are tender and the sausage is browned, 4–5 minutes. Add the garlic and paprika and cook, stirring, for 30 seconds. Stir in the marjoram, tomatoes, wine, red pepper flakes, and hot sauce. Bring to a simmer over medium heat, breaking up the tomatoes with the back of a spoon. Season with salt and pepper. Cook, uncovered, until the liquid is reduced by about one-third, 5–6 minutes.

Add the mussels to the pot, discarding any that do not close to the touch. Cover and cook over medium heat until the mussels open, 4–5 minutes. Discard any mussels that failed to open. Stir in the cilantro and parsley.

Transfer the mussels to a warmed serving bowl and serve at once.

The traditional cooking vessel for this Portuguese coastal classic is a *cataplana*, an oval metal pot that is hinged on one side and held together with clamps. A Dutch oven will work just as well. Small clams, such as Manila, can be used in place of the mussels or added to the mix. Portuguese *chourico* or linguica are the sausages of choice, though Spanish chorizo is a fine substitute. Adjust the hot pepper sauce to the heat of the sausage.

Sri Lankan Fish Stew

Coconut milk adds a soothing touch of the tropics to this mildly spiced dish, and tamarind paste contributes a sour-sweet flavor. You can make the stew with any mild, firm fish fillets, but rosy-hued salmon looks especially pretty in contrast to the creamy golden sauce.

In a large frying pan over medium heat, warm the canola the oil. Add the onion and garlic and sauté until they start to turn tender, about 3 minutes. Add the cayenne, coriander, turmeric, cumin, black pepper, fennel seeds, cinnamon, and cloves and sauté until the spices are fragrant and evenly coat the onion and garlic, about 30 seconds. Add the tomatoes and sauté until they start to release their juices, about 1 minute. Stir in the coconut milk, dissolved tamarind paste, sugar, and ³/₄ teaspoon salt. Bring to a boil and deglaze the pan, stirring and scraping up the browned bits on the bottom of the pan with a wooden spoon.

STOVE TOP: Transfer the coconut-milk mixture to a large, heavy-bottomed saucepan or Dutch oven. Partially cover and cook over low heat for 25 minutes. Uncover and add the fish. Partially cover and cook until the fish is flaky but still very moist and the sauce is thickened, about 20 minutes longer.

SLOW COOKER: Transfer the coconut-milk mixture to a slow cooker. Cook until the sauce is thick but still fluid, 3 hours on the low-heat setting. Uncover and add the fish. Cover and cook until the fish is flaky but still very moist and the sauce is thickened, about 30 minutes longer.

Transfer the fish and sauce to warmed plates and serve at once.

2 tablespoons canola oil

1 yellow onion, chopped

3 cloves garlic, minced

¹/₂ teaspoon cayenne pepper

¹/₂ teaspoon ground coriander

¹/₂ teaspoon ground turmeric

¹/₄ teaspoon ground cumin

¹/₄ teaspoon freshly ground black pepper

¹/₄ teaspoon fennel seeds

Pinch of ground cinnamon

Pinch of ground cloves

2 tomatoes, chopped

1 can (13¹/₂ oz/420 ml) unsweetened coconut milk

1 tablespoon tamarind paste dissolved in 3 tablespoons warm water

1 teaspoon sugar

Salt

2 lb (1 kg) halibut, salmon, or sea bass fillets, cut into serving pieces

Tuna Steaks with Cannellini Beans

2 cups (14 oz/440 g) dried
cannellini beans

4 tablespoons (2 fl oz/60 ml)
olive oil

4 teaspoons chopped fresh
rosemary

Salt and freshly ground
pepper

4 tuna steaks, each about
6 oz (185 g) and ¾ inch
(2 cm) thick

1 red bell pepper (capsicum),
seeded and coarsely chopped

1 yellow onion, coarsely
chopped

4 cloves garlic, minced

⅔ cup (5 fl oz/160 ml)
dry white wine such as
sauvignon blanc

1½ cups (12 fl oz/375 ml)
vegetable broth

Pick over the beans, removing any misshapen beans or grit. Rinse under cold running water. Put the beans in a bowl, add enough cold water to cover by at least 2 inches (5 cm), and let stand at room temperature overnight. Alternatively, for a quick soak, put the beans in a saucepan, add enough water to cover by at least 2 inches, bring to a boil, remove from the heat, cover, and let soak for 1 hour. Drain and rinse the beans.

In a large saucepan, combine the beans with enough cold water to cover by 1–2 inches (2.5–5 cm). Bring to a boil over high heat, reduce the heat to low, partially cover, and simmer gently until the beans are very tender, about 2 hours. Drain and set aside.

In a large frying pan over medium-high heat, warm 2 tablespoons of the olive oil. In a small bowl, stir together 2 teaspoons of the rosemary, ½ teaspoon salt, and ½ teaspoon pepper. Season the tuna on both sides with the rosemary mixture. Add the tuna to the pan and sear, turning once, until lightly browned on each side, about 5 minutes total. Transfer to a plate and set aside.

Add the remaining 2 tablespoons oil to the pan and reduce the heat to medium. Add the bell pepper and onion and sauté until the onion is barely tender, 3–4 minutes. Add the garlic and sauté for 30 seconds. Add the beans, wine, broth, and remaining 2 teaspoons rosemary. Cover, reduce the heat to medium-low, and cook until the flavors begin to blend, about 10 minutes. Arrange the tuna on top of the beans, cover, and cook until opaque throughout, 8–10 minutes. Season to taste with salt and pepper.

Transfer to the tuna steaks to a cutting board and slice on the bias. Divide the beans among warmed plates and top each serving with an equal amount of tuna. Serve at once.

Creamy cannellini beans, a type of white kidney bean, is the perfect accompaniment to a meaty fish such as tuna. After a quick searing, the tuna is cooked with the beans just long enough to infuse the beans. If you wish, add one or two rosemary sprigs to the pot when you cook the beans.

Brazilian Seafood Stew

Assembled in layers, this spicy-and-sweet stew seems like a metaphor for Brazil's medley of cultures. If you prefer, substitute large, ripe-but-firm bananas for the less sweet, blander plantains. Serve over steamed white rice.

Combine the fish and scallops in a nonreactive bowl. Squeeze the juice from the lime wedges over the fish and scallops, add the wedges to the bowl, and toss gently. Cover with plastic wrap and marinate in the refrigerator for 30 minutes.

Meanwhile, in a large frying pan over medium-high heat, warm the olive oil. Add the onion and garlic and sauté until they start to turn tender, about 3 minutes. Add the tomatoes, bell pepper, red pepper flakes, 1 1/2 teaspoons salt, and 1/2 teaspoon pepper, and sauté until the tomatoes begin release their juices and the peppers start to soften, 3–5 minutes.

STOVE TOP: Transfer the tomato mixture to a large Dutch oven. Arrange the fish and scallops on top, nestling them into the mixture. Neatly arrange the plantain and yam slices over the seafood, overlapping them. Pour the coconut milk evenly over the top, then sprinkle with the brown sugar and cilantro. Partially cover and cook over low heat until the fish is opaque throughout and the plantains and yams are tender, 45–60 minutes.

SLOW COOKER: Transfer the tomato mixture to a slow cooker. Arrange the fish and scallops on top, nestling them into the mixture. Neatly arrange the plantain and yam slices over the seafood, overlapping them. Pour the coconut milk evenly over the top, then sprinkle with the brown sugar and cilantro. Cover and cook until the fish is opaque throughout and the plantains and yams are tender, 2 hours on the high-heat setting or 4 hours on the low-heat setting.

Arrange the layers of fruit, seafood, and vegetables in warmed bowls and serve at once.

1 lb (500 g) firm white fish fillets such as Chilean sea bass, black cod, or halibut, cut into 1 1/2-inch (4-cm) chunks

1 lb (500 g) large sea scallops

1 lime, cut into wedges

2 tablespoons olive oil

1 large yellow onion, finely chopped

3 cloves garlic, minced

2 large tomatoes, chopped

1 yellow bell pepper (capsicum), seeded and chopped

1/2 teaspoon red pepper flakes

Salt and freshly ground pepper

2 large, ripe plantains, peeled and thinly sliced on the diagonal

1 large yam, peeled and thinly sliced on the diagonal

1 can (13 1/2 fl oz/420 ml) unsweetened coconut milk

2 tablespoons firmly packed dark brown sugar

3/4 cup (3/4 oz/20 g) coarsely chopped fresh cilantro (fresh coriander)

Vietnamese Clay Pot Fish

½ cup (4 oz/125 g) sugar

¼ cup (2 fl oz/60 ml) canola oil

3 cloves garlic, minced

3 shallots, minced

1-inch (2.5-cm) piece fresh ginger, peeled and grated

2 small fresh red or green Thai chiles or other small hot chiles, halved lengthwise, seeded, and thinly sliced

¼ cup (2 fl oz/60 ml) fish sauce (see note)

¼ cup (2 fl oz/60 ml) soy sauce

2 lb (1 kg) firm, mild white fish fillets such as black cod, halibut, or Chilean sea bass, cut into 1-inch (2.5-cm) chunks

Freshly ground pepper

In a small, heavy-bottomed saucepan over medium-high heat, combine the sugar and ¼ cup (2 fl oz/60 ml) water. Cook, stirring occasionally, until the sugar melts. Bring to a boil, stirring frequently, until the mixture turns caramel brown, 12–15 minutes. Watch carefully so that it doesn't burn. Remove from the heat and, taking care to avoid splatters, stir in ¼ cup water until thoroughly blended. Set aside.

In a large frying pan over medium-high heat, warm the oil. Add the garlic, shallots, ginger, and chiles and sauté until just tender, 1–2 minutes. Stir in the fish sauce, soy sauce, reserved caramel, and 1 cup (8 fl oz/250 ml) water. Bring to a boil, stirring occasionally.

STOVE TOP: Transfer the caramel mixture to a large Dutch oven. Partially cover and cook over low heat until the sauce is syrupy but still very fluid, about 15 minutes. If the sauce becomes too thick, stir in ½ cup (4 fl oz/125 ml) water. Uncover and add the fish chunks, gently turning to coat with the sauce. Cover and cook, turning the fish once at the midway point, until opaque throughout, about 15 minutes longer. Season with salt and pepper.

SLOW COOKER: Transfer the caramel mixture to a slow cooker. Cover and cook until the sauce is syrupy but still very fluid, 1–1½ hours on the low-heat setting. If the sauce gets too thick, stir in ½ cup (4 fl oz/125 ml) water. Uncover and add the fish chunks, gently turning to coat with the sauce. Cover and cook, turning the fish once at the midway point, until opaque throughout, about 25 minutes longer. Season with pepper.

Transfer the fish and sauce to warmed plates and serve at once.

In this Vietnamese classic, two seemingly contradictory flavors—intensely sweet caramel and briny fish sauce—reach a pleasing harmony by gently simmering together, along with aromatic seasonings. Fish fillets, added during the final minutes of cooking, not only soak up the flavors but also acquire a deep, glossy mahogany color. Look for Vietnamese fish sauce, made from anchovies and called *nuoc mam*, in Asian markets or well-stocked food stores; similar Thai fish sauce, called *nam pla*, may also be used.

Cioppino

This famous San Francisco fisherman's stew has as many recipes as there are good cooks and restaurants in the city. Most include local Dungeness crab, but beyond that the seafood additions depend on the catch of the day and the whim of the cook. Following this philosophy, use whatever seafood is best in your area. If you can't find Dungeness crab, which is usually available outside Northern California already cooked, substitute good fresh lump crabmeat.

In a large Dutch oven over medium heat, warm the olive oil. Add the onions and bell peppers and sauté until just tender, 4–5 minutes. Add the garlic and sauté for 30 seconds. Add the bay leaves, tomatoes, and red and white wines, and bring to a simmer. Partially cover, reduce the heat to medium-low, and cook until thickened slightly, about 15 minutes.

Remove and discard the bay leaves. Add the oregano, thyme, fish, and clams, discarding any clams that do not close to the touch. Cover and cook over medium-low heat for 5 minutes. Add the crab and shrimp, cover, and cook until the shrimp and fish are opaque throughout and the clams have opened, 3–4 minutes. Discard any clams that failed to open. Stir in the hot sauce and season to taste with salt and pepper.

Divide among warmed bowls and serve at once.

¼ cup (2 fl oz/60 ml) olive oil

2 yellow onions, chopped

2 red bell peppers (capsicums), seeded and chopped

4 cloves garlic, minced

2 bay leaves, broken in half

2 cans (14½ oz/455 g each) diced tomatoes

¾ cup (6 fl oz/180 ml) dry red wine such as Chianti

½ cup (4 fl oz/125 ml) dry white wine such as sauvignon blanc

2 tablespoons chopped fresh oregano

2 tablespoons chopped fresh thyme

¾ lb (375 g) firm white fish fillets such as halibut or monkfish, cut into 1-inch (2.5-cm) chunks

1 lb (500 g) littleneck or other small clams, scrubbed

1 lb (500 g) Dungeness crab claws, or ½ lb (250 g) Dungeness or other lump crabmeat, picked over for shells

20 large shrimp (prawns), peeled and deveined

¼–½ teaspoon hot pepper sauce such as Tabasco

Salt and freshly ground pepper

Poultry

About Poultry

Slow Cooked chicken and duck are ingredients in some long time favorite dishes such as chicken with dumplings, chicken fricassee, and braised duck. When available, always look for organic or free-range chickens, as the texture and flavor do make a difference.

In the United States, poultry sold in retail outlets has been visually inspected for wholesomeness by a mandatory system run by the United States Department of Agriculture (USDA). In addition, some processors choose to have their chickens (and most other birds) graded by the USDA for appearance and meatiness.

Whole birds should look plump, and their skin should be free of discoloration or feathers. The color of the skin depends on the breed and on the diet. Most poultry skin is naturally white, but some growers feed their chickens marigold petals, for example, which give the skin a yellow tint that appeals to many consumers. Skinless cuts should look plump and moist.

Raw poultry labeled "fresh" has never been chilled below 26°F (−4°C), the temperature at which flesh freezes solid. Poultry stored at 0°F (−18°C) or less is labeled "frozen" or "previously frozen." No labeling is required for poultry that is held at temperatures between these two extremes. So if unfrozen poultry is important to you, make sure it says "fresh" on the label. Any liquid you see in the package is usually water that was absorbed by the bird when it was chilled during processing.

Today's chickens are a lot more tender than the farmyard hens and roosters that used to end up in the pot for Sunday dinner. The tough birds that were the original ingredients of traditional chicken recipes such as Summer Coq au Vin (page 145) required long and slow cooking. Favorite poultry recipes like Braised Garlic Chicken (page 123), Chicken Fricasse with Wild Mushroom (page 139), Chicken Adobo (page 120), and Chicken and Sausage Gumbo (page 124) were originally slow-cooked and savory braises designed to make tough old hens and well-muscled roosters succulent and tender. These days we slow-cook chicken for the complex, rich flavors of these old fashioned recipes. Using today's slow cooking techniques we can easily make the old time recipes and put these traditional favorites back on our tables with a minimum of fuss and bother.

When you purchase chicken these days, I think it's worth it to pay a little more for organic and free range birds. They really do have more flavor and don't have the hormones and additives of mass produced poultry. Some cooks prefer to remove the skin before cooking chicken to reduce the fat level of the finished dish. And it is healthier, I suppose. But I love the color, taste, and texture that skin gives to a braised or slow roasted chicken.

Braised duck is absolutely delicious, luscious and tender, with an intense flavor and toothsome texture. But there is the problem of the high fat content. So when you braise duck, be sure to remove all visible fat before you brown it. Taking off the skin is an option, of course, but the taste of the duck's skin really does add to the flavor of the dish. After you brown the duck, it's important to pour off almost all the fat, leaving just a little for browning the aromatics. When the dish is finished and before you thicken the sauce, skim off all the fat you can from the surface of the sauce. Follow the directions in our Braised Duck Legs with Port (page 121), Duck Ragù (page 140) or Allspice Duck with Braised Bok Choy (page 110).

If you can, make braised chicken or duck the day before you intend to eat it and refrigerate it overnight. This allows you to remove the fat congealed on the surface and the dish taste even better when you reheat and serve it.

USING POULTRY IN SLOW COOKING

You have a lot of choices in today's market for poultry. You can buy a whole bird and cut it up yourself into serving pieces. Or you can buy a cut up chicken or whatever amounts you want of various pieces. Many cooks prefer to buy only breasts and thighs without having to deal with wings and backs and this is certainly convenient. Others prefer to include the whole cut up bird in the stew or braise.

And then there's the question of skin mentioned above. You can buy bone-in chicken breasts with skin or boneless, skinless breasts, bone-in legs and thighs with skin or boneless, skinless chicken thighs. It's your and your family's choice. Our recipes give specific suggestions here, but follow your own preferences.

When buying duck for braising, however, don't buy the whole duck and try to cut it up yourself. It's too complicated and there is just too much waste. If you want roast duck, then of course buy the whole bird. But for a braise, buy duck breasts and legs with thighs attached. Purchase boneless Musccovy duck breasts (which the French call magrets) when you can find them. They are meatier and have less fat than the most common domestic duck, the Peking.

Chicken with Shallots and Balsamic Vinegar

Shallots are most often used minced, in salad dressings, marinades, or sauces. The purple-hued bulb has a flavor somewhere between onion and garlic and is slow-cooked whole in this recipe. Red wine and balsamic vinegar provide an acidic touch that marries well with the sweetness of the shallots. Don't let the amount of shallots used here alarm you. Shallots lose much of their potency once cooked. Halved Cornish game hens can be used in place of the chicken.

Using a paring knife, cut a shallow X in the root end of each shallot. Set aside.

Season the chicken all over with salt and pepper. In a large, deep frying pan over medium-high heat, melt the butter with the canola oil. Working in batches if necessary, add the chicken and cook, turning frequently, until browned, about 5 minutes. Remove from the pan and set aside.

Pour off all but 2 tablespoons of the fat in the pan. Add the shallots and sauté over medium-high heat until lightly browned, about 5 minutes. Add the wine, broth, and vinegar. Raise the heat to high, bring to a boil, and deglaze the pan, stirring and scraping up the browned bits on the bottom pf the pan with a wooden spoon.

STOVE TOP: Transfer the chicken to a large Dutch oven and add the shallot mixture. Cover and cook over medium-low heat until the chicken is tender and opaque throughout, about 40 minutes. Uncover, raise the heat to high, bring to a boil, and cook, turning the chicken and the shallots occasionally to prevent scorching, until the liquid has thickened slightly, 5–10 minutes.

SLOW COOKER: Transfer the chicken to a slow cooker and add the shallot mixture. Cover and cook until the chicken is tender and opaque throughout, 3 hours on the high-heat setting or 6 hours on the low-heat setting. Uncover, set the temperature to the high setting if necessary, and cook, stirring often, until the liquid has thickened slightly, about 15 minutes.

Transfer the chicken and shallots to a warmed platter and top with any remaining sauce. Serve at once.

2 lb (1 kg) shallots

1 chicken, about 2 lb (1 kg), cut into serving pieces

Salt and freshly ground pepper

2 tablespoons unsalted butter

2 tablespoons canola oil

¼ cup (2 fl oz/60 ml) dry red wine such as Burgundy

½ cup (4 fl oz/125 ml) chicken broth

¼ cup (2 fl oz/60 ml) balsamic vinegar

Allspice Duck with Braised Bok Choy

3 tablespoons canola oil

Salt and freshly ground pepper

4 lb (2 kg) boneless duck breasts, trimmed of excess skin and fat

2 yellow onions, finely chopped

2 cloves garlic, minced

1-inch (2.5-cm) piece fresh ginger, peeled and grated

1½ tablespoons ground allspice

1 cinnamon stick, 3 inches (7.5 cm)

1 star anise, broken into pieces

1½ cups (12 fl oz/375 ml) chicken broth

¼ cup (2 oz/60 g) firmly packed dark brown sugar

¼ cup (2 fl oz/60 ml) soy sauce

3 tablespoons hoisin sauce

6 baby bok choy, about 2 lb (1 kg) total weight, each cut lengthwise into quarters

In a large frying pan over medium-high heat, warm the canola oil. In a small bowl, combine 1½ teaspoons salt and 1 teaspoon pepper. Rub the mixture all over the duck breasts. Place in the pan, skin side down, and cook until well browned, 4–5 minutes per side. Remove from the pan and set aside.

Pour off all but a thin coating of fat in the pan. Add the onions, garlic, ginger, allspice, cinnamon, and star anise and sauté over medium-high heat until the onions begin to soften, about 3 minutes. Add the broth and deglaze the pan, stirring and scraping up the browned bits on the bottom of the pan with a wooden spoon. Stir in the sugar, soy sauce, and hoisin sauce and bring to a boil.

STOVE TOP: Transfer the duck breasts to a large Dutch oven. Pour the broth mixture over the duck. Partially cover and cook over very low heat for 1 hour. Uncover and use a large, shallow spoon or a ladle to skim as much fat as possible from the surface. Arrange the bok choy around the duck breasts, pushing it slightly into the cooking liquid. Partially cover and cook until the duck is very tender and the sauce is thick, about 30 minutes longer.

SLOW COOKER: Transfer the duck breasts to a slow cooker. Pour the broth mixture over the duck. Cover and cook until the duck is very tender and the sauce is thick, 2 hours on the high-heat setting or 4½ hours on the low-heat setting. Uncover and use a large shallow spoon or a ladle to skim as much fat as possible from the surface. Arrange the bok choy around the duck breasts, pushing it slightly into the cooking liquid. Cover and cook until the duck is very tender and the sauce is thick, about 30 minutes longer.

Slice the duck breasts on the diagonal and arrange the slices on warmed plates with the bok choy. Spoon any remaining sauce on top and serve at once.

Duck is a popular banquet dish at Asian meals. Slow cooking duck breasts with sweet and savory spices beautifully complements their rich flavor and texture. Serve with Steamed Jasmine Rice (page 262).

Chicken and Dumplings

You can easily make this dish over a couple of days. The first day, cook the chicken and strain the broth, then refrigerate the broth and chicken overnight. The fat will congeal on top, making it easy to remove, and pulling the meat off the bones will be a snap. Make the sauce in advance if desired, but leave mixing the dumpling dough until the last minute.

STOVE TOP: Place the chicken in a large Dutch oven. Pour in enough cold water to cover by 1 inch (2.5 cm) and add the carrots, onion, celery, and bay leaf. Bring to a boil over high heat. Reduce the heat to medium, partially cover, and simmer gently until the chicken is falling off the bones, about 2 hours. Remove from the pot and set aside to cool. When the chicken is cool enough to handle, remove the meat and shred into large pieces.

Strain the broth into a large saucepan and wipe the Dutch oven clean. Bring to a boil, reduce the heat to medium-high, and cook until reduced to 6 cups (48 fl oz/1.5 l), about 10 minutes.

In the Dutch oven over medium-high heat, melt the butter. Add the flour and whisk until smooth. Pour in the reduced broth, raise the heat to high, and bring to a boil. Cook, whisking constantly, until smooth and thickened, 8–10 minutes. Add the chicken and season with salt and pepper. Reduce the heat to medium-high and keep at a steady simmer.

SLOW COOKER: Place the chicken in a slow cooker. Pour in enough cold water to cover by 1 inch (2.5 cm) and add the carrots, onion, celery, and bay leaf. Cover and cook until the chicken is falling off the bones, 3–4 hours on the high-heat setting or 6–7 hours on the low-heat setting. Remove from the cooker and set aside to cool. When the chicken is cool enough to handle, remove the meat and shred into large pieces.

Strain the broth into a large saucepan. Bring to a boil, reduce the heat to medium-high, and cook until reduced to 6 cups (48 fl oz/1.5 l), about 10 minutes.

In a large saucepan over medium-high heat, melt the butter. Add the flour and whisk until smooth. Pour in the reduced broth, raise the heat to high, and bring to a boil. Cook, whisking constantly, until smooth and thickened, 8–10 minutes. Add the chicken and season with salt and pepper. Transfer to the slow cooker and set the temperature to high.

Make the dumplings: In a bowl, stir together the flour, baking powder, parsley, and 1/2 teaspoon salt. Add the butter and, using your fingers or a pastry cutter, work the butter into the dry ingredients until the mixture has the texture of small peas. Gently stir in the milk and egg to form a sticky batter. Drop heaping spoonfuls of the dough into the simmering sauce and chicken, reduce the heat to low, cover, and cook until the dumplings are fluffy, about 15 minutes on the stove top and 30 minutes in the slow cooker.

1 chicken, 3 1/2–4 lb (1.75–2 kg), trimmed of excess skin and fat

2 carrots, cut into 1-inch (2.5-cm) pieces

1 yellow onion, quartered

1 rib celery, cut into 2-inch (5-cm) pieces

1 bay leaf

4 tablespoons (2 oz/60 g) unsalted butter

1/4 cup (1 1/2 oz/45 g) all-purpose (plain) flour

Salt and freshly ground pepper

For the Dumplings

1 1/2 cups (7 1/2 oz/235 g) all-purpose (plain) flour

3 teaspoons baking powder

2 tablespoons flat-leaf (Italian) parsley

Salt

2 tablespoons unsalted butter, cut into small pieces and chilled

1/2 cup (4 fl oz/125 ml) milk

1 egg

Vietnamese Chicken Curry

3 tablespoons canola oil

3 lb (1.5 kg) skinless,
bone-in chicken thighs

3 cloves garlic, minced

2 shallots, minced

3 tablespoons Madras-style
curry powder

1 tablespoon firmly packed
dark brown sugar

1 teaspoon red pepper flakes

Freshly ground pepper

2 lemongrass stalks, trimmed
and cut into 1-inch (2.5-cm)
pieces

1-inch (2.5-cm) piece fresh
ginger, peeled and cut into
4 slices

1 cup (8 fl oz/250 ml)
chicken broth

1 can (13½ fl oz/420 ml)
unsweetened coconut milk

2 tablespoons fish sauce

3 carrots, cut into 1-inch
(2.5-cm) chunks

1 sweet potato, about ¾ lb
(375 g), peeled and cut into
1-inch (2. 5-cm) chunks

3 tablespoons finely shredded
fresh basil

In a large frying pan over medium-high heat, warm the canola oil. Working in batches if necessary, cook the chicken thighs until nicely browned, about 4 minutes per side. Remove from the pan and set aside.

Add the garlic and shallots to the pan and sauté over medium-high heat just until fragrant, about 30 seconds. Add the curry powder, brown sugar, red pepper flakes, 1 teaspoon pepper, the lemongrass, and ginger and sauté until the spices are fragrant and well blended with the garlic and shallots, about 30 seconds. Add the broth and deglaze the pan, stirring and scraping up the browned bits on the bottom of the pan with a wooden spoon. Stir in the coconut milk and fish sauce and bring to a boil.

STOVE TOP: Transfer the coconut-milk mixture to a large Dutch oven. Add the chicken thighs, carrots, and sweet potato, pushing them into the mixture. Partially cover and cook over low heat until the chicken is opaque throughout and the chicken and vegetables are very tender, about 1 hour.

SLOW COOKER: Transfer the coconut-milk mixture to a slow cooker. Add the chicken thighs, carrots, and sweet potato, pushing them into the mixture. Cover and cook until the chicken is opaque throughout and the chicken and vegetables are very tender, 3 hours on the high-heat setting and 6 hours on the low-heat setting.

Transfer the chicken, vegetables, and sauce to a warmed platter. Garnish with the basil and serve at once.

Like many curries of Southeast Asia, those of Vietnam show a strong tropical influence, evident here in the use of coconut milk as the primary cooking liquid. Steamed Jasmine Rice (page 262) is an excellent side dish.

Chicken Tagine with Olives and Lemon

The colorful Moroccan stew offers a tantalizing combination of spicy, sweet, salty, and tangy flavors. For the most authentic presentation, serve it on a platter or individual plates atop a bed of Couscous (page 261), the steamed Moroccan grain-sized pasta.

On a plate, stir together the flour, 1 teaspoon salt, and $^{1}/_{2}$ teaspoon pepper. Turn the chicken pieces in the seasoned flour, shaking off any excess. In a large frying pan over medium-high heat, warm the olive oil. Working in batches if necessary, and cook, turning often, until golden brown, about 10 minutes. Remove from the pan and set aside.

Add the onion and garlic to the pan and sauté over medium-high heat for about 30 seconds. Add the paprika, cumin, ginger, cinnamon, and coriander and sauté until the spices are fragrant and evenly coat the onion-garlic mixture, about 1 minute. Add the broth-saffron mixture and deglaze the pan, stirring and scraping up the browned bits on the bottom of the with a wooden spoon. Bring to a boil.

STOVE TOP: Transfer the broth mixture to a large Dutch oven. Add the chicken pieces, arranging the thighs on the bottom and the breasts on top. Cover and cook over low heat until the chicken is tender and opaque throughout, about 1 $^{1}/_{2}$ hours. About 30 minutes before the chicken is done, scatter the olives over the chicken and sprinkle with the lemon juice and zest.

SLOW COOKER: Transfer the broth mixture to a slow cooker. Add the chicken pieces, arranging the thighs on the bottom and the breasts on top. Cover and cook until the chicken is tender and opaque throughout, 2 $^{1}/_{2}$–3 hours on the high-heat setting or 5–6 hours on the low-heat setting. About 1 hour before the chicken is done, scatter the olives over the chicken and sprinkle with the lemon juice and zest.

Transfer the chicken to warmed plates, garnish with the mint, and serve at once.

3 tablespoons all-purpose (plain) flour

Salt and freshly ground pepper

3 tablespoons olive oil

3$^{1}/_{2}$ lb (1.75 kg) skinless, bone-in chicken breasts and thighs

1 yellow onion, finely chopped

4 cloves garlic, minced

2 teaspoons hot paprika

1 teaspoon ground cumin

1 teaspoon ground ginger

$^{1}/_{2}$ teaspoon ground cinnamon

$^{1}/_{2}$ teaspoon ground coriander

1$^{1}/_{2}$ cups (12 fl oz/375 ml) chicken broth

$^{1}/_{8}$ teaspoon saffron threads, crumbled and dissolved in the chicken broth

2 cups (8 oz/500 g) pitted green olives, coarsely chopped

$^{1}/_{4}$ cup (2 fl oz/60 ml) fresh lemon juice

2 tablespoons grated lemon zest

3 tablespoons finely chopped fresh mint

Chicken Korma

¼ cup (2 fl oz/60 ml) canola oil

1 yellow onion, finely chopped

2 cloves garlic, minced

2-inch (5-cm) piece fresh ginger, peeled and grated

2-inch (5-cm) piece cinnamon stick

2 bay leaves

1 tablespoon ground coriander

1 teaspoon ground turmeric

½ teaspoon cayenne pepper

½ teaspoon ground cumin

1½ cups (12 fl oz/375 ml) chicken broth

1 cup (8 fl oz/250 ml) canned tomato sauce

1 tablespoon sugar

Salt

2 lb (1 kg) skinless, boneless chicken breasts, cut into strips ½ inch (12 mm) wide

½ cup (4 fl oz/125 ml) buttermilk

½ cup (3 oz/90 g) roasted cashew nuts

3 tablespoons chopped fresh cilantro (fresh coriander)

In a large frying pan over medium-high heat, warm the canola oil. Add the onion and sauté until it begins to soften, about 3 minutes. Add the garlic, ginger, cinnamon, bay leaves, coriander, turmeric, cayenne, and cumin and sauté until the spices are fragrant and evenly coat the chopped onion, about 1 minute. Stir in the broth, tomato sauce, sugar, and 1 teaspoon salt and deglaze the pan, stirring and scraping up the browned bits on the bottom of the pan with a wooden spoon. Bring to a boil.

STOVE TOP: Transfer the broth-spice mixture to a large Dutch oven. Add the chicken strips and stir to coat. Partially cover and cook over low heat until the chicken is very tender and the sauce is thickened, about 1 hour.

SLOW COOKER: Transfer the broth-spice mixture to a slow cooker. Add the chicken strips and stir to coat. Cover and cook until the chicken is very tender and the sauce is thickened, 3 hours on the high-heat setting or 6 hours on the low-heat setting.

About 15 minutes before the chicken is done, combine the buttermilk and cashews in a blender or food processor. Blend or process until the nuts are finely puréed and combined with the buttermilk. Add to the chicken and stir to blend with the chicken and sauce. Continue cooking until the sauce is completely heated through and thick, about 5 minutes. Remove and discard the cinnamon and bay leaves.

Divide the chicken and sauce among warmed bowls, garnish with the cilantro, and serve at once.

One of the richest-tasting, yet mildest curries, this northern Indian specialty is beloved for its creamy sauce, which includes puréed cashew nuts. Different versions may use yogurt or cream as part of the final enrichment, but this recipe features buttermilk, a lighter, but no less authentic choice. Serve with steamed white rice to soak up the sauce.

Chicken Adobo

2 yellow onions, halved and thinly sliced

1-inch (2.5-cm) piece fresh ginger, peeled and cut into 4 slices

6 cloves garlic, crushed

3½ lb (1.75 kg) skinless, bone-in chicken thighs, trimmed of excess fat

Salt and freshly ground pepper

¾ cup (6 fl oz/180 ml) white wine vinegar

½ cup (4 fl oz/125 ml) soy sauce

1 tablespoon sugar

2 limes, cut into wedges

OVEN: Preheat the oven to 350°F (180°C). Evenly spread half of the onion slices in the bottom of a large Dutch oven. Top with the ginger and garlic, distributing them evenly. Arrange the chicken thighs in a single layer over the onions and seasonings. Sprinkle with 1 teaspoon pepper and ¼ teaspoon salt and top with the remaining onion slices. Drizzle with the vinegar and soy sauce and sprinkle with the sugar. Cover and cook until the onions are soft and the chicken is opaque throughout and very tender, about 2 hours.

SLOW COOKER: Evenly spread half of the onion slices in the bottom of a slow cooker. Top with the ginger and garlic, distributing them evenly. Arrange the chicken pieces in a single layer over the onions and seasonings. Sprinkle with 1 teaspoon pepper and ¼ teaspoon salt and cover the chicken evenly with the remaining onion slices. Drizzle with the vinegar and soy sauce, and sprinkle with the sugar. Cover and cook until the onions are soft and the chicken is opaque throughout and very tender, 4 hours on the high-heat setting or 8 hours on the low-heat setting.

Remove and discard the ginger and garlic cloves. Transfer the chicken and sauce to warmed plates. Serve at once with the lime wedges.

One of the classic dishes of the Philippines, adobo—which takes its name from the Spanish for "marinade"—combines both Iberian and Asian influences. If you like, include chicken breasts, although dark meat holds up better to the robust seasonings. Serve this easily assembled recipe with Saffron Risotto (page 263) to soak up the flavorful juices.

Braised Duck Legs with Port and Figs

Duck meat is so rich that it goes exceptionally well with intense fruity flavors such as those of port wine and figs. Since duck is very fatty, be sure to trim away as much visible fat as possible before cooking and to skim off all the liquid fat you can at the end of cooking. The duck can be prepared a day in advance and stored in the braising liquid. Before serving, remove all the solidified fat and reheat the duck in a Dutch oven, adding the figs and honey and continuing with the final step of reducing the sauce before serving.

In a small bowl, stir together the coriander, allspice, 1½ teaspoons salt, and ¾ teaspoon pepper. Rub the spice mixture all over the duck legs. In a large frying pan over high heat, warm the olive oil. Working in batches if necessary, add the duck legs, skin side down, and cook until brown, about 5 minutes per side. Remove from the pan and set aside.

Pour off most of the fat in the pan. Add the port, taking care to avoid splattering, and deglaze the pan, stirring and scraping up the browned bits on the bottom of the pan with a wooden spoon. Bring to a boil and cook until reduced by about half, about 10 minutes. Stir in the broth and bring to a boil.

OVEN: Preheat the oven to 325°F (165°C). Transfer the duck legs to a large Dutch oven. Pour the port mixture over the duck. Add the onion quarters, bay leaves, garlic, juniper berries, orange zest, rosemary, and thyme. Cover and cook for 1½ hours. Uncover and use a large, shallow spoon or a ladle to skim as much of the fat as possible from the surface. Immerse the dried figs in the cooking liquid around the duck legs and drizzle with the honey. Cover and cook until the duck is tender, about 30 minutes longer.

SLOW COOKER: Transfer the duck legs to a slow cooker. Pour the port mixture over the duck. Add the onion quarters, bay leaves, garlic, juniper berries, orange zest, rosemary, and thyme. Cover and cook for 2½ hours on the high-heat setting or 5½ hours on the low-heat setting. Uncover and use a large, shallow spoon or a ladle to skim as much of the fat as possible from the surface. Immerse the dried figs in the cooking liquid around the duck legs and drizzle with the honey. Cover and cook until the duck is tender, about 30 minutes longer.

Transfer the duck and dried figs to a warmed serving dish, and cover loosely with aluminum foil to keep warm. Pour the cooking liquid into a saucepan over medium-high heat and simmer briskly until reduced to a light syrupy consistency, about 10 minutes.

Divide the duck legs and figs among warmed plates. Spoon the sauce over and around the duck and garnish with the chives. Serve at once.

1½ teaspoons ground coriander

½ teaspoon ground allspice

Salt and freshly ground pepper

6 duck legs, trimmed of excess skin and fat

¼ cup (2 fl oz/60 ml) olive oil

1½ cups (12 fl oz/375 ml) ruby port

1 cup (8 fl oz/250 ml) chicken broth

1 yellow onion, quartered and each quarter stuck with 1 clove

2 bay leaves

2 cloves garlic, crushed

6 juniper berries, slightly crushed

3 strips orange zest, each about 4 inches (10 cm) long

2 teaspoons fresh rosemary leaves

2 teaspoons fresh thyme leaves

18 dried figs, halved

2 tablespoons honey

2 tablespoons chopped fresh chives

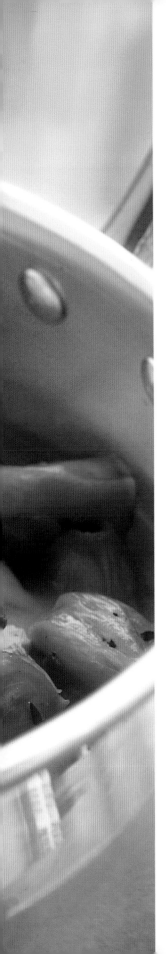

Braised Garlic Chicken

Four whole heads of garlic might sound excessive, but as it cooks, the garlic mellows and thickens, adding depth of flavor to the pan juices that are served over the chicken. There is no need to peel the garlic since it will be softened after cooking and then strained. The pulp of the cooked garlic imparts a wonderful flavor and helps thicken the sauce.

Season the chicken all over with salt and pepper. In a large frying pan over medium-high heat, warm the canola oil. Working in batches if necessary, add the chicken and cook, turning frequently, until well browned, 7–10 minutes. Remove from the pan and set aside.

Pour off all but 2 tablespoons of the fat in the pan. Add the garlic cloves and sauté over medium-high heat until lightly browned, about 3 minutes. Pour in the wine and deglaze the pan, stirring and scraping up the browned bits on the bottom of the pan with a wooden spoon.

STOVE TOP: Transfer the chicken to a Dutch oven. Sprinkle with the thyme and add the garlic mixture. Cover and cook until the chicken is tender and opaque throughout, about 45 minutes.

SLOW COOKER: Transfer the chicken to a slow cooker. Sprinkle with the thyme and add the garlic mixture. Cover and cook until the chicken is tender and opaque throughout, 3 hours on the low-heat setting.

Transfer the chicken to a platter and cover loosely with aluminum foil to keep warm. Set a fine-mesh sieve over a saucepan and strain the pan juices. Press on the garlic cloves to extract as much liquid and pulp as possible. Bring to a simmer over medium-high heat and season to taste with salt and pepper. Transfer the chicken to a warmed platter and top with the sauce. Serve at once.

1 chicken, 3–4 lb (1.5–2 kg), cut into 8 serving pieces, trimmed of excess skin and fat

Salt and freshly ground pepper

2 tablespoons canola oil

4 heads garlic, separated into cloves, unpeeled

¼ cup (2 fl oz/60 ml) dry white wine such as chardonnay or sauvignon blanc

1 tablespoon chopped fresh thyme

Chicken and Sausage Gumbo

1 chicken, 3–4 lb (1.5–2 kg),
cut into 8 serving pieces,
trimmed of excess skin
and fat

Salt and freshly ground black
pepper

2 tablespoons unsalted butter

2 tablespoons canola oil,
plus ⅓ cup (3 fl oz/80 ml)

1 yellow onion, finely
chopped

1 small green bell pepper
(capsicum), seeded and
chopped

1 small red bell pepper
(capsicum), seeded and
chopped

1 ribs celery, chopped

2 cloves garlic, minced

⅓ cup (2 oz/60 g)
all-purpose (plain) flour

3 cups (24 fl oz/750 ml)
chicken broth

¾ lb (375 g) Andouille or
other smoked sausage,
cut into slices ½ inch
(12 mm) thick

1 lb (500 g) okra, trimmed
and cut into slices ½ inch
(12 mm) thick

¼ teaspoon cayenne pepper

Season the chicken all over with salt and black pepper. In a frying pan over medium-high heat, melt the butter with the 2 tablespoons canola oil. Working in batches if necessary, add the chicken and cook, turning frequently, until browned, about 10 minutes. Remove from the pan and set aside.

Pour off all but 1 tablespoon of the fat in the pan. Add the onion, bell peppers, and celery and sauté over medium-high heat until softened, about 5 minutes. Add the garlic and cook for 1 minute longer. Set aside.

In a small, heavy saucepan over medium-high heat, warm the ⅓ cup oil. Add the flour and cook, whisking frequently, until the mixture turns light brown, about 5 minutes. Add the broth, raise the heat to high, bring to a boil, and cook, whisking constantly, until thickened, 5–7 minutes.

STOVE TOP: Pour the broth mixture into a Dutch oven. Add the chicken, the bell-pepper mixture, and the sausage. Cover and cook until the chicken is opaque throughout and the sausage is cooked through, about 45 minutes. Uncover and use a large, shallow spoon or a ladle to skim as much fat as possible from the service. Add the okra, cover, and cook until tender, about 10 minutes longer. Stir in the cayenne and season to taste with salt and black pepper.

SLOW COOKER: Pour the broth mixture into a slow cooker. Add the chicken, the bell-pepper mixture, and the sausage. Cover and cook until the chicken is opaque throughout and the sausage is cooked through, 2½–3½ hours on the high-heat setting or 5½–7½ hours on the low-heat setting. Uncover and use a large, shallow spoon or a ladle to skim as much fat as possible from the service. Add the okra, cover, and cook until tender, about 30 minutes longer. Stir in the cayenne and season to taste with salt and black pepper.

Divide the gumbo among warmed bowls. Serve at once.

Gumbo rivals jambalaya as the quintessential Creole classic. The stew has many variations but a common ingredient is okra, a vegetable that originated in Africa. Okra is prized not only for its earthy flavor but also for its ability to thicken a sauce or stew. Andouille is a spicy sausage that is considered another gumbo staple, although other fresh sausages are wonderful alternatives.

Chicken Cacciatore

Cacciatore means "hunter's style" in Italian. Here we use an old-fashioned preparation that once relied on the hunter bringing home the chicken to cook for dinner. Creamy Polenta (page 261) is a great accompaniment.

Season the chicken pieces all over with salt and pepper. In a nonreactive bowl, stir together 2 tablespoons of the olive oil, the lemon juice, garlic, and thyme. Add the chicken pieces and turn to coat. Cover and marinate in the refrigerator, turning the chicken frequently, for at least 1 hour or up to overnight.

Remove the chicken from the marinade and pat dry with paper towels; discard the marinade. In a large frying pan over medium-high heat, melt the butter with the remaining 1 tablespoon oil. Working in batches if necessary, add the chicken and cook, turning frequently, until browned, about 10 minutes. Remove from the pan and set aside.

Pour off all but 1 tablespoon of the fat in the pan and return to medium-high heat. Add the onion and sauté until softened, 3–5 minutes. Add the mushrooms and continue cooking, stirring often, until they begin to soften, 6–8 minutes. Stir in the tomatoes, capers, anchovy paste (if using), and broth. Raise the heat to high and deglaze the pan, stirring and scraping up the browned bits on the bottom of the pan with a wooden spoon. Bring to a boil.

OVEN: Preheat the oven to 350°F (180°C). Transfer the chicken to a Dutch oven and add the tomato mixture. Cover and cook in the oven until the chicken is tender and opaque throughout, about 45 minutes. Transfer the chicken to a platter and cover loosely with aluminum foil to keep warm. Bring the juices in the pot to a boil over high heat on the stove top. Boil rapidly until reduced and thickened, 3–5 minutes. Season to taste with salt and pepper.

SLOW COOKER: Transfer the chicken to a slow cooker and add the tomato mixture. Cover and cook until the chicken is tender and opaque throughout, 6 hours on the low-heat setting. Transfer the chicken to a platter and cover loosely with aluminum foil to keep warm. Set the temperature to the high setting, bring the juices to a strong simmer, and cook, uncovered, until reduced and thickened, 5–10 minutes. Season to taste with salt and pepper.

Transfer the chicken to a warmed platter, top with the sauce, and serve at once.

1 chicken, 3½–4 lb (1.75–2 kg), cut into 8 serving pieces, trimmed of excess skin and fat

Salt and freshly ground pepper

3 tablespoons olive oil

1 tablespoon fresh lemon juice

1 clove garlic, minced

1 tablespoon chopped fresh thyme

2 tablespoons unsalted butter

1 yellow onion, thinly sliced

½ lb (250 g) fresh mushrooms, brushed clean, stems removed, and large caps halved or quartered

1 can (28 oz/875 g) whole plum Roma tomatoes

2 tablespoons capers, rinsed, drained, and chopped

1 teaspoon anchovy paste (optional)

¼ cup (2 fl oz/60 ml) chicken broth

½ lb (250 g) fresh mushrooms, brushed clean, stems removed, and large caps halved or quartered

Chicken Marsala

3 tablespoons all-purpose (plain) flour

Salt and freshly ground pepper

3 tablespoons unsalted butter

3 tablespoons olive oil

6 skinless, boneless chicken breast halves, about 6 oz (185 g) each

4 shallots, minced

¼ lb (125 g) pancetta, diced

2¼ cups (18 fl oz/560 ml) Marsala

1 cup (8 fl oz/250 ml) chicken broth

2 teaspoons dried oregano

½ lb (250 g) cremini or button mushrooms, brushed clean, stems removed, and caps cut into slices ¼ inch (6 mm) thick

½ cup (4 oz/125 g) mascarpone

3 tablespoons finely chopped fresh chives

On a plate, stir together the flour, 1 teaspoon salt, and ½ teaspoon pepper. One at a time, turn the chicken breasts in the flour mixture, gently shaking off any excess. In a large frying pan over medium-high heat, melt 1½ tablespoons of the butter with 1½ tablespoons of the olive oil. Working in batches if necessary, add the chicken breasts and cook, turning once, until golden on both sides, about 5 minutes total. Remove from the pan and set aside.

Add the shallots and pancetta to the pan and sauté over medium-high heat until lightly browned, 2–3 minutes. Add 2 cups (16 fl oz/500 ml) of the Marsala to the pan and raise the heat to high. Cook, stirring, until the wine is reduced and thickened, 7–10 minutes. Add the broth and oregano and return to a boil.

STOVE TOP: Transfer the chicken to a large Dutch oven and add the Marsala mixture. Cover and cook over low heat until the chicken is opaque throughout and very tender, about 30 minutes. Meanwhile, melt the remaining 1½ tablespoons butter with the remaining 1½ tablespoons oil in a large frying pan over high heat. Add the mushroom slices and sauté until the edges begin to brown, about 5 minutes. Stir in the mascarpone, bring to a boil, and season generously with salt and pepper. Add the mushroom mixture and the remaining ¼ cup (2 fl oz/60 ml) Marsala to the Dutch oven. Cook, covered, until the chicken is cooked through and the sauce has thickened, about 30 minutes longer.

SLOW COOKER: Transfer the chicken to a slow cooker and add the Marsala mixture over the chicken. Cover and cook until the chicken is opaque throughout and very tender, 2½ hours on the high-heat setting or 5 hours on the low-heat setting. About 30 minutes before the chicken is done, melt the remaining 1½ tablespoons butter with the remaining 1½ tablespoons oil in a large frying pan over high heat. Add the mushroom slices and sauté until the edges begin to brown, about 5 minutes. Stir in the mascarpone, bring to a boil, and season generously with salt and pepper. Add the mushroom mixture and the remaining ¼ cup (2 fl oz/60 ml) Marsala to the slow cooker. Cover and cook until the chicken is cooked through and the sauce has thickened, about 20 minutes.

Serve at once, spooning the mushrooms and sauce over the chicken and garnishing with the chives.

Chicken with a creamy Marsala sauce is a standard of old-school Italian restaurants, where you might find it prepared or finished tableside in a chafing dish. Cooking it at a more leisurely pace in a slow cooker or on the stove top eliminates much of the fuss and produces very tender, flavorful results. Substituting tangy Italian mascarpone, a soured cream cheese, for the usual cream adds a sophisticated touch.

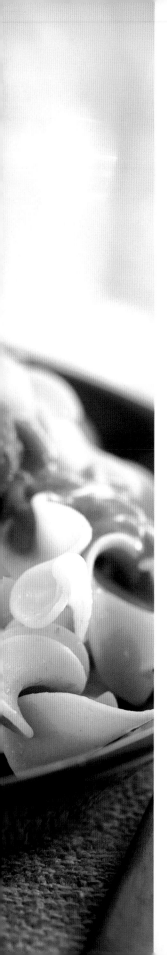

Chicken Paprika

The old-world combination of chicken and paprika, served with buttered noodles, has long been considered a classic. The deep, rich color and slighly piquant flavor of paprika are at once mellow and intense. Use a good Hungarian brand for the best results.

Season the chicken all over with salt and pepper. In a frying pan over medium-high heat, melt the butter with the canola oil. Working in batches if necessary, add the chicken and cook, turning frequently, until browned, about 10 minutes. Remove from the pan and set aside.

Pour off all but 1 tablespoon of the fat in the pan. Add the onions and bell pepper and sauté over medium-high heat until softened, about 5 minutes. Stir in the broth, paprika, and tomatoes and deglaze the pan, stirring and scraping up the browned bits on the bottom of the pan with a wooden spoon.

STOVE TOP: Transfer the chicken to a Dutch oven and add the tomato mixture. Cover and cook over medium heat until the chicken is tender and opaque throughout, about 45 minutes. Transfer the chicken to a platter and cover loosely with aluminum foil to keep warm. Bring the cooking liquid to a boil over high heat and cook, uncovered, until slightly thickened, about 2 minutes. Remove from the heat, stir in the sour cream, and season to taste with salt and pepper.

SLOW COOKER: Transfer the chicken to a slow cooker and add the tomato mixture. Cover and cook until the chicken is tender and opaque throughout, 6 hours on the low-heat setting. Transfer the chicken to a platter and cover loosely with aluminum foil to keep warm. Set the temperature to high, bring the cooking liquid to a boil, and cook, uncovered, until slightly thickened, about 10 minutes. Turn off the cooker, stir in the sour cream, and season to taste with salt and pepper.

Divide the egg noodles and chicken among warmed plates, top with the sauce, and serve at once.

1 chicken, 3–4 lb (1.5–2 kg), cut into 8 serving pieces, trimmed of excess skin and fat

Salt and freshly ground pepper

2 tablespoons unsalted butter

2 tablespoons canola oil

2 yellow onions, finely chopped

1 green bell pepper (capsicum), seeded and finely chopped

1/2 cup (4 fl oz/125 ml) chicken broth

2 tablespoons sweet paprika

2 tomatoes, seeded and chopped

1/2 cup (4 oz/125 g) sour cream

Buttered Egg Noodles (page 264)

Teriyaki Chicken Thighs

8 chicken thighs, 2½–3 lb (1.25–1.5 kg) total weight

Salt and freshly ground pepper

1 clove garlic, minced

2-inch (5-cm) piece fresh ginger, peeled and finely chopped

½ cup (4 fl oz/125 ml) soy sauce

1 teaspoon Asian sesame oil

2 tablespoons unsalted butter

2 tablespoons canola oil

¼ cup (2 fl oz/60 ml) mirin

1 tablespoon sugar

Sliced green (spring) onions for garnish

Season the chicken thighs generously with salt and pepper. In a nonreactive bowl, stir together the garlic, ginger, soy sauce, and sesame oil. Add the chicken thighs and turn to coat. Cover and marinate in the refrigerator, turning frequently, for at least 1 hour or up to overnight.

Remove the chicken from the marinade and pat dry with paper towels; discard the marinade. In a large frying pan over medium-high heat, melt the butter with the canola oil. Working in batches if necessary, add the chicken and cook, turning frequently, until browned, about 5 minutes.

STOVE TOP: Transfer the chicken to a Dutch oven. Add the mirin and sugar and turn the thighs a few times to coat. Cover and cook over low heat until the chicken is opaque throughout, about 30 minutes. Uncover and cook, turning often, until the thighs are glazed, about 10 minutes longer.

SLOW COOKER: Transfer the chicken to a slow cooker. Add the mirin and sugar and turn the thighs a few times to coat. Cover and cook until the chicken is opaque throughout, 1½ hours on the high-heat setting or 2½ hours on the low-heat setting. Uncover, set the temperature to high if necessary, and cook, turning often, until most of the liquid has evaporated and the thighs are glazed, about 20 minutes longer.

Transfer the chicken to a warmed platter, garnish with the green onions, and serve at once.

Teriyaki is a combination of two Japanese words, *teri*, meaning "luster," and *yaki*, "to grill or broil." Here, a marinade of teriyaki seasonings flavor the rich dark meat of the chicken thighs, which are well suited to long, slow cooking. Mirin, a sweetened rice wine, helps give the meat a lustrous finish. Serve with fragrant rice.

Chinese Red-Cooked Chicken

The Chinese term "red-cooked" refers to the deep mahogany color that the chicken meat and skin take on when slowly simmered in a well-seasoned mixture of soy sauce, broth, and rice wine or sherry. A last-minute brushing of dark toasted sesame oil gives the dish extra fragrance, flavor, and a lovely sheen

Place the chicken on a cutting board with the breast side down. Using poultry shears or a large, sharp knife, cut along one side of the backbone. Pull the bird open slightly and cut down the other side of the backbone to free it (reserve for making stock or discard). Turn the chicken so it is breast side up and open it as flat as possible. Press firmly to break the breastbone and flatten the chicken. Trim any excess skin and fat.

STOVE TOP: Place the chicken skin side up in the bottom of a large Dutch oven. Scatter the orange zest, star anise, cinnamon, and ginger around the chicken and sprinkle with the brown sugar. Pour in the soy sauce and 1 cup (8 fl oz/ 250 ml) of the broth. Bring to a boil over high heat, reduce the heat to very low, partially cover, and cook until the chicken is opaque throughout and very tender, about 45 minutes.

SLOW COOKER: Place the chicken skin side up in the bottom of a slow cooker. Scatter the orange zest, star anise, cinnamon, and ginger around the chicken and sprinkle evenly with the brown sugar. Pour in the soy sauce and 1 cup (8 fl oz/250 ml) of the broth. Cover and cook until the chicken is tender and opaque throughout, 3½ hours on the high-heat setting or 7 hours on the low-heat setting.

Transfer the chicken to a platter, brush with the sesame oil, and cover loosely with aluminum foil to keep warm. Pour the cooking liquid into a saucepan add the Chinese rice wine. In a small cup, stir the cornstarch into the remaining 1 cup broth until completely dissolved. Stir into the cooking liquid and cook over medium heat until the sauce thickens, about 5 minutes. Remove and discard the zest strips, star anise, cinnamon, and ginger.

Divide the chicken and sauce among warmed plates and serve at once.

1 chicken, about 4 lb (2 kg)

4 strips orange zest, each about 3 inches (7.5 cm) long

2 star anise

2 cinnamon sticks, each 3 inches (7.5 cm) long

2-inch piece fresh ginger, peeled and thinly sliced

2 tablespoons firmly packed dark brown sugar

1¼ cups (10 fl oz/310 ml) soy sauce

2 cups (16 fl oz/500 ml) chicken broth

2 tablespoons Asian sesame oil

½ cup (4 fl oz/125 ml) Chinese rice wine or dry sherry

2½ tablespoons cornstarch (cornflour)

Chicken Mole

2 ancho chiles, seeded and torn into pieces

2 pasilla chiles, seeded and torn into pieces

1 chicken, 3–4 lb (1.5–2 kg), cut into 8 serving pieces, trimmed of excess skin and fat

Salt and freshly ground pepper

2 tablespoons canola oil

1 yellow onion, chopped

1 clove garlic, minced

¼ cup (2 fl oz/60 ml) dry white wine such as chardonnay or sauvignon blanc

2 tomatoes, seeded and chopped

½ cup (3 oz/90 g) almonds

½ cup (3 oz/90 g) raisins

6 peppercorns

1 teaspoon ground cinnamon

1 tablespoon sesame seeds

2 teaspoons coriander seeds

2 tablespoons unsalted butter

½ cup (4 fl oz/125 ml) chicken broth

1 oz (30 g) unsweetened chocolate, coarsely chopped

Put the chiles in a small bowl and add enough boiling water to cover. Let soak for 20 minutes. Drain and set aside.

Meanwhile, season the chicken generously with salt and pepper. In a large frying pan over medium-high heat, warm the canola oil. Working in batches if necessary, add the chicken and cook, turning frequently, until browned, about 10 minutes.

Pour off all but 1 tablespoon of the fat in the pan. Add the onion and sauté over medium-high heat until softened, about 5 minutes. Add the garlic and cook for 1 minute. Add the drained chiles, wine, tomatoes, almonds, and raisins and bring to a simmer. Transfer the chile mixture to a food processor or blender. Add the peppercorns, cinnamon, sesame seeds, and coriander seeds. Process or blend until a thick purée forms.

Place the frying pan over medium-high heat and melt the butter. Add the purée and cook until bubbling, about 2 minutes. Pour in the broth. Add the chocolate and stir until melted.

OVEN: Preheat the oven to 350°F (180°C). Transfer the chicken to a large Dutch oven. Pour in the chocolate mixture. Cover and cook in the oven until the chicken is tender and opaque throughout, about 45 minutes.

SLOW COOKER: Transfer the chicken to a slow cooker. Pour in the chocolate mixture. Cover and cook until the chicken is tender and opaque throughout, 3 hours on the low-heat setting.

Transfer the chicken to a warmed platter, top with the mole, and serve at once.

Slow cooking enhances this exotic blend of chiles, spices, bitter chocolate, and aromatic flavorings. Like many traditional dishes, this Mexican favorite evolved over generations. Serve with Spanish rice and warmed corn tortillas to soak up the sauce.

Chicken Fricassee with Wild Mushrooms

The term fricassee, which derives from Latin words for "fry" and "break up," is widely interpreted in a range of chicken stew recipes. Some feature cream sauces, others tomatoes, and most have lively aromatic seasonings. This version includes both shallots and garlic, along with the earthy flavor of both dried and fresh mushrooms, of which most "wild" varieties are now commercially cultivated. The white wine and broth in which the chicken cooks is thickened with a touch of tomato paste and enriched with just a little cream. Serve with Mashed Potatoes (page 260).

Put the dried morels in a small bowl and add enough hot water to cover. Let soak for 20 minutes. Remove the morels from the soaking water, squeezing out any excess liquid, and cut the morels in half lengthwise.

Meanwhile, on a plate, stir together the flour, 1 tablespoon salt, and 1/2 teaspoon pepper. Turn the chicken pieces in the seasoned flour, shaking off any excess. In a large frying pan over medium-high heat, warm 3 tablespoons of the olive oil. Working in batches if necessary, add the chicken and cook, turning frequently, until browned, about 10 minutes. Remove from the pan and set aside.

Add the shallots and garlic to the pan and sauté over medium-high heat for about 30 seconds. Add the tomato paste and sugar, stir well to combine, and cook for about 30 seconds longer. Add the wine and deglaze the pan, stirring and scraping up the browned bits on the bottom of the pan with a wooden spoon. Add the broth and bring to a boil.

STOVE TOP: Transfer the broth-wine mixture to a large Dutch oven. Add the chicken, arranging the dark meat on the bottom and the breasts on top. Add the carrots, parsley and rosemary sprigs, and bay leaf, tucking them among the chicken pieces. Scatter the morels over the chicken, cover, and cook over low heat until the chicken is opaque throughout and very tender, about 1 hour.

SLOW COOKER: Transfer the broth-wine mixture to a slow cooker. Add the chicken, arranging the dark meat on the bottom and the breasts on top. Add the carrots, parsley and rosemary sprigs, and bay leaf, tucking them among the chicken pieces. Scatter the morels over the chicken, cover, and cook until the chicken is tender and opaque throughout, 2 1/2–3 hours on the high-heat setting or 5–6 hours on the low-heat setting.

About 30 minutes before the chicken is done, in a large frying pan over high heat, melt the butter with the remaining 1 tablespoon olive oil. Add the fresh mushrooms and sauté until their edges start to brown, about 5 minutes. Season with salt and pepper. Add the mushroom mixture to the chicken, and cook, covered, until the mushrooms are tender, about 20 minutes. Stir in the cream.

Remove and discard the rosemary sprig and bay leaf. Serve at once, spooning the mushroom and carrots over the chicken.

1/2 oz (15 g) dried morel mushrooms

3 tablespoons all-purpose (plain) flour

Salt and freshly ground pepper

4 tablespoons (2 fl oz/60 ml) olive oil

1 chicken, about 4 lb (2 kg), cut into 8 serving pieces

4 large shallots, thinly sliced

4 cloves garlic, minced

2 tablespoons tomato paste

1 teaspoon sugar

1/2 cup (4 fl oz/125 ml) dry white wine such as chardonnay

1/2 cup (4 fl oz/125 ml) chicken broth

2 carrots, cut into 1/2-inch (12-mm) pieces

1 sprig fresh flat-leaf (Italian) parsley

1 sprig fresh rosemary

1 bay leaf

3 tablespoons unsalted butter

6 oz (185 g) fresh wild mushrooms such as shiitake or oyster, stems removed, and caps cut into thin slices 1/4 inch (6 mm) thick

1/2 cup (4 fl oz/125 ml) heavy (double) cream

Duck Ragù

3 tablespoons olive oil

Salt and freshly ground pepper

3 lb (1.5 kg) skinless, boneless duck pieces, preferably legs and thighs, trimmed of excess fat

1 red onion, diced

2 shallots, minced

2 cloves garlic, minced

1 teaspoon red pepper flakes

1 carrot, diced

1 rib celery, diced

2 tablespoons tomato paste

1½ cups (12 fl oz/375 ml) dry red wine such as Chianti or Valpolicella

1 can (28 oz/875 g) diced plum (Roma) tomatoes, preferably San Marzano

1 teaspoon sugar

1 oz (30 g) dried porcini mushrooms

1 teaspoon dried thyme

½ teaspoon fennel seeds

Buttered Egg Noodles (page 264)

In a large frying pan over medium-high heat, warm the olive oil. In a small bowl, combine ¾ teaspoon salt and ½ teaspoon pepper. Rub the mixture all over the duck pieces. Working in batches if necessary, add the duck and cook, turning frequently, until browned, about 10 minutes. Remove from the pan and set aside.

Add the onion, shallots, and garlic to the pan and cook over medium-high heat until they start to soften, about 3 minutes. Stir in the red pepper flakes and sauté for about 30 seconds. Add the carrot, celery, and tomato paste, stir to combine, and continue to cook for about 2 minutes. Add the red wine and deglaze the pan, stirring and scraping up the browned bits on the bottom of the pan with a wooden spoon. Stir in the tomatoes, sugar, porcini, thyme, and fennel seeds and bring to a boil.

STOVE TOP: Transfer the duck to a Dutch oven. Pour the tomato mixture over the duck. Cover and cook over very low heat until the duck is very tender and the sauce is thick, about 2½ hours. Transfer the duck to a cutting board. Using a fork and a sharp knife, cut and shred the meat into bite-sized pieces. Return the duck to the sauce, cover, and cook until heated through, about 10 minutes. Season to taste with salt and pepper.

SLOW COOKER: Transfer the duck to a slow cooker. Pour the tomato mixture over the duck. Cover and cook until the duck is very tender and the sauce is thick, 3½ hours on the high-heat setting or 7½ hours on the low-heat setting. Transfer the duck to a cutting board. Using a fork and a sharp knife, shred the meat into bite-sized pieces. Return the duck to the sauce, cover, and cook until heated through, about 10 minutes. Season to taste with salt and pepper.

Divide the egg noodles and ragù among warmed bowls and serve at once.

The rich taste and robust texture of duck meat works perfectly in this rustic yet elegant Italian stew, which is traditionally served as a sauce for bite-sized al dente pasta shapes or gnocchi. The ragù can be made 2 days in advance.

Chicken with Pumpkin-Seed Mole

This vivid, fresh-tasting version of a traditional green mole sauce proves that authentic Mexican food does not have to be spicy hot, although you can certainly raise the heat level by using four chiles instead of just two. Well-stocked markets and health-food stores sell bags of shelled pumpkin seeds, known in Spanish as *pepitas*. Serve the chicken and sauce over red, Spanish-style rice and garnish with dollops of sour cream for an attractive presentation featuring the colors of the Mexican flag.

In a large frying pan over medium-high heat, warm the olive oil. Add the onion and sauté until it starts to turn tender, about 3 minutes. Stir in the garlic and chiles and sauté for about 30 seconds. Add the pumpkin seeds and cook, stirring, until they darken in color, about 5 minutes. Stir in the broth, tomatillos, cilantro, oregano, and 1 teaspoon salt, and bring to a boil.

Ladle about one-half of the pumpkin-seed mixture into a blender or food processor and pulse a few times. Add the remaining mixture and blend or process until it forms a uniformly coarse purée.

STOVE TOP: Transfer the purée to a large Dutch oven. Add the chicken pieces, arranging the thighs on the bottom and the breasts on top. Partially cover and cook over low heat until the chicken is opaque throughout and tender, about 1 hour.

SLOW COOKER: Transfer the purée to a slow cooker. Add the chicken pieces, arranging the thighs on the bottom and the breasts on top. Cover and cook until the chicken is opaque throughout and tender, 2 hours on the high-heat setting or 4 hours on the low-heat setting.

Transfer the chicken to warmed plates. Spoon the pumkin-seed sauce over the chicken, garnish with cilantro leaves and the sour cream, and serve at once.

1/4 cup (2 fl oz/60 ml) olive oil

1 white onion, chopped

2 cloves garlic, chopped

3 jalapeño chiles, halved, seeded, and coarsely chopped

1 1/2 cups (6 oz/185 g) pumpkin seeds

1 1/2 cups (12 fl oz/375 ml) chicken broth

3/4 lb (375 g) tomatillos, husks removed and coarsely chopped

3/4 cup (3/4 oz/20 g) loosely packed fresh cilantro (fresh cilantro) leaves, plus more for garnish

1 teaspoon dried oregano

Salt

3 lb (1.5 kg) skinless, boneless chicken thighs or breasts

1/4 cup (2 fl oz/60 ml) sour cream

Summer Coq au Vin

3 tablespoons all-purpose
(plain) flour

Salt and freshly ground white
pepper

3 tablespoons olive oil

1 chicken, about 4 lb (2 kg),
cut into 8 serving pieces,
trimmed of excess skin
and fat

4 shallots, minced

2 cups (16 fl oz/500 ml)
dry white wine such as
chardonnay

1 cup (8 fl oz/250 ml)
chicken broth

3 sprigs fresh flat-leaf
(Italian) parsley

2 sprigs fresh thyme

$\frac{1}{2}$ lb (250 g) summer squash
such as yellow crookneck
zucchini (courgettes), cut into
bite-sized pieces

3 carrots, about $\frac{1}{4}$ lb (125 g)
total weight, peeled and cut
into bite-sized pieces

$\frac{1}{4}$ lb (125 g) frozen pearl
onions, or 1 yellow onion,
chopped

$\frac{1}{4}$ lb (125 g) sugar snap
peas, trimmed

Use white wine instead of the usual red to make this lesser-known, but still traditional version of the French classic. It transforms the slowly simmered stew into a lighter, fresher-tasting dish perfect for a summertime dinner. If you like, garnish each serving with large croutons made by sautéing pieces of crustless, good-quality white bread until golden in a little olive oil with minced garlic. Serve the dish with the same variety of white wine you used to cook it.

On a plate, stir together the flour, 1 teaspoon salt, and $\frac{1}{2}$ teaspoon white pepper. Turn the chicken pieces in the seasoned flour, shaking off any exccess. In a large frying pan over medium-high heat, warm the olive oil. Working in batches if necessary, add the chicken and cook, turning frequently, until browned, about 10 minutes. Remove from the pan and set aside.

Add the shallots to the pan and cook over medium-high heat for about 30 seconds. Add the wine and deglaze the pan, stirring and scraping up the browned bits on the bottom of the pan with a wooden spoon. Pour in the broth and bring to a boil.

STOVE TOP: Transfer the wine-shallot mixture to a large Dutch oven. Add the chicken, arranging the dark meat on the bottom and the breasts on top. Tuck the parsley and thyme sprigs among the chicken pieces. Cover and cook over low heat until the chicken is tender and opaque throughout, about 40 minutes. Uncover and add the squash, carrots, onions, and sugar snap peas, pushing them into the cooking liquid around the chicken pieces. Cover and cook until the vegetables are cooked through, about 20 minutes longer.

SLOW COOKER: Transfer the wine-shallot mixture to a slow cooker. Add the chicken, arranging the dark meat on the bottom and the breasts on top. Tuck the parsley and thyme sprigs among the chicken pieces. Cover and cook for 2–2$\frac{1}{2}$ hours on the high-heat setting or 4$\frac{1}{2}$–5$\frac{1}{2}$ hours on the low-heat setting. Uncover and add the squash, carrots, onions, and sugar snap peas, pushing them into the cooking liquid around the chicken pieces. Cover and cook until the vegetables are cooked through, about 20 minutes longer.

Transfer the chicken and vegetables to a warmed platter and serve at once.

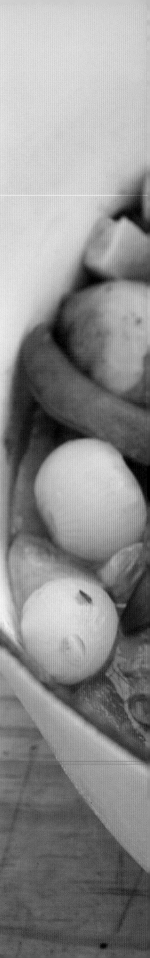

Chicken with Tomatoes and Olives

A hearty wine, one that can stand up to the strong, full flavors of tomatoes and olives, extra space is best for this dish. Couscous with Almonds and Raisins makes a good accompaniment (page 261).

Season the chicken all over with salt and pepper. Set aside.

In a small saucepan, combine the wine, shallots, garlic, peppercorns, and thyme. Bring to a boil over high heat and cook, stirring frequently, until reduced to about $1/2$ cup (4 fl oz/125 ml), about 20 minutes.

STOVE TOP: Place the chicken in a Dutch oven. Add the wine mixture and the chopped tomatoes. Cover and cook over medium heat, turning frequently, until the chicken is very tender and opaque throughout, about 40 minutes.

SLOW COOKER: Place the chicken in a slow cooker. Add the wine mixture and the chopped tomatoes. Cover and cook until the chicken is very tender and opaque throughout, $1–1^{1}/2$ hours on the high-heat setting or 3 hours on the low-heat setting.

Transfer the chicken to a platter. Set a fine-mesh sieve over a small bowl and strain the cooking juices. You should have about 1 cup (8 fl oz/250 ml). Whisk in the tomato paste.

Pour the juices into a large frying pan and bring to a boil over medium-high heat. In a small bowl, combine the butter and flour. Using your fingers or a fork, mix until a crumbly paste forms. Add the butter mixture to the pan and cook, whisking constantly, until a thick sauce forms, 7–10 minutes. Season to taste with salt and pepper, and stir in the olives. Add the chicken, turn to coat with the sauce, and cook over medium-low heat until warmed through, about 5 minutes.

Divide the chicken among warmed plates, spoon the sauce over the top, and serve at once.

3 lb (1.5 kg) chicken legs and thighs, 12 pieces total

Salt and freshly ground pepper

2 cups (16 fl oz/500 ml) hearty red wine such as Côtes du Rhone

2 shallots, minced

1 clove garlic, minced

6 peppercorns

3 or 4 sprigs fresh thyme

3 tomatoes, seeded and chopped

1 tablespoon tomato paste

1 tablespoon unsalted butter, cut into small pieces

1 tablespoon all-purpose (plain) flour

1 cup (4 oz/125 g) brined black or green olives, pitted and coarsely chopped

Spanish Chicken Stew

1 chicken, 3–4 lb (1.5–2 kg), cut into 8 serving pieces, trimmed of excess skin and fat

Salt and freshly ground pepper

2 tablespoons unsalted butter

2 tablespoons canola oil

2 red or yellow bell peppers (capsicums), seeded and finely chopped

1 yellow onion, thinly sliced

1 clove garlic, minced

2 tomatoes, seeded and chopped

2 teaspoons smoked hot paprika

1 can (15 oz/470 g) chickpeas (garbanzo beans)

¾ cup (5 oz/155 g) pitted green olives

½ cup (2 oz/60 g) sliced (flaked) almonds, toasted, plus more for garnish

Season the chicken all over with salt and pepper. In a large frying pan over medium-high heat, melt the butter with the canola oil. Working in batches if necessary, add the chicken and cook, turning frequently, until browned, about 10 minutes. Remove from the pan and set aside.

Pour off all but 1 tablespoon of the fat in the pan. Add the bell peppers and onion and sauté until softened, about 5 minutes. Add the garlic and cook for 1 minute. Stir in the tomatoes and paprika.

STOVE TOP: Transfer the chicken to a Dutch oven. Add the bell pepper mixture. Cover and cook over medium-low heat until the chicken is tender and opaque throughout, about 40 minutes. Uncover and add the chickpeas, olives, and ½ cup almonds. Cover and cook until the chickpeas are warmed through, about 10 minutes longer.

SLOW COOKER: Transfer the chicken to a slow cooker. Add the bell pepper mixture. Cover and cook until the chicken is tender and opaque throughout, 5½ hours on the high-heat setting or 3 hours on the low-heat setting. Uncover and add the chickpeas, olives, and ½ cup almonds. Cover and cook until the chickpeas are warmed through, about 30 minutes longer.

Arrange the chicken on a warmed platter or individual plates. Garnish with sliced almonds and serve at once.

Olives and almonds are staples of Spanish cuisine. Here, they are combined with chicken and slow-cooked with peppers, tomatoes, and garlic for a powerful, full-flavored dish. Potatoes, brought back from the New World by early Spanish and Portuguese explorers round out the meal. Serve with Roasted Potatoes (page 260) for an authentic accompaniment.

Pork

About Pork

Slow cooking pork shoulder or spareribs results in silky smooth and luscious flavors that are unforgettable. Cooking pork stews and braises the day before you intend to serve them gives you a chance to remove the fat before re-heating and serving the dish.

Slow roasted or braised pork becomes exceptionally succulent and luscious after long cooking. The collagen and connective tissue in the tougher cuts of pork used for braising and the layer of fat just under the skin dissolve into gelatin that bastes and moistens the meat. This gives slow cooked pork a rich and satisfying quality that's has to do as much with texture as with taste. Wine tasters talk about the mouth feel and sensuous texture of a well aged cabernet and use words like velvety and silky to describe this. Long cooked pork has the same quality: unctuous and rich and supremely tender. A good example of this rich and silky texture can be found in Brined Pork Belly with herbs (page 189).

USING PORK IN SLOW COOKING

Bone-in and boneless meats can be slow cooked sucessfully. Bone-in cuts cook faaster than boned—especially true for pork chops—because the bone helps spread the heat throughout the meat more quickly.

Whatever cut you decide on make sure you have a look at i before you buy it to check for coloring. when looking at large cuts look for servings that have small flecks or thing "streams" of fat, rather than large deposits or "rivers."

Leaner meats which, by nature, have less fat, usually need added moisture. You can accomodate this byt tying the meat together tightly and slowing simmering in aromatic liquid until the meat is very tender and cooked through. For added flavor, you can also treat the meat with a marinade, for example, allowing the seasonings to penetrate it for a time before it is placed on the heat.

If you do not have time for a long marinade, surrounding the pork with vegetables while it cooks, will help keep the moisture in while also providing a side dish.

The tougher and fattier cuts from the shoulder (see Stuffed Braised Pork Shoulder, page 169), shank, ribs, and leg are perfect for pit roasting, braising and stewing. If you want the juiciness and rich flavor of old fashioned pork, keep the temperature low and stew or braise the meat under you can pull it apart with your fingers (see Pulled Pork, page 178).

CHOOSING A CUT

The best cuts for slow cooking pork come from the much used muscles of the shoulder, leg, and side of the animal. These get more exercise and therefore develop more collagen and connective tissue that will harden and dry out with high heat, but gets soft and succulent when cooked long and slow in moist heat. They also seem to gain in meatiness and flavor, with a characteristic sweetness that the blander loin and tenderloin often lack.

The shoulder is the preferred cut for slow roasting, braising, or stewing. The shoulder is a large cut primal cut, which is usually divided into smaller cuts before selling. You should look for bone-in or boneless shoulder sold in 4 to 8 pound pieces; these cuts are often called shoulder butt roast or shoulder arm (see Beer-Braised Pork Roast, page 187). If in doubt, ask the butcher, but most shoulder cuts should have the word shoulder somewhere in the name. If you want to cut up pork for a stew or a braise, this is the most efficient cut to use (see Carnitas, page 162, Caribbean Pork Stew with Plantains, page 166, and Posole: Pork with Red Chiles and Hominy, page 173). Pork shoulder is fattier than loin, however, so be sure to cut off and discard all exterior fat. Always be sure to trim the pieces to an equal size so that the cooking times are accurate

Pork loin chops, like beef porterhouse steaks, have both the loin and the tenderloin, spearated by the rib bone. Ham is usually smoked, but fresh ham or pork leg can be delicious when slow roasted or braised. Most hams are sold cut in half into the butt end or the shank end, but whole fresh hams can sometimes be found. Fresh ham is a good choice for cutting up into stew; it has less fat and is a bit more tender than the shoulder.

Ribs are also delicious when slow roasted, braised or stewed, but you need to distinguish types of pork ribs to know how to cook them correctly. Baby back ribs are cut from the back of the loin area and are quite tender. They can be cooked by grilling or broiling and are not usually slow roasted, braised, or stewed. Country style ribs (see page 159), however, cut from the shoulder of the animal, are a great choice for slow roasting, braising, or stewing. They are very meaty and flavorful and are delicious when cooked long and slow. Pork ribs, in general, are a very faty cut of meat, so take the time to remove all external fat before cooking. Spareribs are cut from the side or flank of the pig. These should be slow roasted either in the oven or in a covered barbecue for hours at low temperature. If you use a sauce on any pork ribs, brush it on the ribs towards the end of cooking to avoid charring.

Roast Pork with Apricots

This rich and creamy dish tastes as good as it looks. The concentrated essense of dried fruit is a classic complement for almost any pork dish. This roast cooks slowly with apricots for a memorable dish. If you like, use prunes in place of the apricots. If you do, omit the orange juice and add a couple tablespoons of fresh lemon juice.

On a plate, stir together the flour, $\frac{1}{2}$ teaspoon salt, and $\frac{1}{4}$ teaspoon pepper. Turn the pork in the seasoned flour, shaking off any excess. In a large frying pan over medium-high heat, warm the oil. Cook the pork, turning frequently, until browned on all sides, about 5 minutes. Remove from the pan and set aside.

Pour off all but 1 tablespoon of the fat in the pan. Add the onion and sauté until softened, 3–5 minutes. Add the garlic and sauté for 1 minute. Pour in the broth and deglaze the pan, stirring and scraping up the browned bits on the bottom of the pan with a wooden spoon.

STOVE TOP: Transfer the pork to a Dutch oven and pour in the broth mixture. Add the apricots, orange juice, and thyme. Cover and cook until the pork is very tender and an instant-read thermometer inserted in the center reads 140°F (60°C), about $1\frac{1}{2}$ hours.

SLOW COOKER: Transfer the pork to a slow cooker and pour in the broth mixture. Add the apricots, orange juice, and thyme. Cover and cook until the pork is very tender and an instant-read thermometer inserted in the center reads 140°F (60°C), 2–3 hours on the high-heat setting or 4–6 hours on the low-heat setting.

Transfer the pork to a cutting board and cover loosely with aluminum foil to keep warm. Using a slotted spoon, remove the apricots and set aside. Use a large, shallow spoon or a ladle to skim as much fat as possible from the surface of the cooking liquid. Strain the juices into a large saucepan. Bring to a boil over high heat and cook, stirring ocassionally, until reduced and concentrated, about 10 minutes. Stir the mustard into the sauce and add the apricots. Season to taste with salt and pepper.

Cut the pork loin, across the grain into thin slices and arrange the slices on a warmed platter. Serve at once with the sauce and apricots.

$\frac{1}{4}$ cup ($1\frac{1}{2}$ oz/45 g) all-purpose (plain) flour

Salt and freshly ground pepper

1 boneless pork loin roast, about $2\frac{1}{2}$ lb (1.25 kg)

2 tablespoons canola oil

1 yellow onion, thinly sliced

1 clove garlic, minced

1 cup (8 fl oz/250 ml) chicken broth

3 cups (18 oz/560 g) dried apricots

$\frac{1}{2}$ cup (4 fl oz/125 ml) fresh orange juice

2 tablespoons chopped fresh thyme

2 tablespoons Dijon mustard

Orange-Braised Ham

1 cured ham from the shank end, 7–8 lb (3.5–4 kg)

2 cups (16 fl oz/500 ml) fresh orange juice

1 tablespoon grated orange zest

1 cup (7 oz/220 g) firmly packed brown sugar

1 cinnamon stick, 3-inch (7.5-cm), broken in half

6 cloves

6 peppercorns

Using a large, sharp knife, remove the skin from the ham if necessary and shave away all but a ¹/₂-inch (12-mm) layer of the fat. Score the top and sides of the ham at 1-inch (2.5-cm) intervals to form a diamond pattern.

In a saucepan over medium heat, combine the orange juice and zest, brown sugar, cinnamon, cloves, and peppercorns. Cook, stirring frequently, until the mixture is thick and syrupy, about 15 minutes. Set aside.

OVEN: Preheat the oven to 350°F (180°C). Place a flat rack in a large roasting pan. Transfer the ham to the rack, arranging it fat side up. Bake the ham, basting it every 20 minutes with the orange mixture, until the ham is warmed through and the fat is glistening, about 1 hour.

SLOW COOKER: Place the ham fat side up in a slow cooker. Cover and cook for 6 hours on the low-heat setting. Uncover and remove some of the fat in the bottom of the cooker. Pour the glaze over the ham, cover, and cook until the juices in the cooker are bubbling and the top of the ham is glistening, about 2 hours longer.

Transfer the ham to a cutting board, cover loosely with aluminum foil, and let rest for 15 minutes. Using a sharp knife and working against the grain, cut the ham into thin slices, arrange on a warmed platter, and serve at once.

A ham glistening with spicy orange glaze makes a deceptively dramatic dish, especially considering how simple it is to make. Cutting a diamond pattern cut into the skin takes just minutes and cooks into an elegant finish.

Country-Style Pork Ribs

Country-style ribs are cut from the loin end of the hog, right behind the upper part of the pork shoulder. They are much meatier than spareribs or baby back ribs and are often treated like pork chops.

Place the ribs in a large pot and add enough cold water to cover. Bring to a boil over high heat. Reduce the heat to medium and simmer, skimming off any scum that rises to the top, for 30 minutes. Drain the ribs and pat dry with paper towels.

In a small saucepan, combine the ketchup, vinegar, lemon juice, soy sauce, brown sugar, garlic, cayenne, pineapple juice, and tomatoes. Bring to a boil over high heat, reduce the heat to medium-low, and simmer, stirring ocassionally, until reduced by half and thickened, about 20 minutes. Strain the sauce, pushing firmly on the solids to extract as much liquid as possible. You should have about 2 cups (16 fl oz/500 ml) of sauce.

OVEN: Preheat the oven to 350°F (180°C). Arrange the ribs in a Dutch oven and top with the sauce. Turn to coat and cover. Cook, turning the ribs occasionally, until they are very tender, about 1 1/2 hours. Uncover and cook until the ribs are evenly glazed and deep brown in color, about 45 minutes longer.

SLOW COOKER: Arrange the ribs in a slow cooker, and top with the sauce. Turn to coat and cover. Cook for 4 hours on the low-heat setting. Uncover and cook until most of the sauce has boiled off and the ribs are are evenly glazed and deep brown in color, about 2 hours longer.

Divide the ribs and sauce among warmed plates and serve at once.

2 1/2 lb (1.25 kg), bone-in, country-style pork ribs

1 cup (8 fl oz/250 ml) tomato ketchup

2 tablespoons red wine vinegar

2 tablespoons fresh lemon juice

2 tablespoons soy sauce

2 tablespoons firmly packed dark brown sugar

1 clove garlic, minced

1/2 teaspoon cayenne pepper, or more to taste

3/4 cup (6 fl oz/180 ml) pineapple juice

2 tomatoes, seeded and chopped

Wine-Braised Sausages with Polenta

1 small fennel bulb, about ¼ lb (125 g)

1¼ lb (625 g) sweet Italian sausages

1 cup (8 fl oz/250 ml) dry red wine such as Chianti

3 tablespoons olive oil

1 small yellow onion, chopped

3 large cloves garlic, minced

1 large bunch broccoli rabe, about 1 lb (500 g), stems trimmed

1 cup (8 fl oz/250 ml) chicken broth

Creamy Polenta (page 261) for serving

⅓ cup (1½ oz/45 g) freshly grated Parmesan cheese

Cut off the stalks and feathery leaves from the fennel bulb. Peel away the outer layer of the bulb if it is tough, and cut away any discolored areas. Cut the bulb lengthwise into thin slices, trimming any tough base portions. Set aside.

Prick each sausage in several places with a fork. Place the sausages in a small Dutch oven. Add ½ cup (4 fl oz/125 ml) of the wine and bring to a boil over medium-high heat. Cover, reduce the heat to medium-low, and cook the sausages for 5 minutes. Uncover, raise the heat to medium-high, and cook, turning the sausages occasionally, until they are browned and the liquid is evaporated, 8–10 minutes. Remove from the pan and set aside.

Pour off all but 2 tablespoons of the drippings in the pot, add the olive oil, and reduce the heat to medium. Add the onion and fennel and sauté just until tinged with gold and softened, 4–5 minutes. Stir in the garlic and sauté for 30 seconds. Return the sausages to the pot and add the broccoli rabe, broth, and remaining ½ cup wine. Cover, reduce the heat to medium-low, and cook until the broccoli rabe is tender and the sausages are cooked through, 8–10 minutes.

Arrange the polenta on a warmed platter. Ladle the sausages and vegetables over the polenta, sprinkle with the Parmesan, and serve at once.

Broccoli rabe is well suited for braising, which mellows its sharp flavor and tenderizes its tough stems. Serving the sausages, vegetables, and abundant broth over soft polenta makes a simple, quick, yet quite elegant supper.

Italian Braised Pork

In this traditional Italian recipe, the natural sugars in the milk complement the sweetness of the pork, and the liquid cooks down to form a thick sauce that begins to caramelize slightly toward the end of cooking. What results is tender meat served with a simple, yet very flavorful sauce. Serve with Mashed Potatoes (page 260) or Herbed Rice Pilaf (page 262).

Season the pork generously with salt and pepper. Set aside.

In a large frying pan over medium heat, warm the olive oil. Add the bacon and cook, stirring often, until browned, 2–3 minutes. Transfer to a paper towel–lined plate and set aside.

Raise the heat to medium-high. Add the pork to the fat in the pan and cook, turning occasionally, until evenly browned on all sides, about 10 minutes. Remove from the pan and set aside. Pour off the fat in the pan and return to medium-high heat. Add 3 cups (24 fl oz/750 ml) of the milk and deglaze the pan, stirring and scraping up the browned bits on the bottom of the pan with a wooden spoon. Bring to a boil.

STOVE TOP: Transfer the pork to a large Dutch oven and add the garlic. Pour in the milk mixture and add the reserved bacon. Partially cover and cook over very low heat until the pork is tender and the milk has reduced and thickened, about 2 hours. During the final 30 minutes of cooking, check the milk level and, if necessary, heat some of the remaining milk and add to the pork.

SLOW COOKER: Transfer the pork to a slow cooker and add the garlic. Pour in the milk mixture and add the reserved bacon. Cover and cook until the pork is tender and the milk has reduced and thickened, 3 hours on the high-heat setting or 6 hours on the low-heat setting. During the last 1 or 2 hours of cooking, check the milk level and, if necessary, heat some of the remaining milk and add to the pork.

Transfer the pork to a cutting board and cover loosely with aluminum foil to keep warm. Remove and discard the garlic cloves. Raise the heat to high, and cook the remaining liquid, whisking constantly until it forms a thick sauce, about 5 minutes on the stove top or 10 minutes in the slow cooker.

Cut the pork loin crosswise into slices about 1/2 inch (12 mm) thick. Arrange the pork slices on a warmed platter, top with the sauce, and serve at once.

1 boneless pork loin roast, 2–2½ lb (1–1.25 kg)

Salt and freshly ground pepper

2 tablespoons olive oil

3 slices bacon, about 3 oz (90 g) total weight, roughly chopped

3–4 cups (24–32 fl oz/ 750 ml–1 l) whole milk

2 cloves garlic

Carnitas

Salt and freshly ground pepper

1 boneless pork shoulder roast, 3–4 lb (1.5–2 kg)

¼ cup (2 fl oz/60 ml) olive oil

1 yellow onion, finely chopped

2 cloves garlic, minced

1½ cups (12 fl oz/375 ml) Mexican, lager-style beer

Grated zest and juice of 1 large orange

Grated zest and juice of 1 lime

1 tablespoon dried oregano

For Serving

Warm corn or flour tortillas

Lime wedges

Chopped yellow onion

Hot or mild salsa

Chopped fresh cilantro (fresh coriander)

In a small bowl, combine 2 teaspoons salt and 1 teaspoon pepper. Season the pork roast generously with the mixture. Set aside.

In a large frying pan over medium-high heat, warm the olive oil. Add the pork, and cook, turning frequently until browned on all sides, about 10 minutes. Remove from the pan and set aside.

Pour off all but a thin layer of fat in the pan. Add the onion and garlic and sauté just until they begin to soften, 1–2 minutes. Add the beer and deglaze the pan, stirring and scraping up the browned bits on the bottom of the pan with a wooden spoon.

OVEN: Preheat the oven to 350°F (180°C). Transfer the pork to a large Dutch oven and pour in the beer mixture. Add the orange and lime zests and juices and the oregano. Cover and cook until the pork is very tender, about 2½ hours.

SLOW COOKER: Transfer the pork to a slow cooker and pour in the beer mixture. Add the orange and lime zests and juices and the oregano. Cover and cook until the pork is very tender, 5 hours on the high-heat setting or 10 hours on the low-heat setting.

Transfer the pork to a cutting board and cover loosely with aluminum foil to keep warm. Use a large, shallow spoon or a ladle to skim as much fat as possible from the surface of the cooking liquid. Using a large, sharp knife and a fork, coarsely cut and shred the pork into small bite-sized pieces. Arrange the meat on a warmed platter or individual plates, moisten it lightly with the cooking juices, and serve at once with the tortillas, lime wedges, chopped onion, salsa, and cilantro.

The popular "little meats" of Mexican cooking are traditionally made by slowly simmering large chunks of well-seasoned, sometimes marinated pork shoulder in hot lard, then coarsely chopping the meat and eating it wrapped in warm tortillas. In the following version, the fat content of the finished dish is dramatically diminished by simmering the meat in flavorful citrus juices. The results taste marvelously authentic.

Pork Loin Roast with Root Vegetables

Parsnips, young turnips, and celery root add an undertone of sweetness to the caramelized vegetables surrounding this tender roast, and the onion cooks down and thickens the pan juices into a rich sauce. These earthy vegetables, which pair so well with pork, are best in cold weather when a hearty roast is a welcome part of any good meal.

Season the pork generously with salt and pepper. In a large frying pan over medium-high heat, warm the canola oil. Add the pork and cook, turning frequently, until browned on all sides, about 10 minutes. Remove from the pan and set aside.

Pour off all but 2 tablespoons of the fat in the pan. Add the onion and sauté over medium-high heat until softened and lightly browned, about 5 minutes. Add the garlic and cook for 1 minute. Set aside.

OVEN: Preheat the oven to 325°F (165°C). Place the carrots, parsnips, potatoes, turnips, and celery root in a Dutch oven. Add the onion mixture, season generously with salt and pepper, and stir well to combine. Place the pork on top of the vegetables. Pour in the 1 cup broth. Cover and cook until the pork is very tender and the vegetables are softened, about 2 hours. Check the pork and vegetables periodically, and if more liquid is needed to prevent scorching, add another 1/2 cup (4 fl oz/125 ml) broth.

SLOW COOKER: Transfer the pork to a slow cooker. Add the onion mixture and the carrots, parsnips, potatoes, turnips, and celery root. Season generously with salt and pepper. Pour in the 1 cup broth. Cover and cook until the pork is very tender and the vegetables are fully cooked, 6–8 hours on the low-heat setting.

Transfer the pork to a warmed platter and surround with the vegetables. Use a large, shallow spoon or a ladle to skim as much fat as possible from the surface of the cooking liquid. Spoon the cooking juices over the pork and serve at once.

1 boneless pork loin roast, about 2 lb (1 kg)

Salt and freshly ground pepper

2 tablespoons canola oil

1 yellow onion, thinly sliced

1 clove garlic, minced

2 carrots, peeled, halved lengthwise, and cut into 2-inch (5-cm) pieces

2 parsnips, peeled and cut into 2-inch (5-cm) pieces

2 Yukon gold potatoes, peeled and cut into 2-inch (5-cm) pieces

2 or 3 young white turnips, about 2 lb (1 kg) total weight, peeled and quartered

1 small celery root (celeriac), peeled, halved, and quartered

1 cup (8 fl oz/250 ml) chicken broth, plus more if needed

1 tablespoon chopped fresh rosemary

Caribbean Pork Stew with Plantains

3 tablespoons all-purpose (plain) flour

Salt and freshly ground pepper

¼ cup (2 fl oz/60 ml) canola oil

2 lb (1 kg) boneless pork shoulder, trimmed of excess fat and cut into 1-inch (2.5-cm) cubes

1 yellow onion, chopped

2 cloves garlic, minced

1 teaspoon red pepper flakes

½ teaspoon ground ginger

¼ teaspoon ground cinnamon

1 bay leaf

1½ cups (12 fl oz/375 ml) fresh orange juice

2 tablespoons firmly packed dark brown sugar

3 firm, ripe plantains or large, firm, slightly underripe bananas, cut into ¾-inch (2-cm) pieces

2 tablespoons chopped fresh chives

On a plate, stir together the flour, 1 teaspoon salt, and 1 teaspoon pepper. Turn the pork cubes in the seasoned flour, shaking off any excess. In a large frying pan over medium-high heat, warm the canola oil. Working in batches to avoid overcrowding, sauté until browned on all sides, about 5 minutes. Remove from the pan and set aside.

Add the onion to the pan and sauté over medium-high heat until tender but not yet browned, about 3 minutes. Add the garlic, red pepper flakes, ginger, cinnamon, and bay leaf and sauté until fragrant, about 30 seconds. Pour the orange juice and deglaze the pan, stirring and scraping up the browned bits on the bottom of the pan with a wooden spoon. Stir in the brown sugar until dissolved and bring to a boil.

STOVE TOP: Transfer the pork cubes to a large Dutch oven and pour in the orange juice mixture. Cover and cook over very low heat for 2–2½ hours. Uncover and use a large, shallow spoon or a ladle to skim as much fat as possible from the surface of the cooking liquid. Add the plantain chunks, pushing them down into the cooking liquid. Cover and cook until the pork is very tender and a slightly thickened sauce has formed, about 30 minutes.

SLOW COOKER: Transfer the pork cubes to a slow cooker and pour in the orange juice mixture. Cover and cook for 3½ hours on the high-heat setting or 7½ hours on the low-heat setting. Uncover and use a large, shallow spoon or a ladle to skim as much fat as possible from the surface of the cooking liquid. Add the plantain chunks, pushing them down into the cooking liquid. Cover and cook until the pork is very tender and a slightly thickened sauce has formed, about 30 minutes.

Divide the stew among warmed plates, garnish with the chives, and serve at once.

The sweet-and-spicy flavors of the Caribbean go especially well with the rich, sweet taste of pork. Plantains, which resemble overgrown bananas, have a starchier, less sweet flavor. Look for ripe plantains that have slightly blackened peels. If they are unavailable, substitute slightly underripe bananas that still have some green along the ridges of their peels. You can also add cubes of yam or chunks of fresh pineapple to the stew. Serve over Steamed Jasmine Rice (page 262).

Braised Stuffed Pork Shoulder

An economical cut of pork becomes a special-occasion, family-style main course in this traditional French country recipe. Feel free to vary the stuffing, adding other herbs or some grated Parmesan cheese or chopped ham. You can also add some crushed tomatoes and dried oregano to the cooking liquid for a thicker, Italian-style sauce.

Lay the pork shoulder on a cutting board with the boned side facing up. Starting at the center and using a sharp knife, cut through the thickest part of the meat, working from the center to the sides and cutting parallel to the board, to create 2 flaps of meat. When opened, the butterflied pork should measure about 12 by 16 inches (30 by 40 cm).

In a bowl, stir together the bread, egg, garlic, parsley, basil, oregano, dried thyme, 1/4 teaspoon salt, and a pinch of pepper. Spread on the pork, leaving a border of about 1/4 inch (6 mm) on the long edges and about 1 inch (2.5 cm) on the short edges. Starting at a short edge, roll up the meat. Securely tie the roll at regular intervals with kitchen string.

In a large frying pan over medium-high heat, warm the olive oil. Season the pork generously with salt and pepper. Cook the pork, turning occasionally, until browned on all sides, about 10 minutes. Remove from the pan and set aside.

Add the wine to the pan and deglaze over medium-high heat, stirring and scraping up the browned bits on the bottom of the pan with a wooden spoon. Stir in the broth and bring to a boil.

OVEN: Preheat the oven to 350°F (180°C). Place the pork in a large Dutch oven. Add the broth mixture and thyme sprigs. Cover and cook until the pork is tender, about 2 hours.

SLOW COOKER: Place the pork in a slow cooker. Add the broth mixture and thyme sprigs. Cover and cook until the pork is very tender, 4 hours on the high-heat setting or 8 hours on the low-heat setting for 8 hours.

Transfer the pork to a cutting board and cover loosely with aluminum foil to keep warm. Remove and discard the thyme sprigs. Pour the cooking liquid into a saucepan, bring to a boil over high heat, and cook until it thickens slightly to a sauce consistency, about 10 minutes. Taste and, if necessary, adjust the seasonings with salt and pepper if necessary.

Using a sharp knife, cut the pork crosswise into slices about 1/2 inch (12 mm) thick, removing the strings as you slice. Arrange the slices on warmed plates, top with the sauce, and serve at once.

1 boneless pork shoulder, about 4 lb (2 kg)

1 thick slice good-quality white sandwich bread, coarsely crumbled

1 egg, lightly beaten

2 cloves garlic, minced

2 tablespoons chopped fresh flat-leaf (Italian) parsley

1 tablespoon finely shredded fresh basil leaves

1/2 teaspoon dried oregano

1/2 teaspoon dried thyme

Salt and freshly ground pepper

1/4 cup (2 fl oz/60 ml) olive oil

1 cup (8 fl oz/250 ml) dry white wine such as sauvignon blanc

1 cup (8 fl oz/250 ml) chicken broth

2 sprigs fresh thyme

Pork Shoulder with Sauerkraut and Apples

1 boneless pork shoulder roast, 4–5 lb (2–2.5 kg)

Salt and freshly ground pepper

2 tablespoons unsalted butter

2 tablespoons canola oil

1 yellow onion, thinly sliced

3 Golden Delicious apples, peeled, halved, and cored

1 tablespoon thyme

1/2 cup (4 fl oz/125 ml) dry white wine such as chardonnay

2 lb (1 kg) sauerkraut, squeezed dry

1/4 cup (2 oz/60 g) firmly packed dark brown sugar

1 tablespoon caraway seeds

Lay the pork flat, boned side up, on a cutting board. Using a sharp knife, trim away any large pockets of fat. Starting at the thinner end of the meat, roll up the pork and securely tie the roll at regular intervals with kitchen string. Season the pork generously with salt and pepper.

In a frying pan over medium-high heat, melt the butter with the canola oil. Add the pork and cook, turning frequently, until browned on all sides, about 10 minutes. Remove from the pan and set aside.

Add the onion, apples, and thyme to the pan and sauté over medium-high heat until the onion and apples are lightly browned, about 5 minutes. Remove from the pan and set aside. Pour off the fat in the pan. Add the wine and deglaze the pan, stirring and scraping up the browned bits on the bottom of the pan with a wooden spoon.

OVEN: Preheat oven to 325°F (165°C). Cover the bottom of a large Dutch oven with the sauerkraut. Sprinkle with the brown sugar and caraway seeds. Place the pork on top and surround with the apple mixture. Pour in the wine mixture. Cover and cook until the pork is fork-tender and shreds easily, 4–5 hours.

SLOW COOKER: Cover the bottom of a slow cooker with the sauerkraut. Sprinkle with the brown sugar and caraway seeds. Place the pork on top and surround with the apple mixture. Pour in the wine mixture. Cover and cook until the pork is fork-tender and shreds easily, 8–10 hours on the low-heat setting.

Transfer the pork to a cutting board. Using a sharp knife, cut the pork crosswise into slices about 1/2 inch (12 mm) thick, removing the strings as you slice. Place the sauerkraut on a large platter and top with the pork slices. Surround with the apples and serve at once.

Here, the sharp flavor of sauerkraut and the slight sweetness of Golden Delicious apples augment the richness of pork. The apples and pork shoulder also benefit from long, slow cooking. If you have access to a butcher, ask to have the shoulder trimmed and tied for you.

Posole

There's something eloquently simple and satisfying about this slowly simmered, main-course soup, a standby in kitchens in both Mexico and the American Southwest. It takes its name from the Spanish word for hominy, giant kernels of slaked corn. Since canned precooked hominy is so widely available, and the results are almost indistinguishable from dried hominy cooked at home, most cooks today start with the canned product. Leftover posole tastes just as good or even better reheated the next day.

STOVE TOP: Place the pork, hominy, onions, garlic, broth, chile powder, oregano, cumin, 1 1/2 teaspoons salt, and 1/2 teaspoon pepper in a large Dutch oven. Stir to combine. Bring to a boil over medium-high heat, reduce the heat to very low, partially cover, and cook until the pork is very tender, about 3 hours.

SLOW COOKER: Place the pork, hominy, onions, garlic, broth, chile powder, oregano, cumin, 1 1/2 teaspoons salt, and 1/2 teaspoon pepper in a slow cooker. Stir to combine. Cover and cook until the pork is very tender, 4 hours on the high-heat setting or 8 hours on the low-heat setting.

Season the posole to taste with salt and pepper. Arrange the cabbage, onions, radishes, avocado, red pepper flakes, oregano, and lime wedges in small bowls. Ladle the posole into warmed bowls and serve at once. Pass the accompaniments at the table.

3 lb (1.5 kg) boneless pork shoulder, trimmed of excess fat and cut into 1-inch (2.5-cm) chunks

4 cans (15 1/2 oz/485 g each) white hominy, drained, rinsed, and drained again

2 yellow onions, finely chopped

6 cloves garlic, minced

4 cups (32 fl oz/1 l) chicken broth

4 tablespoons medium-hot chile powder

1 tablespoon dried oregano

1 1/2 teaspoons ground cumin

Salt and freshly ground pepper

For Serving

1 head green or white cabbage, quartered, cored, and thinly shredded

2 yellow onions, finely chopped

1 small bunch red radishes, coarsely chopped

2 firm, ripe avocados, halved, pitted, peeled, and diced

Red pepper flakes

Dried oregano

3 limes, cut into wedges

Pork Chops and Mushrooms in Cream Sauce

4 bone-in center-cut pork chops, each 6–8 oz (185–250 g) and about ³⁄₄ inch (2 cm) thick

Salt and freshly ground pepper

3 tablespoons unsalted butter

2 leeks, white and pale green parts only, thinly sliced

1 lb (500 g) assorted fresh mushrooms such as cremini, brushed clean, stems removed, and caps sliced

¹⁄₄ cup (2 fl oz/60 ml) Madeira

1 tablespoon Worcestershire sauce

2 tablespoons chopped fresh tarragon

¹⁄₂ cup (4 fl oz/125 ml) heavy (double) cream

¹⁄₄ cup (2 fl oz/60 ml) chicken broth

Season the pork chops generously with salt and pepper. In a large frying pan over medium-high heat, melt 2 tablespoons of the butter. Add the pork chops and cook until browned on both sides, 5–6 minutes. Remove from the pan and set aside.

Return the pan to medium-high heat and melt the remaining 1 tablespoon butter. Add the leeks, reduce the heat to medium, and sauté until soft and golden, 3–4 minutes. Add the mushrooms and cook, stirring often, until the mushrooms are softened and beginning to release their liquid, about 4 minutes. Stir in the Madeira, Worcestershire sauce, and 1 tablespoon of the tarragon. Cook, stirring frequently, for 2 minutes. Stir in the cream and broth.

Return the pork chops and any accumulated juices to the pan. Spoon the mushroom mixture over the pork chops, cover, reduce the heat to medium-low, and cook until the pork chops are tender, about 10 minutes.

Stir in the remaining 1 tablespoon tarragon and season to taste with salt and pepper. Serve the pork chops at once, topped with the mushrooms and sauce.

Pork chops, which are very lean and tend to dry out quickly, stay moist when braised, even for a short time. Bourbon gives a heady flavor to the sauce, but Madeira or port will work equally well. Accompany with Roasted Potatoes (page 260) and steamed asparagus.

Chile Verde

Literally "green chile," this traditional stew from Mexico and the American Southwest couldn't be simpler to make, combining bite-sized pieces of lean pork stew meat with mild green chiles and green tomatillos. Many home cooks add just a little ripe red tomato, which enriches the flavor without interfering with the dish's signature color. Serve as an appetizer or as a main course over steamed rice.

Place the pork cubes in a large bowl. Sprinkle with 2 teaspoons salt and 1 teaspoon pepper and toss to coat well.

STOVE TOP: Transfer the pork to a large Dutch oven. Add the mild green chiles, tomatillos, onion, garlic, jalapeño, broth, tomatoes, oregano, and cumin and stir briefly to combine. Bring to a boil over high heat, reduce the heat to very low, partially cover, and cook until the pork is very tender and a thick sauce has formed, 2–3 hours.

SLOW COOKER: Transfer the pork to a slow cooker. Add the mild green chiles, tomatillos, onion, garlic, jalapeño, broth, tomatoes, oregano, and cumin and stir briefly to combine. Cover and cook until the pork is very tender and a thick sauce has formed, 4 hours on the high-heat setting or 8 hours on the low-heat setting.

Ladle the chile verde into warmed bowls and serve at once. Pass the corn tortillas, sour cream, and cilantro at the table.

4 lb (2 kg) boneless pork shoulder, trimmed of excess fat cut into 1-inch (2.5-cm) cubes

Salt and freshly ground pepper

4 cans, (7 oz/220 g each) diced, roasted mild green chiles

2 cans, (12 oz/375 g each) whole tomatillos, drained and broken up by hand

1 large yellow onion, finely chopped

4 cloves garlic, minced

1 large jalapeño chile, seeded and minced

2 cups (16 fl oz/500 ml) chicken broth

3/4 lb (375 g) firm, ripe tomatoes, finely chopped

1 tablespoon dried oregano

2 teaspoons ground cumin

Warmed corn tortillas, torn into bite-sized pieces, for garnish

Sour cream for garnish

Chopped fresh cilantro (fresh coriander) for garnish

Pulled Pork

1 boneless pork shoulder roast, about 3 lb (1.5 kg)

Salt and freshly ground pepper

2 tablespoons canola oil

1 yellow onion, chopped

1 clove garlic, minced

1/2 cup (4 fl oz/125 ml) chicken broth

2 cups (16 fl oz/500 ml) bottled or homemade barbecue sauce, plus more for serving

3 tablespoons yellow mustard

1/4 cup (2 fl oz/60 ml) honey

Soft sandwich rolls, split and toasted, for serving

Cole Slaw (page 265) for serving

Lay the pork flat, side surface up, on a cutting board. Using a sharp knife, trim away any large pockets of fat. Starting at the thinner end of the meat, roll up the pork. Securely tie the roll at regular intervals with kitchen string. Season the pork all over with salt and pepper.

In a large frying pan over medium-high heat, warm the canola oil. Add the pork and cook, turning frequently, until browned on all sides, about 10 minutes. Remove from the pan and set aside.

Pour off all but 2 tablespoons of the fat in the pan. Add the onion and sauté over medium-high heat until softened, 3–5 minutes. Add the garlic and cook for 1 minute. Add the broth and season to taste with salt and pepper.

STOVE TOP: Transfer the pork to a Dutch oven and add the broth mixture. Cover and cook over medium heat, turning the pork occasionally, until tender, about 2 hours. Transfer the pork to a platter and let cool. Cut away the string and pull the pork into shreds, removing all the fat and gristle. Return the pork to the pot. Add the 2 cups barbecue sauce, the mustard, honey, 1/2 teaspoon salt, and 1/4 teaspoon pepper. Stir well, raise the heat to high, and cook, uncovered, and stirring frequently, until the flavors are well blended and the sauce has thickened, about 30 minutes.

SLOW COOKER: Transfer the pork to a slow cooker and add the broth mixture. Cover and cook until the pork is very tender, 8–10 hours on the low-heat setting. Transfer the pork to a platter and let cool. Cut away the strings and pull the pork into shreds, removing all the fat and gristle. Return the pork to the cooker. Add the 2 cups barbecue sauce, the mustard, the honey, 1/2 teaspoon salt, and 1/4 teaspoon pepper. Stir well, set the temperature to high, and cook, uncovered, and stirring frequently, until the flavors are well blended and the sauce has thickened, about 30 minutes.

Serve the pork on the rolls, topped with the coleslaw. Pass the additional barbecue sauce at the table.

This pork is cooked so long and becomes so tender that it can easily be pulled into shreds using two forks, hence the name of this favorite recipe from the American South. Sweetened iced tea is the beverage of choice.

Maple-Braised Pork Chops

With its sweet-and-tangy combination of flavors, this popular home-style recipe from New England is a cousin to the well-loved barbecued or pulled pork of the American South. If you like, tuck some wedges of apple among the chops during the last half hour or so of cooking.

On a plate, stir together the flour, ³/₄ teaspoon salt, and ¹/₂ teaspoon pepper. Turn the pork chops in the seasoned flour, shaking off any excess. In a large frying pan over medium-high heat, warm the canola oil. Working in batches if necessary, cook the pork chops until golden brown, about 4 minutes per side. Remove from the pan and set aside.

Pour off all but a thin coating of fat in the pan and return it to medium-high heat. Add the onion, garlic, and chile powder and sauté until fragrant, about 30 seconds. Pour in the broth and deglaze the pan, stirring and scraping up the browned bits on the bottom of the pan with a wooden spoon. Stir in the maple syrup, vinegar, and Worcestershire sauce and bring to a boil.

STOVE TOP: Transfer the pork chops to a large Dutch oven. Pour the maple syrup mixture over the chops to cover them. Partially cover and cook over very low heat until the pork chops are very tender and the sauce is thick, about 2 hours.

SLOW COOKER: Transfer the pork chops to a slow cooker. Pour the maple syrup mixture over the chops to cover them. Cover and cook until the chops are very tender and the sauce is thick, 4 hours on the high-heat setting or 8 hours on the low-heat setting.

Arrange the chops on warmed plates. Top with the sauce, garnish with the chives, and serve at once.

3 tablespoons all-purpose (plain) flour

Salt and freshly ground pepper

4 bone-in pork loin chops, each about 12 oz (375 g) and 1¹/₂ inches (4 cm) thick

3 tablespoons canola oil

1 small yellow onion, finely chopped

1 clove garlic, minced

2 teaspoons chile powder

³/₄ cup (6 fl oz/180 ml) chicken broth

³/₄ cup (6 fl oz/180 ml) maple syrup

3 tablespoons apple cider vinegar

2 tablespoons Worcestershire sauce

2 tablespoons finely chopped fresh chives

Ale-Braised Sausages with Bell Peppers

2 tablespoons olive oil

2 lb (1 kg) cooked sausages such as kielbasa, sliced

1 large yellow onion, thinly sliced

1 large red bell pepper (capsicum), seeded and sliced

2 tablespoons all-purpose (plain) flour

1 cup (8 fl oz/250 ml) ale

½ cup (4 fl oz/125 ml) apple cider

3 tablespoons chopped fresh thyme

1½ cups (12 fl oz/375 ml) chicken broth

Salt and freshly ground pepper

Mashed Potatoes (page 260) for serving

In a Dutch oven over medium-high heat, warm the olive oil. Add the sausages and cook, stirring and turning often, until browned, 4–5 minutes. Transfer to a plate and set aside.

Add the onion and bell pepper to the pot, reduce the heat to medium, and sauté until tender and golden, about 5 minutes. Add the flour and cook, stirring, until golden, 1–2 minutes. Whisk in the ale and cider until the mixture is smooth and bubbly. Add the thyme and broth, whisking to blend, and bring to a simmer.

Return the sausages to the pot. Cover, reduce the heat to medium-low, and cook until the flavors are blended, about 15 minutes. Uncover and simmer until the sauce is slightly reduced, about 5 minutes. Season to taste with salt and pepper.

Divide the sausages and sauce among warmed plates and serve at once with mashed potatoes alongside.

You can vary this recipe depending on the type of sausage and ale you choose. Mashed potatoes are the perfect foil for the hearty sauce and big flavors. Kielbasa is a garlicky, fully cooked Polish sausage which is available made with pork or beef, but a combination of the two is the most tasty.

Pork Vindaloo

The name of this dish, *vindaloo*, is reputedly a Hindu reinterpretation of the Portuguese *vinho de alho*, "wine of garlic," reflecting Portugal's influence on the cooking of its former colony, Goa, on the western coast of the India. Although vindaloo-style curries are legendary for their incendiary spiciness, this version is not overwhelmingly hot and aims to present a well-balanced flavor. If you're a fanatic for heat, add more cayenne. Serve with steamed white rice or Herbed Rice Pilaf (page 262) to provide a soothing accompaniment.

Place the pork cubes in a bowl, sprinkle with 1 teaspoon salt and 1 teaspoon black pepper, and toss to coat. In a large frying pan over medium-high heat, warm the canola oil. Working in batches, add the pork and cook until well browned on all sides, 6–7 minutes. Remove from the pan and set aside.

Add the onions to the pan, raise the heat to high, and sauté until browned, 10–12 minutes. Add the garlic, ginger, cayenne, mustard seeds, cumin, paprika, turmeric, cinnamon, and cloves and sauté until the spices are fragrant and evenly coat the chopped onion, about 1 minute. Pour in the vinegar and deglaze the pan, stirring and scraping up the browned bits on the bottom of the pan with a wooden spoon. Stir in the broth and bring to a boil.

STOVE TOP: Transfer the pork to a large Dutch oven and pour in the broth mixture. Partially cover and cook over low heat until the pork is very tender and the sauce has thickened, 1 1/2–2 hours.

SLOW COOKER: Transfer the pork to a slow cooker and pour in the broth mixture. Cover and cook until the pork is very tender and the sauce has thickened, 3 hours on the high-heat setting or 6 hours on the low-heat setting.

Divide the pork among warmed plates and serve at once.

2 1/2–3 lb (1.25–1.5 kg) boneless pork shoulder, trimmed of excess fat and cut into 1-inch (2.5-cm) cubes

Salt and freshly ground black pepper

1/2 cup (4 fl oz/125 ml) canola oil

2 yellow onions, finely chopped

8 cloves garlic, minced

2-inch (5-cm) piece fresh ginger, peeled and grated

1 1/2 teaspoons cayenne pepper

1 1/2 teaspoons brown mustard seeds

1 1/2 teaspoons ground cumin

1 1/2 teaspoons hot paprika

1 1/2 teaspoons ground turmeric

1/2 teaspoon ground cinnamon

Pinch of ground cloves

1/3 cup (3 fl oz/80 ml) white wine vinegar

1 cup (8 fl oz/250 ml) chicken broth

Braised Pork Chops with Turnips and Greens

½ teaspoon hot paprika

Salt and freshly ground pepper

6 bone-in pork loin chops, each about 14 oz (440 g) and 1½ inches (4 cm) thick

6 slices smoked bacon, about 6 oz (185 g) total weight, cut crosswise into ½-inch (12-mm) pieces

2 yellow onions, thinly sliced

4 cloves garlic, minced

½ teaspoon red pepper flakes

½ teaspoon caraway seeds

1 cup (8 fl oz/250 ml) dark beer

1 cup (8 fl oz/250 ml) chicken broth

⅓ cup (3 fl oz/80 ml) rice vinegar

1 tablespoon molasses

1 tablespoon firmly packed dark brown sugar

1 lb (500 g) turnip greens, mustard greens, or kale, stems removed and leaves cut crosswise into ribbons 1 inch (2.5 cm) wide

¾ lb (375 g) small turnips, peeled and each cut into 8 wedges

In a small bowl, combine the paprika, ¾ teaspoon salt, and ½ teaspoon pepper. Season the pork chops all over with the mixture. Set aside.

In a large frying pan over medium-high heat, sauté the bacon pieces until they have shriveled and rendered several tablespoons of fat and have just started to brown, about 3 minutes. Using a slotted spoon, transfer to a paper towel-lined plate and set aside.

Working in batches, add the pork chops to the pan and cook, turning frequently, until browned on all sides, about 10 minutes. Remove from the pan and aside.

Pour off all but a thin layer of fat in the pan. Add the onions and sauté over medium-high heat just until they begin to brown, about 5 minutes. Stir in the garlic, red pepper flakes, and caraway seeds and sauté for about 30 seconds. Pour in the beer and deglaze the pan, stirring and scraping up the browned bits on the bottom of the pan with a wooden spoon. Stir in the broth, rice vinegar, molasses, and brown sugar and bring to a boil. Add the greens and reserved bacon and stir gently to combine.

STOVE TOP: Transfer the beer mixture to a large Dutch oven. Add the pork chops, burying them among the greens. Partially cover and cook over very low heat for about 1 hour. Uncover and add the turnip wedges, placing them between the chops. Partially cover and cook until the pork chops are very tender, about 1 hour longer.

SLOW COOKER: Transfer the beer mixture to a slow cooker. Add the pork chops, burying them among the greens. Cover and cook for 3 hours on the high-heat setting or 7 hours on the low-heat setting. Uncover and add the turnip wedges, placing them between the chops. Cover and cook until the pork chops are very tender, about 1 hour longer.

Transfer the pork chops to a warmed platter, spooning the greens and turnips around them. Use a large, shallow spoon or a ladle to skim as much fat as possible from the surface of the cooking liquid. Taste and adjust the seasonings with salt and pepper if necessary. Spoon the cooking juices over the pork and vegetables and serve at once.

Pork and slightly bitter greens are natural companions. In this sweet-and-tangy recipe from the American South, slow simmering mellows the flavor of the greens and cooks the meat to fork tenderness. Wedges of turnip simmered in the cooking juices add their own delicate, yet down-to-earth flavor. This recipe calls for four pork chops so big and meaty that they will likely serve six unless those at table are especially hearty eaters.

Beer-Braised Pork Roast

In this recipe the pleasantly astringent flavor of beer permeates the pork during slow cooking. The butt, used here, is the top end of a whole leg of the pig. The shoulder, although a little fattier and with more connective tissue, makes a good alternative for beer-braising. Serve with braised red cabbage or sautéed green vegetables.

Season the pork generously with salt and pepper. In a large frying pan over medium-high heat, warm the canola oil. Add the pork and cook, turning frequently, until browned on all sides, about 10 minutes. Remove from the pan and set aside.

Pour off all but 1 tablespoon of the fat in the pan. Add the onions and carrot and sauté over medium-high heat until softened, about 5 minutes. Add the garlic and cook for 1 minute. Stir in the tomato paste and cook, stirring frequently, until the mixture starts to become dry, about 2 minutes. Add the flour and cook, stirring constantly to prevent scorching, for 2 minutes. Pour in the beer and deglaze the pan, stirring and scraping up the browned bits on the bottom of the pan with a wooden spoon. Cook until the liquid starts to thicken, about 10 minutes. Stir in the cider, broth, vinegar, and thyme. Season to taste with salt and pepper and bring to a boil.

OVEN: Preheat the oven to 300°F (150°C). Transfer the pork to a Dutch oven. Add the beer mixture. Cover and cook in the oven for about 3 hours. Uncover and cook, basting frequently with the cooking liquid, until the pork is tender, about 1 hour longer.

SLOW COOKER: Transfer the pork to a slow cooker. Add the beer mixture. Cover and cook for 6–8 hours on the low-heat setting. Uncover, set the temperature to high, and cook, basting frequently with the cooking liquid, until the pork is tender, about 1 hour longer.

Transfer the pork to a cutting board and cover loosely with aluminum foil to keep warm. Use a large, shallow spoon or a ladle to skim as much fat as possible from the surface of the cooking liquid. Cut the pork against the grain into thin slices. Arrange the slices on a warmed platter, spoon the cooking juices over the top, and serve at once.

1 pork butt roast, about 4 lb (2 kg), trimmed

Salt and freshly ground pepper

2 tablespoons canola oil

2 yellow onions, thinly sliced

1 carrot, chopped

2 cloves garlic, minced

1 tablespoon tomato paste

3 tablespoons all-purpose (plain) flour

1 bottle (12 fl oz/375 ml) dark beer or ale

½ cup (4 fl oz/125 ml) apple cider

1 cup (8 fl oz/250 ml) chicken broth

1 tablespoon apple cider vinegar

5–6 sprigs fresh thyme

Brined Pork Belly

Look for pork belly often times called side pork at Asian or other ethnic markets. Brining boosts the flavor, and braising renders out the fat, leaving the meat meltingly tender.

In a large bowl, combine the water, sugar, and salt. Set aside, stirring occasionally, until the sugar and salt dissolve. Stir in the sage and peppercorns. Add the pork belly and cover with plastic wrap. Refrigerate, turning occasionally to ensure the meat is covered with the brine, at least 3 hours or overnight

Discard the brine. Rinse the pork under cold running water to remove excess salt. Pat dry with paper towels.

Preheat the oven to 325°F (165°C). In a large enameled cast iron Dutch oven, heat 2 tablespoons of olive oil over medium-high heat. Add the pork, fat-side down, and cook 5 minutes, or until nicely browned. Turn over and cook 4–5 minutes longer. Transfer the meat to a plate. Drain off all but 2 tablespoons of fat from the pan. Scatter onion slices over the bottom, and place the meat on top, fat-side up. Season with pepper to taste. Pour in the chicken stock. Cover and bake for one hour. Use the tip of a sharp knife to score the top fat into a cross-hatch pattern about ¼-inch deep. Return to the oven and bake, covered, until the meat is very tender when pierced with a fork, about 1¼ hours longer. Increase the oven temperature to 450°F. and cook uncovered for 20 minutes, or until the top fat is browned and crisp.

Transfer the pork to a cutting board and let rest 5 to 10 minutes before cutting into strips or other serving-size pieces. Drain the onions and serve on the side, or reserve for another use. If desired, the cooled pork can be refrigerated in its juices. The next day, scrape off and discard any visible fat before reheating, covered, in a low oven.

Brine

4 cups cold water

⅔ cup sugar

⅔ cup coarse sea salt

8 fresh sage leaves

8 whole peppercorns

2lb (1 kg) piece of pork belly, with rinds and bones

1 slab skinless boneless fresh

2 tablespoons olive oil

2 onions, peeled and cut into slices ½-inch thick

Freshly ground pepper

1 cup chicken stock, broth, or water

Pork Tenderloin with Braised Cabbage and Figs

1 savoy cabbage, about 2 lb (1 kg), bruised or discolored outer leaves removed

1/2 cup (2 1/2 oz/75 g) all-purpose (plain) flour

3 small pork tenderloins, about 1 1/4 lb (625 g) each, trimmed of excess fat

2 tablespoons unsalted butter

2 tablespoons canola oil

1 yellow onion, thinly sliced

1/4 cup (2 fl oz/60 ml) dry white wine such as chardonnay

Salt and freshly ground pepper

24 dried Black Mission or Calimyrna figs, stems removed

Replace the figs with prunes or dried apricots if desired. Serve with Mashed Potatoes (page 260), Buttered Egg Noodles (page 264), or glazed sweet potatoes.

Cut the cabbage in half lengthwise and remove the core. Cut the cabbage into very thin slices and set aside.

Spread the flour on a plate. Roll each tenderloin in the flour, shaking off the excess. In a large frying pan over medium-high heat, melt the butter with the canola oil. Cook the tenderloins, turning frequently, until browned on all sides, about 10 minutes. Remove from the pan and set aside.

Pour off all but 2 tablespoons of the fat in the pan. Add the onion and sauté over medium-high heat until softened, 3–5 minutes. Add the cabbage and cook, stirring constantly, until slightly wilted, about 3 minutes. Pour in the wine, raise the heat to high, and deglaze the pan, stirring and scraping up the browned bits on the bottom of the pan with a wooden spoon. Cook until the cabbage is completely wilted, about 2 minutes. Season with salt and pepper.

OVEN: Preheat oven to 350°F (180°C). Transfer the cabbage mixture to a Dutch oven. Arrange the tenderloins on top of the cabbage and add the figs. Cover and cook until a thermometer inserted into the thickest part of a tenderloin registers 140°F (60°C), about 45 minutes.

SLOW COOKER: Transfer the cabbage mixture to a slow cooker. Arrange the tenderloins on top of the cabbage and add the figs. Cover and cook until an instant-read thermometer inserted into the thickest part of a tenderloin registers 140°F (60°C), 4 hours on the low-heat setting.

Transfer the tenderloins to a cutting board and cut into thick slices. Season the cabbage to taste with salt and pepper. Arrange the cabbage and figs on a warmed platter, top with the pork slices, and serve at once.

Cochinita Pibil

One of the most time-honored and impressive specialties of Mexico's Yucatán region is *cochinita pibil*, literally "pit-barbecued little pig." In the dish's most traditional form, a whole pig is cooked in a fire pit that is dug in the earth and lined with banana leaves. The leaves keep the meat moist and add a hint of verdant tropical flavor. The other distinction is the seasonings, including *annatto* seeds, called achiote in Spanish, which contribute an appealingly musty fragrance along with a vibrant, deep red color, and the juice of bitter Seville oranges.

In a large nonreactive bowl, stir together the achiote powder, garlic, oregano, cumin, 1 teaspoon salt, and 1 teaspoon pepper. Add the pork and turn to coat evenly with the achiote mixture, rubbing it thoroughly into the meat with your fingertips.

OVEN: Preheat the oven to 325°F (165°C). Line the bottom and sides of a large Dutch oven with half of the banana leaves, overlapping them. Add the pork, fat side up, and pour in the orange and lemon juices. Cover the pork with the remaining banana leaves, overlapping them and tucking them around the sides of the pot. Cover and cook until the pork is very tender, about 4 hours.

SLOW COOKER: Line the bottom and sides of a slow cooker with half of the banana leaves, overlapping them. Add the pork, fat side up and pour in the orange and lemon juices. Cover the pork with the remaining banana leaves, overlapping them and tucking them around the sides of the cooker. Cover and cook until the pork is very tender, 5 hours on the high-heat setting or 10 hours on the low-heat setting.

Meanwhile, put the onion slices in a nonreactive bowl. Sprinkle with the lime juice and 1/2 teaspoon salt and toss to combine. Cover with plastic wrap and refrigerate until the pork is done, stirring the onions every 1–2 hours.

When the pork is done, remove and discard the top banana leaves. Use a large, shallow spoon or a ladle to skim as much fat as possible from the surface of the cooking liquid. Using a pair of forks, coarsely shred the pork, removing and discarding any excess fat.

Arrange the tortillas, avocado slices, salsa, lime wedges, and marinated onion slices on one platter and the shredded pork on another. Serve at once, letting guests assemble their own tacos with the pork, spooning a little of the cooking juices over the meat and garnishing with the onion, avocado, salsa, and a squeeze of lime.

3 tablespoons achiote powder

4 cloves garlic, minced

2 teaspoons dried oregano

1 teaspoon ground cumin

Salt and freshly ground pepper

1 boneless pork shoulder roast, about 3 lb (1.5 kg)

2 large banana leaves, rinsed, trimmed, and cut into 6–8 rectangles about 9 by 12 inches (23 by 30 cm) each

2/3 cup (5 fl oz/160 ml) fresh orange juice

1/2 cup (4 fl oz/125 ml) fresh lemon juice

1 large red onion, halved and thinly sliced

Juice of 2 limes

For Serving

Warmed corn or flour tortillas

2 firm, ripe avocados, halved, pitted, peeled, and cut lengthwise into thin slices

Tomato or chile salsa

Lime wedges

Pork-Stuffed Cabbage Rolls

For the Cabbage Rolls

1 green cabbage, about 2 lb (1 kg), bruised or discolored outer leaves discarded

1 lb (500 g) lean ground (minced) pork

1/2 cup (2 1/2 oz/75 g) cooked rice

1 egg

3 green (spring) onions, white and pale green parts, thinly sliced

1/4 teaspoon freshly grated nutmeg

Salt and freshly ground pepper

4 slices bacon, about 1/4 lb (125 g) total weight

1 yellow onion, chopped

1 rib celery, chopped

1 carrot, chopped

1 teaspoon caraway seeds

1 can (28 oz/875 g) crushed tomatoes

1 cup (8 fl oz/250 ml) chicken broth

1/4 cup (1 1/2 oz/45 g) small raisins

1 tablespoon red wine vinegar

Make the cabbage rolls: Bring a large pot of water to a boil. Using a sharp paring knife, cut out the core from the cabbage. Lower the cabbage into the boiling water and cook until the leaves soften, about 5 minutes. Remove and set aside to cool. When the cabbage is cool enough to handle, gently peel off 12 large outer leaves. Drain the leaves and let cool. Coarsely chop enough of the remaining cabbage to make 1/4 cup (1 oz/30 g).

In a bowl, combine the chopped cabbage, pork, rice, egg, green onions, nutmeg, 3/4 teaspoon salt, and 1/2 teaspoon pepper. Using your hands, gently but thoroughly blend the ingredients. Divide the pork filling among the cabbage leaves. Fold the core end of each leaf over the filling, then fold in the sides and roll up the leaf. Set aside

Preheat the oven to 325°F (165°C). In a large Dutch oven over medium heat, cook the bacon slices, turning, until crisp, about 5 minutes. Transfer to a paper towel–lined plate. When drained, crumble the bacon and set aside.

Add the onion, celery, and carrot to the pan and sauté over medium heat until the vegetables are tender and tinged with gold, about 5 minutes. Stir in the caraway seeds, tomatoes, broth, raisins, and vinegar. Place the cabbage rolls, seam sides down, in a single layer in the pan, spooning some of the liquid over the rolls. Cover and cook in the oven until the cabbage rolls are tender and the pork filling is cooked through, 1–1 1/2 hours.

Transfer the cabbage rolls to warmed bowls. Ladle the cooking juices over the top, garnish with the crumbled bacon, and serve at once.

Various renditions of this eastern European staple are found in Poland, Hungary, and Austria. Here, the sweet-and-sour balance of the pork stuffing and braising liquid highlights the traditional flavors. The stuffed cabbage can be prepared a few hours ahead and reheated. Serve with Buttered Egg Noodles (page 264).

Albondigas

In this classic Mexican soup, pork meatballs are cooked in an aromatic broth. The hearty soup can be as spicy as you wish, depending on the variety of chile powder used. Warm corn tortillas or Corn Bread (page 264) and a salad complete the meal. Masa harina is sold in well-stocked stores and in the Latin American markets.

Make the meatballs: In a bowl, stir together the masa harina and chicken broth to make a paste. Add the pork, egg, onion, garlic, oregano, chile powder, cumin, 1 teaspoon salt, and ½ teaspoon pepper. Using your hands, gently but thoroughly blend the ingredients. Form the mixture into small meatballs about 1 inch (2.5 cm) in diameter. Set aside.

In a large saucepan over medium heat, warm the canola oil. Add the onion and sauté until softened and tinged with gold, about 5 minutes. Add the garlic and sauté for 30 seconds. Stir in the cumin and chipotles in adobo. Cook, stirring frequently for 30 seconds, then stir in the broth and tomatoes and bring to a simmer.

Drop the meatballs into the broth mixture and return to a simmer. Cover, reduce the heat to medium-low, and cook without stirring until the meatballs are firm, 15–20 minutes.

Uncover and stir in the lime juice. Season to taste with salt and pepper. Stir in the cilantro. Ladle into warmed shallow bowls and serve at once.

For the Meatballs

¼ cup (1½ oz/45 g) masa harina, or ¼ cup (1 oz/30 g) dried bread crumbs

¼ cup (2 fl oz/60 ml) chicken broth

1 lb (500 g) lean ground (minced) pork

1 egg

1 yellow onion, finely chopped

2 cloves garlic, minced

1 tablespoon chopped fresh oregano

2 teaspoons ancho chile powder

½ teaspoon ground cumin

Salt and freshly ground pepper

2 tablespoons canola oil

1 yellow onion, chopped

2 cloves garlic, minced

1 teaspoon ground cumin

1½ teaspoons minced chipotle chiles in adobo

6 cups (48 fl oz/1.5 l) chicken broth

1 can (14½ oz/455 g) diced tomatoes

1 tablespoon fresh lime juice

Salt and freshly ground pepper

3 tablespoons chopped fresh cilantro (fresh coriander)

Smothered Pork Chops with Caramelized Onions

½ cup (2½ oz/75 g) all-purpose (plain) flour

Salt and freshly ground pepper

6 boneless pork loin chops, each 6–8 oz (185–250 g) and about 1 inch (2.5 cm) thick

2 tablespoons unsalted butter

2 tablespoons canola oil

2 yellow onions, thinly sliced

2 cloves garlic, minced

½ teaspoon sugar

2 cups (16 fl oz/500 ml) chicken broth

On a plate, stir together the flour, 1 teaspoon salt, and ¼ teaspoon pepper. Turn the pork chops in the seasoned flour, shaking off any excess. In a large frying pan over medium-high heat, melt the butter with the canola oil. Cook the pork chops until browned, about 5 minutes per side. Remove from the pan and set aside.

Add the onions and garlic to the pan and sprinkle with the sugar. Cook over medium-high heat, stirring frequently, until lightly browned and caramelized, about 15 minutes. Pour in the broth and deglaze the pan, stirring and scraping up the browned bits on the bottom of the pan with a wooden spoon.

OVEN: Preheat the oven to 325°F (165°C). Transfer the pork chops to a large Dutch oven and add the onion mixture. Cover and cook until the chops are very tender, about 1 hour.

SLOW COOKER: Transfer the pork to a slow cooker and add the onion mixture. Cover and cook until the chops are very tender, 6–8 hours on the low-heat setting.

Transfer the pork chops to warmed individual plates. Top with the onions and serve at once.

This traditional American comfort food is divine when served with fluffy Mashed Potatoes (page 260) seasoned with lots of freshly ground pepper. A modest sprinkling of sugar helps caramelize the onions quickly and evenly, but be sure not to rush cooking them. The added depth of flavor from the caramelized onions makes this simple dish more than the sum of its parts.

Beef and Lamb

About Beef and Lamb

Beef chuck from the shoulder and lamb shoulder are preferred cuts for slow cooking and braising, although other cuts such as beef round or rump and leg of lamb are also delicious when cooked slowly in a flavorful stock or sauce.

With the exception of flank, skirt, and hanger steaks, which come from the belly of the steer, steaks are cut from the back of the animal, usually from the loin and rib portions. Most steaks are tender enough to grill over direct heat, which creates a caramelized crust and juicy interior. The less tender steaks from the belly tend to have a "beefier" flavor than those from the less used muscles along the back; these steaks benefit from a marinade before grilling to increase their tenderness.

When choosing steaks, seek out bright red meat with light marbling (internal fat), a fine texture, and nearly white outer fat. The exterior fat should be minimal, although you can always trim it later. The more marbling, the more tender and juicy the beef will be, so keep this in mind when you are balancing a meal for health reasons. Look for many small deposits of fat, which resemble the light streaks in a dark marble floor, rather than a few large globs.

Use the same criteria for choosing meat for choosing ribs as you would for steaks: vibrant red meat with good marbling. Pass up beef that is turning brown or has large pieces of fat. For best results with kabobs, choose a large piece of meat and cut it into cubes just before using.

When selecting ground (minced) beef, seek out a nice piece of chuck with 15 to 20 percent fat, ask the butcher to grind it for you, and then cook it the same day. Better yet, if you have access to a meat grinder, grind it yourself just before you plan to use it. Not only will this create a flavorful burger, but it will also reduce the likelihood that a breeding ground for dangerous bacteria will develop.

When shopping for roasts, look for well-trimmed external fat and a good amount of internal marbling. The meat should appear slightly moist and be a good, even red color. Smell the meat to make sure that it has a clean, fresh aroma with no off odor. Most large cuts will appear fine-grained, with the exception of brisket and tri-tip, which will have a coarser texture.

USING BEEF AND LAMB IN SLOW COOKING

The best cuts for stewing, braising, or slow roasting come from the chuck or shoulder, the rump or round, the brisket or foreleg, and the flank or ribs of the animal.

Brisket is an excellent cut for braised or stewed beef. It is a favorite of Western barbecue cooks (see Barbecue-Style Brisket, page 234) who slow roast it to tender perfection. Brisket is a large cut and is usually sold as brisket first cut or flat and brisket front cut. The first cut or flat is leaner, but the brisket front cut includes the deckle, a lusciously marbled piece of meat much loved by brisket fanciers (see Brisket with Yams and Potatoes, page 213).

The round or rump is often used in braises either as round steak or as a pot roast. The round has plenty of flavor but is lacking in fat. If cooked slowly in liquid or moist heat, round can be very tasty. Eye of the round is a popular cut, but as always with round, cook it slowly in plenty of liquid to ensure juiciness.

Flank steak is a cut that can be marinated and grilled when it is often called London broil. When pounded and rolled as in our recipe for Braciole (page 253) it is delicious when braised. Short ribs cut from the flank are wonderfull when braised to tender perfection in wine or stock. They are quite fatty though, so be sure to trim off all external fat and to remove fat from the gravy before thickening it.

The shank is a very tough muscle in any animal and is very high in collagen and connective tissue. In fact, the hoof and shank and bones of animals are used to make gelatin and glue. This high collagen level means that beef shank or veal shank (see Osso Buco, page 214) or Braised Lamb Shanks (page 256) are all very tough unless cooked slowly for a long time in a savory liquid. But when they are cooked this way they are absolutely delicious. Osso bucco and lamb shank are among the most popular dishes in restaurants and demonstrate the luscious juiciness that can be achieved by long and slow cooking.

Lamb shoulder and leg of lamb are both delicious when roasted, but can be braised with very good results. Roast shoulder can be a bit chewey, but braising it makes it fork tender and delicious while also producing a delightful gravy. Leg of lamb (see Stuffed Leg of Lamb, page 255) makes a fine braise and is very flavorful and tender after long slow cooking.

All beef should rest for 3 to 15 minutes after cooking, depending on size, to allow the juices to redistribute throughout the meat, thus ensuring juiciness and full flavor. The internal temperature could rise as much as 5° to 10°F (3° to 6°C) as the meat sits. Keep this in mind and remove beef from the grill when it is some degrees shy of the desired temperature. You can always cook beef a little more if needed.

Pappardelle Bolognese

If you prefer a thicker, drier, more even-textured Bolognese sauce in the classic Italian style, cook the sauce in the oven. For a sauce with a bit more liquid, use the slow cooker. Fresh thyme adds depth of flavor and fragrance. If the fresh herb is unavailable, substitute $\frac{1}{2}$ teaspoon dried thyme.

In a large frying pan over medium-high heat, warm the olive oil. Add the onion and celery and sauté until softened, about 5 minutes. Add the garlic and cook for 1 minute. Stir in the beef, veal, and pork and cook, stirring and breaking up the meat with a wooden spoon, until no longer pink, about 5 minutes. Add the wine and cook, stirring frequently, until it has almost evaporated, 2–3 minutes. Pour in the broth, stir in the tomato paste and parsley, and season with salt and pepper.

OVEN: Preheat the oven to 350°F (180°C). Transfer the meat mixture to a Dutch oven. Cover and cook, stirring occasionally, until thickened, about 1$\frac{1}{2}$ hours. If the sauce looks too dry after 1 hour, add $\frac{1}{2}$ cup (4 fl oz/125 ml) water.

SLOW COOKER: Transfer the meat mixture to a slow cooker. Cover and cook until thickened, 8–10 hours on the low-heat setting.

About 20 minutes before the sauce is done, bring a large pot three-fourths full of water to a boil. Add 2 tablespoons salt and the pasta and cook according to the package directions until al dente. Drain the pasta and return to the pot. Add $\frac{1}{2}$ cup of the sauce and toss gently to coat. Divide the pasta among warmed bowls and top with additional sauce. Sprinkle with some of the Parmesan and serve at once. Pass the remaining cheese at the table.

2 tablespoons olive oil

1 yellow onion, chopped

1 rib celery, thinly sliced

1 clove garlic, minced

$\frac{1}{2}$ lb (250 g) ground (minced) beef

$\frac{1}{2}$ lb (250 g) ground (minced) veal

$\frac{1}{2}$ lb (250 g) ground (minced) pork

$\frac{1}{2}$ cup (4 fl oz/125 ml) dry white wine such as chardonnay

2 cups (16 fl oz/500 ml) beef broth

2 tablespoons tomato paste

1 tablespoon chopped fresh flat-leaf (Italian) parsley

Salt and freshly ground pepper

1 lb (500 g) fresh pappardelle or fettuccine

$\frac{1}{2}$ cup (2 oz/60 g) shaved or grated Parmesan cheese

Italian Braised Short Ribs

3 tablespoons all-purpose (plain) flour

Salt and freshly ground pepper

5$\frac{1}{2}$–6 lb (2.75–3 kg) beef short ribs, English cut

$\frac{1}{4}$ cup (2 fl oz/60 ml) olive oil

2 oz (60 g) pancetta, chopped

2 yellow onions, finely chopped

4 cloves garlic, minced

1 teaspoon red pepper flakes

2 carrots, chopped

2 tablespoons tomato paste

1 tablespoon sugar

1 cup (8 fl oz/250 ml) dry red wine such as Chianti or valpolicella

1 can (14$\frac{1}{2}$ oz/455 g) diced plum (Roma) tomatoes

1 cup (8 fl oz/250 ml) beef broth

$\frac{1}{4}$ cup (2 fl oz/60 ml) balsamic vinegar

2 bay leaves

2 sprigs fresh rosemary

2 sprigs fresh thyme

1 tablespoon dried oregano

On a plate, stir together the flour, 1 teaspoon salt, and $\frac{1}{2}$ teaspoon pepper. Turn the ribs in the seasoned flour, shaking off any excess. In a large frying pan over medium-high heat, warm the olive oil. Working in batches if necessary, cook the ribs, turning occasionally, until evenly browned, about 10 minutes. Remove from the pan and set aside.

Add the pancetta to the pan and sauté, stirring often, until the fat is rendered, about 5 minutes. Add the onions and sauté until beginning to soften, about 3 minutes. Stir in the garlic and red pepper flakes and sauté until fragrant, about 30 seconds. Add the carrots, tomato paste, and sugar and cook, stirring frequently, until well blended, about 1 minute. Add the wine and deglaze the pan, stirring and scraping up the browned bits on the bottom of the pan with a wooden spoon. Bring the wine to a boil; stir in the tomatoes, broth, and vinegar; and return to a boil.

OVEN: Preheat the oven to 350°F (180°C). Transfer the ribs to a large Dutch oven. Add the tomato-broth mixture and the bay leaves, rosemary and thyme sprigs, and oregano. Cover and cook until the short ribs are very tender, about 2 hours. When the ribs are done, use a large, shallow spoon or a ladle to skim as much fat as possible from the surface of the cooking liquid. Season to taste with salt and pepper.

SLOW COOKER: Transfer the ribs to a slow cooker. Add the tomato-broth mixture and the bay leaves, rosemary and thyme sprigs, and oregano. Cover and cook until the ribs are very tender, 3 hours on the high-heat setting or 6 hours on the low-heat setting. When the ribs are done, use a large, shallow spoon or a ladle to skim as much fat as possible from the surface of the cooking liquid. Season to taste with salt and pepper.

Transfer the ribs to warmed individual plates, spoon the cooking juices over and around them, and serve at once.

Rich, meaty short ribs go well with the robust flavors of traditional Italian cooking, and slow cooking coaxes them to fall-off-the-bone tenderness. For an extra flourish, garnish each serving with some of the *gremolata* traditionally sprinkled over Osso Buco (page 214).

Springtime Veal Stew

Mild-tasting, tender veal combines with springtime vegetables in this exemplar of seasonal cooking.·Feel free to add or substitute different vegetables of your choosing. This recipe also works great with spring lamb.

Place the veal cubes in a large bowl. Sprinkle with 1 teaspoon salt and $^1/_2$ teaspoon pepper and toss to coat evenly. In a large frying pan over medium-high heat, melt the butter with the olive oil. Working in batches to avoid overcrowding, sauté the veal until evenly browned on all sides, 5–7 minutes. Remove from the pan and set aside.

Add the shallots and prosciutto to the pan and sauté over medium-high heat for about 1 minute. Pour in the wine and deglaze the pan, stirring and scraping up the browned bits on the bottom of the pan with a wooden spoon. Stir in the broth and bring to a boil.

STOVE TOP: Transfer the veal and any accumulated juices to a large Dutch oven. Add the broth mixture. Tuck the thyme sprigs among the veal cubes. Cover and cook over very low heat for 1$^1/_2$ hours. Add the carrots, cover, and cook until the veal is tender, about 20 minutes. Add the asparagus and peas and continue to cook, covered, until the vegetables are tender, about 10 minutes longer. Stir in the cream and cook until the sauce is heated through, about 5 minutes. Season to taste with salt and pepper.

SLOW COOKER: Transfer the veal and any accumulated juices to a slow cooker. Add the broth mixture. Tuck the thyme sprigs among the veal cubes. Cover and cook until the veal is very tender, 2$^1/_2$ hours on the high-heat setting or 5$^1/_2$ hours on the low-heat setting. Add the carrots, cover, and cook until the veal is tender, about 20 minutes. Add the asparagus and peas and continue to cook, covered, until the vegetables are tender, about 10 minutes longer. Stir in the cream and cook until the sauce is heated through, about 5 minutes. Season to taste with salt and pepper.

Divide the veal, vegetables, and sauce among warmed bowls and serve at once.

3 lb (1.5 kg) boneless veal shoulder, cut into 2-inch (5-cm) cubes

Salt and freshly ground pepper

2 tablespoons unsalted butter

1 tablespoon olive oil

6 shallots, minced

2 oz (60 g) prosciutto, minced

$^1/_2$ cup (4 fl oz/125 ml) dry white wine such as sauvignon blanc

1 cup (8 fl oz/250 ml) chicken broth

3 sprigs fresh thyme

2 large carrots, diced

1 bunch asparagus, trimmed and cut into 1-inch (2.5-cm) pieces

1 cup (6 oz/185 g) frozen baby peas

1 cup (8 fl oz/250 ml) heavy (double) cream

Meatballs in Tomato Sauce

For the Meatballs

2 lb (1 kg) ground (minced) beef, pork, and veal

1 egg

1 small yellow onion, finely chopped

$1/2$ cup (1 oz/30 g) fresh bread crumbs or panko

$1/4$ cup (1 oz/30 g) pine nuts, toasted

$1/4$ cup (1 oz/30 g) grated Parmesan or Romano cheese

2 tablespoons chopped fresh flat-leaf (Italian) parsley

1 tablespoon chopped fresh oregano

1 tablespoon chopped fresh basil

Salt and freshly ground pepper

2 tablespoons olive oil

1 yellow onion, chopped

3 cloves garlic, minced

1 can (28 oz/875 g) diced tomatoes in purée

1 can ($14^{1}/_{2}$ oz/455 g) chipotle chiles in adobo

$1/2$ cup (4 fl oz/125 ml) dry white wine such as sauvignon blanc

2 tablespoons chopped fresh basil

Make the meatballs: In a large bowl, combine the ground meats, egg, onion, bread crumbs, pine nuts, cheese, parsley, oregano, basil, $3/4$ teaspoon salt, and $1/2$ teaspoon pepper. Using your hands, gently but thoroughly blend the ingredients. Form the mixture into meatballs about $1^{1}/_{2}$ inches (4 cm) in diameter. Set aside.

In a small Dutch oven over medium heat, warm the olive oil. Add the onion and sauté until softened, 4–5 minutes. Add the garlic and sauté for 30 seconds. Stir in the diced tomatoes, chipotles in adobo, and wine and bring to a boil. Drop the meatballs into the sauce, gently spooning the sauce over them. Bring to a simmer, reduce the heat to medium-low, cover, and cook until the meatballs are firm and cooked through, 20–30 minutes.

Remove from the heat and let stand for 5 minutes. Stir in the basil. Divide the meatballs and tomato sauce among warmed plates and serve at once.

Using a trio of meats is perfect for these tender meatballs. Beef adds hearty flavor, while pork and veal provide a natural sweetness. It is best to use an equal amount of each for the perfect blend. Unlike most recipes that call for browning the meatballs, this one braises them in an herbed tomato sauce. The meatballs and sauce can be prepared a day ahead, refrigerated, and reheated before serving.

Beef Brisket with Yams and Prunes

Braised beef brisket is the quintessential Jewish holiday dish for Passover or Rosh Hashanah. It also makes a festive main course at any time of year for any faith. The sweet-sour yam-and-prune mixture that cooks with the brisket is one of many versions of the traditional accompaniment known as *tsimmes*, a Yiddish word that also means "mess," capturing its appealingly chunky character. You can substitute carrots for the yams and dried apricots for the prunes. Many fans of braised brisket swear that it's even better reheated the next day.

Using a small, sharp knife, trim away most of the excess fat from the surface of the brisket. In a small bowl, stir together the paprika, 1 teaspoon salt, and ¹/₂ teaspoon pepper. Rub the spice mixture evenly over the meat.

In a large frying pan over medium-high heat, warm the olive oil. Add the brisket, fat side down, and cook until browned on both sides, about 10 minutes. Remove from the pan and set aside.

Add the onions to pan and sauté over medium-high heat until they start to brown, 6–8 minutes. Stir in the garlic and sauté for about 1 minute. Pour in the wine and deglaze the pan, stirring and scraping up the browned bits on the bottom of the pan with a wooden spoon. Stir in the broth and ketchup and bring to a boil.

OVEN: Preheat the oven to 375°F (190°C). Place the brisket, fat side up, in a large Dutch oven. Add the onion-broth mixture, spooning some of the onions over the brisket. Add the bay leaves and sprinkle in the thyme. Cover and cook for 1 hour. In a large bowl, combine the prunes, yams, orange juice, and brown sugar, tossing to coat the prunes and yams. Push the prunes and yams into the cooking liquid around the brisket and drizzle the juice-sugar mixture over them. Cover and cook until the brisket is tender, about 2 hours longer.

SLOW COOKER: Place the brisket, fat side up, in a slow cooker. Add the onion-broth mixture, spooning some of the onions over the brisket. Add the bay leaves and sprinkle in the thyme. Cover and cook for 2 hours on the high-heat setting or 6 hours on the low-heat setting. In a large bowl, combine the prunes, yams, orange juice, and brown sugar, tossing to coat the prunes and yams. Push the prunes and yams into the cooking liquid around the brisket and drizzle the juice-sugar mixture over them. Cover and cook for 1 hour on the high-heat setting, or until the brisket is tender. Or cook for 1 hour on the low-heat setting, raise the heat to high, and cook for 1 hour longer, or until the brisket is tender.

Transfer the brisket to a carving board. Cover loosely with aluminum foil to keep warm and let rest for about 15 minutes. Use a large, shallow spoon or ladle to skim as much fat as possible from the surface of the cooking liquid.

Using a large, sharp knife, cut the brisket across the grain into slices ¹/₄–¹/₂ inch (6–12 mm) thick. Arrange the slices on a warmed platter and top with the cooking juices and vegetables. Serve at once.

1 beef brisket, about 3 lb (1.5 kg)

1 tablespoon sweet paprika

Salt and freshly ground pepper

3 tablespoons olive oil

3 yellow onions, thinly sliced

4 cloves garlic, minced

1 cup (8 fl oz/250 ml) dry red wine such as cabernet or zinfandel

1 cup (8 fl oz/250 ml) beef broth

1 cup (8 fl oz/250 ml) tomato ketchup

2 bay leaves

2 teaspoons dried thyme

2 cups (12 oz/375 g) pitted prunes, halved

2¹/₂ lb (1.25 kg) small yams, peeled and cut into 1¹/₂-inch (4-cm) chunks

1 cup (8 fl oz/250 ml) fresh orange juice

³/₄ cup (6 oz/185 g) firmly packed dark brown sugar

Osso Buco

4 veal shanks, 2½–3 lb (1.25–1.5 kg) total weight, each about 2 inches (5 cm) thick

Salt and freshly ground pepper

¼ cup (2 fl oz/60 ml) olive oil

1 small red onion, cut into ¼-inch (6-mm) dice

2 cloves garlic, minced

1 cup (8 fl oz/250 ml) dry white wine such as pinot grigio

1 carrot, cut into ¼-inch (6-mm) dice

1 rib celery, cut into ¼-inch (6-mm) dice

1½ cups (12 fl oz/375 ml) canned crushed plum (Roma) tomatoes

1 cup (8 fl oz/250 ml) chicken broth

2 teaspoon fresh oregano, minced

2 teaspoon fresh thyme

For the *Gremolata*

3 tablespoons finely chopped fresh flat-leaf (Italian) parsley

2 cloves garlic, minced

Grated zest of 1 lemon

Grated zest of 1 orange

Italian-style braised veal shanks are among the most luxurious, yet rustic main courses. This traditional preparation from Milan is almost always served over Saffron Risotto (page 263). *Gremolata*, the final garnish of parsley, garlic, and citrus zest, not only looks colorful but adds an enticing burst of aroma as the fragrances are released by the heat of the veal. The rich, flavorful marrow inside the bones is considered the final delicacy to savor when eating osso buco.

Season the veal shanks all over with 1 teaspoon salt and ½ teaspoon pepper. In a large frying pan over medium-high heat, warm the olive oil. Add the veal shanks and cook until browned on all sides, about 10 mintues. Remove from the pan and set aside.

Add the onion and garlic to the pan and sauté over medium-high heat until they start to turn tender, about 3 minutes. Pour in the wine and deglaze the pan, stirring and scraping up the browned bits on the bottom of the pan with a wooden spoon. Stir in the carrot, celery, tomatoes, broth, oregano, and thyme and bring to a boil.

OVEN: Preheat the oven to 375°F (190°C). Transfer the veal shanks to a large Dutch oven. Pour in the broth and vegetable mixture. Cover and cook until the veal is very tender, about 2 hours.

SLOW COOKER: Transfer the veal shanks to a slow cooker and pour in the broth and vegetable mixture. Cover and cook until the veal shanks are very tender, 3 hours on the high-heat setting or 6 hours on the low-heat setting.

Shortly before the veal is done, make the *gremolata*: In a small bowl, stir together the parsley, garlic, and lemon and orange zests.

Divide the shanks among warmed plates. Spoon the cooking juices and vegetables over the veal, garnish with the *gremolata*, and serve at once.

Stuffed Veal Breast

When sliced, a stuffed breast of veal makes a dramatic presentation. By all means ask a butcher to bone the breast for you, although the task isn't as daunting as it might sound. You'll save money removing the bones yourself and it's good practice for an enthusiastic home cook. A stuffed breast of veal is also delicious served cold. Refrigerate overnight, tightly wrapped in foil, and serve thinly sliced with a crock of good mustard and some vinegary cornichons.

Make the stuffing: In a small frying pan over medium-high heat, melt the butter. Add the onion and cook, stirring frequently, until softened, 3–5 minutes. Remove from the heat and let cool.

In a bowl, combine the ground veal, bread crumbs, garlic, spinach, lemon zest, nutmeg, beaten egg, and reserved onion. Stir well until blended and smooth. Season with salt and pepper.

Lay the veal breast on a cutting board with the skin side down. Season with salt and pepper. Spread a thin layer of the stuffing over the surface of the veal, leaving a border of about 1 inch (2.5 cm) on all sides. Cut the hard-boiled eggs into ¼-inch (6-mm) slices and arrange uniformly over the stuffing. Cut the ham into thin strips and evenly place on top. Gently roll up the meat into a cylinder. Securely tie the roll at regular intervals with kitchen string.

In a large frying pan over medium-high heat, melt the butter with the canola oil. Add the veal and cook, turning frequently, until lightly browned on all sides, 5–7 minutes. Remove from the pan and set aside.

Pour off all but 1 tablespoon of the fat in the pan. Add the onion, carrot, and celery and sauté over medium-high heat until softened, about 5 minutes. Pour in the wine and deglaze the pan, stirring and scraping up the browned bits on the bottom of the pan with a wooden spoon. Stir in the broth and bring to a boil.

OVEN: Preheat the oven to 350°F (180°C). Transfer the veal to a large Dutch oven. Pour in the broth and vegetable mixture. Cover and cook until the veal is tender, 2–2½ hours.

SLOW COOKER: Transfer the veal to a slow cooker. Pour in the broth and vegetable mixture. Cover and cook until the veal is tender, 6 hours on the low-heat setting

Transfer the veal to a cutting board and cover loosely with aluminum foil to keep warm. Using a sharp knife, cut the veal crosswise into slices about ½ inch (12 mm) thick, removing the strings as you cut. Arrange the slices on a warmed platter, spoon the cooking juices on top, and serve at once.

For the Stuffing

2 tablespoons unsalted butter

1 yellow onion, finely chopped

1 lb (500 g) ground (minced) veal

½ cup (1 oz/30 g) fresh bread crumbs

1 clove garlic, minced

½ cup (1 oz/30 g) finely chopped fresh spinach

1 teaspoon grated lemon zest

¼ teaspoon ground nutmeg

1 egg, beaten

Salt and freshly ground pepper

1 boneless veal breast, about 3 lb (1.5 kg).

Salt and freshly ground pepper

2 hard-boiled eggs

4 thin slices boiled ham, about ¼ lb (125 g)

2 tablespoons unsalted butter

2 tablespoons canola oil

1 yellow onion, chopped

1 carrot, chopped

1 rib celery, thinly sliced

½ cup (4 fl oz/125 ml) dry white wine such as chardonnay

1 cup (8 fl oz/250 ml) chicken broth

Roman-Style Braised Oxtails

3 tablespoons all-purpose (plain) flour

Salt and freshly ground pepper

$1/2$ cup (4 fl oz/125 ml) olive oil

4 lb (2 kg) oxtails, cut into individual joints

2 yellow onions, finely chopped

4 cloves garlic, minced

3 oz (90 g) pancetta, chopped

$2/3$ cup (6 oz/185 g) tomato paste

1 tablespoon sugar

$1^{1}/_{2}$ cups (12 fl oz/375 ml) dry red wine such as Chianti

$1^{1}/_{2}$ cups (12 fl oz/375 ml) beef broth

2 carrots, chopped

2 celery stalks, chopped

2 sprigs fresh oregano

On a plate, stir together the flour, 1 teaspoon salt, and $1/2$ teaspoon pepper. In a large frying pan over medium-high heat, warm the olive oil. Working in batches if necessary, roll the oxtails in the seasoned flour, shaking off any excess, and cook, turning occasionally, until browned on all sides, 5–7 minutes. Remove from the pan and set aside.

Add the onions to the pan and sauté over medium-high heat until they begin to soften, about 3 minutes. Stir in the garlic and pancetta and sauté for about 30 seconds. Stir in the tomato paste and sugar and stir to combine, about 1 minute. Add the wine and deglaze the pan, stirring and scraping up the browned bits on the pan bottom with a wooden spoon. Bring the wine to a boil. Stir in the broth and bring to a boil.

STOVE TOP: Transfer the oxtails and any accumulated juices to a large Dutch oven. Add the wine-broth mixture, carrots, celery, and thyme. Cover and cook over very low heat until the oxtails are very tender, about $2^{1}/_{2}$ hours. Uncover and use a large, shallow spoon or a ladle to skim the fat from the sauce. Season to taste with salt and pepper.

SLOW COOKER: Transfer the oxtails and any accumulated juices a slow cooker. Add the wine-broth mixture, carrots, celery, and thyme. Cover and cook until the oxtails are very tender, $3^{1}/_{2}$ hours on the high-heat setting or 7 hours on the low-heat setting. Uncover and use a large, shallow spoon or a ladle to skim the fat from the sauce. Season to taste with salt and pepper.

Transfer the oxtails and sauce to warmed shallow bowls, and serve at once.

This time-honored recipe from Italy's capital highlights the rich, distinctive flavor of oxtail meat, which, in today's market, is likely to be from the same steers that provide the usual cuts of beef. You may have to order the oxtails from your butcher in advance, but they are worth the wait. Pasta is a popular accompaniment. If you make the oxtails a day ahead and refrigerate them, you can remove the meat from the bones with your fingers, skim away the solidified fat from on top of the sauce, and reheat the meat and sauce together to serve over pasta.

Thai Red Curry Beef

Most Thai cooks use bottled curry paste mixtures that make preparing fragrant curries like this one incredibly fast and easy. Serve this liberally sauced dish with lots of Steamed Jasmine Rice (page 262).

Place the beef in a bowl. Sprinkle with 1 teaspoon salt and 1 teaspoon pepper, and toss to coat evenly. In a large frying pan over medium-high heat, warm the canola oil. Working in batches if necessary, sauté the beef until browned on all sides, about 5 minutes. Remove from the pan and set aside.

Add the onion and garlic to the pan and sauté over medium-high heat for 1 minute. Add the curry paste and stir until it is fragrant and coats the onion and garlic, about 30 seconds. Add the coconut milk and deglaze the pan, stirring and scraping up the browned bits on the bottom of the pan with a wooden spoon. Stir in the fish sauce, lime juice, and brown sugar and bring to a boil.

STOVE TOP: Transfer the beef to a large Dutch oven and add the coconut milk mixture. Partially cover and cook over low heat until the beef is tender and the sauce is thick but still fluid, about 2 hours. About 15 minutes before the beef is done, stir the bamboo shoots into the curry.

SLOW COOKER: Transfer the beef to a slow cooker and add the coconut milk mixture. Cover and cook until the beef is very tender and the sauce is thick but still fluid, 3 hours on the high-heat setting or 6 hours on the low-heat setting. About 5 minutes before the beef is done, stir the bamboo shoots into the curry.

Spoon the curry onto warmed individual plates or into a large serving bowl. Garnish with the mint and serve at once.

$2\frac{1}{2}$ lb (1.25 kg) lean stewing beef, such as chuck or round cut into $1\frac{1}{2}$-inch (4-cm) chunks

Salt and freshly ground pepper

3 tablespoons canola oil

1 yellow onion, finely chopped

4 cloves garlic, minced

$\frac{1}{4}$ cup (2 oz/60 g) Thai red curry paste

2 cans ($13\frac{1}{2}$ fl oz/420 ml each) unsweetened coconut milk

2 tablespoons Thai or Vietnamese fish sauce

2 tablespoons fresh lime juice

2 tablespoons packed dark brown sugar

2 cans (8 oz/250 g each) sliced bamboo shoots, drained

3 tablespoons chopped fresh mint

Beef Stroganoff with Mushrooms

3 lb (1.5 kg) chuck steak or round steak, cut crosswise into strips about ¹/₂ inch (12 mm) wide

3 tablespoons all-purpose (plain) flour plus 2 tablespoons

Salt and freshly ground pepper

12 tablespoons (6 oz/180 g) unsalted butter, divided

3 tablespoons olive oil

1 yellow onion, thinly sliced

2 cloves garlic, minced

1 cup (8 fl oz/250 ml) dry red wine such as Cabernet

2 cups (16 fl oz/500 ml) beef broth

2 sprigs fresh thyme

1¹/₂ lb (750 g) assorted fresh mushrooms such as cremini, shiitake, or chanterelle, brushed clean, stems removed, and caps cut into ¹/₂-inch (12-mm) pieces

2 cups (16 fl oz/500 ml) sour cream

¹/₄ cup (2 fl oz/60 ml) dry sherry

2 tablespoons Worcestershire sauce

1¹/₂ teaspoons dry mustard

2 tablespoons chopped fresh flat-leaf (Italian) parsley

In its classic form, this dish is prepared fairly quickly with tender beef filet. This version adapts the preparation to slow cooking an economical cut of steak that needs gentle heat to coax it to absolute tenderness. The cultivated mushrooms add a flavorful touch to the recipe. Serve over Buttered Egg Noodles (page 264).

In a bowl, stir together the 3 tablespoons flour, 1 teaspoon salt, and ¹/₂ teaspoon pepper. In a large frying pan over medium-high heat, melt 6 tablespoons of the butter with 2 tablespoons of the olive oil. Working in batches, roll the steak strips in the seasoned flour and cook, turning occasionally, until browned on all sides, about 5 minutes. Remove from the pan ans set aside.

Add the onion to the pan and sauté over medium-high heat until tender, 3–4 minutes. Add the garlic and sauté for about 30 seconds. Add the wine and broth and bring to a boil, stirring and scraping up the browned bits on the pan bottom with a wooden spoon.

STOVE TOP: Transfer the steak and any accumulated juices to a large Dutch oven. Pour the broth mixture over the steak and add the thyme. Cover and cook over very low heat until the steak is very tender, about 1 hour and 40 minutes. Meanwhile, in a large skillet over high heat, melt the remaining 6 tablespoons butter with the remaining 1 tablespoon oil. Add the mushrooms and sauté until they begin to brown, about 4 minutes. Season lightly with salt and pepper. Add the mushrooms to the steak. In a bowl, stir together the sour cream, sherry, and Worcestershire sauce. Stirring constantly, sprinkle in the remaining 2 tablespoons flour and the dry mustard until thoroughly blended. Add to the mushroom-steak mixture. Continue to cook, covered, until the sauce thickens, about 5 minutes.

SLOW COOKER: Transfer the streak and any accumulated juices to a slow cooker. Pour the broth mixture over the steak and add the thyme. Cover and cook until the steak is tender, 3 hours on the high-heat setting or 6 hours on the low-heat setting. In a large skillet over high heat, melt the remaining 6 tablespoons butter with the remaining 1 tablespoon oil. Add the mushrooms and sauté until they begin to brown, about 4 minutes. Season with salt and pepper. Add the mushrooms to the steak. In a bowl, stir together the sour cream, sherry, and Worcestershire sauce. Stirring constantly, sprinkle in the remaining 2 tablespoons flour and the dry mustard until thoroughly blended. Add to the mushroom-steak mixture. Cover and continue to cook until the sauce thickens, about 5 minutes.

Serve at once, garnished with the parsley.

Shredded Beef Ragù

Leftover beef from a roast or stew put to good use in the following recipe. For a variation, use the same recipe and spread over the bottom of a shallow baking dish that has been rubbed with a cut clove of garlic. Top with a thick layer of fresh breadcrumbs, drizzle with melted butter and bake until the top is browned and crusty for an excellent gratin. If it's the right season, use a couple of peeled, seeded and chopped tomatoes in place of the canned ones called for below. Check the ragu from time to time to make sure there is enough liquid. The sauce should be unctuously rich and not too liquid.

Heat the oil in large Dutch oven over medium heat. Working in batches if necessary, add the beef and cook, stirring occassionally, until no longer pink, about 10 minutes. Remove from the pan and set aside.

Add the onion and cook, stirring, until softened, 3–5 minutes. Stir in the garlic, anchovy paste and oregano. Cook 1 minute longer. Stir in the tomatoes and broth.

STOVETOP: Return the beef to the Dutch oven, reduce the heat to low and cook, uncovered, until the meat is very tender and the sauce has thickened, about 2 hours.

Add the olives and cook just until warmed through, 10 to 15 minutes. Season with salt and pepper.

SLOW COOKER: Transfer the vegetable mixture to a slow cooker, and add the beef. Cook on low for 4 hours.

Uncover and stir in the olives to heat through.

Season to taste with salt and pepper and serve at once.

2 tablespoons olive oil

3 lb (1.5 kg) beef chuck roast, cut into small pieces

1 yellow onion, chopped

1 clove garlic, minced

1 teaspoon anchovy paste

1 tablespoon chopped fresh oregano or 1 teaspoon dried

1 large can (28 oz) crushed tomatoes, with liquid

1 cup (8fl oz/250 ml) beef broth

½ cup (2 oz/60 g) pitted black olives, halved

½ teaspoon red pepper flakes

Salt and freshly ground pepper

American Pot Roast

5 tablespoons (2 oz/60 g) all-purpose (plain) flour

Salt and freshly ground pepper

1 beef chuck roast, 3–4 lb (1.5–2 kg)

2 tablespoons unsalted butter

2 tablespoons canola oil

4 carrots, 2 finely chopped and 2 cut into 1-inch (2.5-cm) pieces

1 yellow onion, chopped

1 rib celery, chopped

3 cups (24 fl oz/750 ml) beef broth

3 Yukon gold potatoes, about 1 lb (500 g) total weight, peeled and quartered

1 cup (6 oz/185 g) frozen pearl onions

1/2 cup (3 oz/90 g) frozen peas

In a large bowl, stir together 3 tablespoons of the flour, 1 teaspoon salt, and 1/2 teaspoon pepper. Turn the roast in the seasoned flour, shaking off any excess. In a large frying pan over medium-high heat, melt the butter with the olive oil. Add the roast and cook, turning occasionally, until browned on all sides, about 10 minutes. Remove from the pan and set aside.

Pour off all but 2 tablespoons of the fat in the pan. Add the chopped carrots, yellow onion, and celery and sauté over medium-high heat until softened, about 5 minutes. Stir in the remaining 2 tablespoons flour and cook for about 1 minute. Pour in the beef stock and deglaze the pan, stirring and scraping up the browned bits on the bottom of the pan with a wooden spoon and bring to a boil.

OVEN: Preheat the oven to 325°F (165°C). Transfer the roast to a large Dutch oven. Pour in the vegetable and broth mixture and cook, turning occasionally, until the meat is very tender, about 3 hours. Uncover and stir in the potatoes, carrot pieces, and pearl onions. Cover and cook for 30 minutes. Uncover and stir in the peas. Cover and cook until all the vegetables are tender, about 15 minutes longer.

SLOW COOKER: Transfer the roast to a slow cooker. Pour in the vegetable and broth mixture and cook for 4 hours on the high-heat setting or 8 hours on the low-heat setting. Uncover and stir in the potatoes, carrot pieces, and pearl onions. Cover and cook for 45 minutes. Uncover and stir in the peas. Cover and cook until all the vegetables are tender, about 15 minutes longer.

Transfer the roast to a cutting board and cover with aluminum foil to keep warm. Strain the cooking liquid through a fine-mesh sieve into a saucepan, discarding the solids. Use a large, shallow spoon or a ladle to skim as much fat as possible from the surface of the cooking liquid. Bring to a boil over high heat and cook until the liquid is slightly thickened, about 10 minutes. Season to taste with salt and pepper.

Two sets of vegetables are used in this stew. The chopped carrots, onion and celery called for in the first part add flavor to the meat and sauce during slow cooking and are strained out before serving. Additional carrots, potatoes, pearl onions and peas are added only during the last hour (or last two hours in the slow cooker) so that they retain a vibrant, fresh taste and color, suitable for serving as an accompaniment to the meat. Such a technique might seem fussy but this all-American pot roast is a glorious, photo-worthy and memorable dish that's worth a little extra effort.

Asian Braised Short Ribs

Seasonings from Chinese, Japanese, Thai, and Vietnamese kitchens give these short ribs a true Pan-Asian character, and the vivid flavors perfectly complement the richness of the meat. You'll find all the ingredients in Asian markets and well-stocked food stores. Serve with Steamed Jasime Rice (page 262).

On a plate, stir together the flour, 1 teaspoon salt, and ½ teaspoon pepper. Turn the short ribs in the seasoned flour, shaking off any excess. In a large frying pan over medium-high heat, warm the canola oil. Working in batches if necessary, cook the ribs, turning occasionally, until evenly browned, 12–15 minutes. Remove from the pan and set aside.

Add the garlic, green onions, ginger, red pepper flakes, and lemongrass to the pan and sauté over medium-high heat until fragrant, about 1 minute. Pour in broth and deglaze the pan, stirring and scraping up the browned bits on the bottom of the pan with a wooden spoon. Stir in the soy sauce, hoisin sauce, vinegar, brown sugar, and chile-garlic sauce. Bring to a boil.

OVEN: Preheat the oven to 350°F (180°C). Transfer the ribs to a large Dutch oven. Add the broth mixture. Cover and cook until the ribs are very tender, about 2 hours. When the short ribs are done, use a large, shallow spoon or a ladle to skim as much as possible from the surface of the sauce.

SLOW COOKER: Transfer the ribs to a slow cooker. Add the broth mixture. Cover and cook until the ribs are very tender, 3 hours on the high-heat setting or 6 hours on the low-heat setting. When the short ribs are done, use a large, shallow spoon as much as possible from the surface of the sauce.

Remove and discard the lemongrass. Transfer the ribs to warmed individual plates, spoon the sauce over and around them, and serve at once.

3 tablespoons all-purpose (plain) flour

Salt and freshly ground pepper

5½–6 lb (2.75–3 kg) beef short rib pieces, Korean-style cut

¼ cup (2 fl oz/60 ml) canola oil

4 cloves garlic, minced

4 green (spring) onions, white and pale green parts, thinly sliced

2 tablespoons minced fresh ginger

1 teaspoon red pepper flakes

1 lemongrass stalk, cut into 4 pieces, halved lengthwise and crushed with a meat pounder

1 cup (8 fl oz/250 ml) beef broth

½ cup (4 fl oz/125 ml) soy sauce

½ cup (4 fl oz/125 ml) hoisin sauce

½ cup (4 fl oz/125 ml) rice vinegar

½ cup (4 oz/125 g) firmly packed dark brown sugar

¼ cup (2 fl oz/60 ml) chile-garlic sauce such as Sriracha

Hungarian Beef Goulash

1 tablespoon canola oil

4 slices bacon, about ¼ lb (125 g) total weight

2 lb (1 kg) beef chuck, cut into 2-inch (5-cm) pieces and patted dry

Salt and freshly ground pepper

2 yellow onions, chopped

2 cloves garlic, minced

1 tablespoon paprika

1 teaspoon caraway seeds

5 sprigs fresh oregano

1 tablespoon tomato paste

1 cup (8 fl oz/250 ml) dry white wine such as chardonnay

1 cup (8 fl oz/250 ml) chicken broth

1 red bell pepper (capsicum), seeded and chopped

6 Yukon gold potatoes, about 2 lb (1 kg) total weight, quartered

½ cup (4 oz/125 g) sour cream

In a large frying pan over medium-high heat, warm the canola oil. Add the bacon and cook, turning frequently, until crisp, about 5 minutes. Transfer to a paper towel–lined plate. When the bacon is cool, coarsely chop and set aside.

Season the beef generously with salt and pepper. Working in batches if necessary, add the beef to the pan and cook over medium-high heat, turning frequently, until browned on all sides, 5–7 minutes. Remove from the pan and set aside.

Pour off all but 2 tablespoons of the fat in the pan. Add the onions and sauté over medium-high heat until softened, 3–5 minutes. Add the garlic and cook for 1 minute. Stir in the paprika, caraway seeds, oregano, tomato paste, wine, and broth and bring to a boil.

OVEN: Preheat the oven to 300°F (150°C). Transfer the beef to a large Dutch oven. Pour in the broth mixture and stir to combine. Cover and cook in the oven until the beef is tender, about 2 hours. Uncover and stir in the reserved chopped bacon, bell pepper, and potatoes. Cover and cook until the potatoes are tender and the sauce is thickened, about 1 hour longer. Season to taste with salt and pepper.

SLOW COOKER: Transfer the beef to a slow cooker. Pour in the broth mixture and stir to combine. Cover and cook until the beef is tender, 6 hours on the low-heat setting. Uncover and stir in the reserved chopped bacon, bell pepper, and potatoes. Cover and cook until the potatoes are tender and the sauce is thickened, about 2 hours longer. Season to taste with salt and pepper.

Divide the goulash among warmed bowls. Garnish with the sour cream and serve at once.

Known as *gulyás* in Hungarian, goulash refers to almost any stew made with beef and seasoned with paprika. Serve with Buttered Egg Noodles (page 264).

Beef and Roasted Garlic Pie

For this rustic pie, a tender beef-and-vegetable stew is topped with creamy mashed potatoes and baked in the oven. The stew gains special distinction from the mellow flavor of roasted garlic, which simmers for hours along with the beef.

Preheat the oven to 400°F (200°C). Using a sharp knife, cut ¼–½ inch (6–12 mm) from the top of the garlic head. Drizzle with 1 tablespoon of the olive oil. Wrap with aluminum foil and bake cloves are very soft, about 30 minutes. Remove the foil and let the garlic cool. Using a small spoon, remove the soft garlic pulp, discarding the skin. Set aside.

On a plate, stir together the flour, 1 teaspoon salt, and 1 teaspoon pepper. Turn the beed chunks in the seasoned flour, shaking off any excess. In a large frying pan over medium-high heat, warm the remaining 3 tablespoons olive oil. Working in batches, cook the beef, turning frequently, until evenly browned on all sides, 5–7 minutes. Set aside.

Add the shallots to the pan and sauté over medium-high heat until softened, about 1 minute. Add the wine and deglaze the pan, stirring and scraping up the browned bits on the bottom of the pan with a wooden spoon. Add the broth and the garlic and bring to a boil, stirring to break up the garlic.

STOVE TOP: Transfer the beef and any accumulated juices to a large Dutch oven. Add the garlic-broth mixture and the carrots, celery, bay leaves, and lemon zest. Cover and cook until the beef is very tender, about 2 hours.

SLOW COOKER: Transfer the beef and any accumulated juices to a slow cooker. Add the garlic-broth mixture and the carrots, celery, bay leaves, and lemon zest. Cover and cook until the beef is very tender, 3 hours on the high-heat setting or 6 hours on the low-heat setting.

Preheat the oven to 350°F (180°C). About 30 minutes before the beef is done, put the potatoes in a large pot filled with enough salted cold water to cover. Bring to a boil over high heat and cook until the potatoes are tender when pierced with a fork, 15–20 minutes. Drain the potatoes and return them to the pot. Add the cream, sprinkle in the Parmesan and mustard powder, and mash the potatoes with a potato masher until smooth. Season generously to taste with salt and pepper.

When the beef is done, remove and discard the bay leaves and lemon zest. Transfer the beef, vegetables, and sauce to a 9-by-12-inch (23-by-30-inch) baking dish. Using a wooden spoon, press down lightly on the meat chunks to break them up slightly and spread them evenly. Spread the mashed potatoes evenly over the top. Bake until the potatoes are golden brown, about 30 minutes.

Using a large spoon, scoop the beef and potatoes into warmed bowls and serve.

1 head garlic

4 tablespoons (2 fl oz/60 ml) olive oil

3 tablespoons all-purpose (plain) flour

Salt and freshly ground pepper

2½ lb (1.25 kg) lean stewing beef, such as chuck or round cut into 1½-inch (4-cm) chunks

4 large shallots, finely chopped

½ cup (4 fl oz/125 ml) dry red wine such as cabernet

1 cup (8 fl oz/250 ml) beef broth

3 carrots, cut into ½-inch (12-mm) pieces

3 ribs celery, cut into ½-inch (12-mm) pieces

2 bay leaves

1 strip lemon zest, about 3 inches (7.5 cm) long

2 lb (1 kg) Yukon gold potatoes, peeled and cut into 1½-inch (4-cm) chunks

1 cup (8 fl oz/250 ml) heavy (double) cream

2 tablespoons freshly grated Parmesan cheese

2 teaspoons dry mustard

Barbecued-Style Brisket

¼ cup (2 oz/60 g) firmly packed dark brown sugar

¼ cup (2 fl oz/60 ml) cider vinegar

2 tomatoes, seeded and chopped

2 cups (16 fl oz/500 ml) beef broth

3 lb (1.5 kg) beef brisket, trimmed of excess fat

Salt and freshly ground pepper

2 tablespoons canola oil

2 yellow onions, thinly sliced

2 cloves garlic, minced

½ teaspoon ground allspice

2 talespoons all-purpose (plain) flour

In a small bowl, stir together the brown sugar, vinegar, tomatoes, and broth. Set aside. Season the brisket generously with salt and pepper. In a large frying pan over medium-high heat, warm the canola oil. Add the brisket fat side down and cook, turning once, until browned on both sides, about 10 minutes. Remove from the pan and set aside.

Pour off all but 2 tablespoons of the fat in the pan. Add the onions and sauté over medium-high heat until softened, about 3 minutes. Add the garlic and cook for 1 minute. Stir in the allspice.

Sprinkle the flour over the onion mixture in the pan and cook over medium heat, stirring frequently, until blended, about 3 minutes. Pour in the reserved broth mixture and stir to combine. Bring to a boil and season with salt and pepper.

OVEN: Preheat the oven to 300°F (150°C). Transfer the brisket to a large Dutch oven. Pour in the broth mixture. Cover and cook until the brisket is very tender, 3–4 hours. Use a large, shallow spoon or a ladle to skim as much fat as possible from the cooking liquid.

SLOW COOKER: Transfer the brisket to a slow cooker. Pour in the broth mixture. Cook until the brisket is very tender, 6–8 hours on low-heat setting. Use a large, shallow spoon or a ladle to skim as much fat as possible from the cooking liquid.

Let the brisket rest, uncovered, in the cooking liquid for 1–2 hours. Transfer to a cutting board. Using a large, sharp knife, cut the brisket across the grain into slices. In a saucepan over medium heat, warm the cooking liquid. Arrange the slices on a warmed platter, top with the cooking juices, and serve at once.

Taken from the breast section under the first five ribs, brisket is sold without the bone and is divided into two sections, the flat cut and the point cut. Ask for the flat cut if possible. It has less fat and is easier to slice than the point cut. Serve with cabbage or boiled potatoes. Horseradish sauce makes an excellent condiment.

Belgian Beef Stew

Carbonnade, the name of this traditional Belgian dish, comes from the Latin root for "carbon." The word reflects that the stew was originally cooked very slowly in a cast-iron pot over the charcoals of an open hearth. It undoubtedly also refers to the caramelized onions and dark beer that give the finished dish a well-burnished color and rich, deep flavor. Serve it with boiled potatoes or Mashed Potatoes (page 260) and ice-cold beer.

In a large frying pan over medium-high heat, warm 2 tablespoons of butter. Add the bacon and cook, turning frequently, until the bacon is crisp, about 5 minutes. Add the onions, sprinkle in the sugar, and sauté until the onions turn a deep caramel brown, about 35 minutes. Stir in the garlic. Remove from the pan and set aside. Wipe the pan clean.

On a plate, stir together the flour, 1 teaspoon salt, and 1 teaspoon pepper. Turn the steak pieces in the seasoned flour, shaking off any excess. In the frying pan over medium heat, melt the remaining 2 tablespoons butter with the olive oil. Working in batches if necessary, cook the steak, turning ocassionally, until browned on all sides, about 10 minutes. Remove from the pan and set aside.

Pour in the beer and deglaze the pan, stirring and scraping up the browned bits on the bottom of the pan with a wooden spoon. Bring to a boil.

STOVE TOP: Transfer the steak and onion mixture to a large Dutch oven. Pour in the beer mixture. Cover and cook over low heat until the meat is very tender, about 2 hours.

SLOW COOKER: Transfer the steak and onion mixture to a large Dutch oven. Pour in the beer mixture. Cover and cook until the meat is very tender, 3 hours on the high-heat setting or 6 hours on the low-heat setting.

Divide the stew among warmed shallow bowls and serve at once.

4 tablespoons (2 oz/60 g) unsalted butter

4 slices bacon, about ¼ lb (125 g) total weight, roughly chopped

4 yellow onions, thinly sliced

2 teaspoons firmly packed dark brown sugar

2 cloves garlic, minced

3 tablespoons all-purpose (plain) flour

Salt and freshly ground pepper

2 tablespoons olive oil

3 lb (1.5 kg) chuck steak or round steak, trimmed of all visible fat and cut into pieces about 3 inches (7.5 cm) wide

2 cups (16 fl oz/500 ml) dark beer

Texas-Style Beef Chili

2 tablespoons olive oil

1 yellow onion, chopped

2 cloves garlic, minced

3 lb (1.5 kg) trimmed chuck roast, cut into ¼-inch (6-mm) cubes

2 tablespoons chile powder

1 teaspoon ground cumin

3 tomatoes, seeded and chopped

2 chipotle chiles in adobo, chopped

1 jalapeño chile, seeded and chopped

1 tablespoon tomato paste

1 cup (8 fl oz/250 ml) beef broth

1 cup (8 fl oz/250 ml) dark beer

1 can (15 oz/470 g) red kidney beans, drained and rinsed

Salt and freshly ground pepper

Chili is the quintessential Texan dish, but there are as many versions as there are chili cooks. Starting with a whole chuck roast and cutting it into small cubes makes for a succulent chili with a rich, beefy flavor. This chunky version gets its smoky flavor from the chipotle chiles. Try serving it with fresh Corn Bread (page 264)

In a large frying pan over medium-high heat, warm the olive oil. Add the onion and sauté until softened, 3–5 minutes. Add the garlic and cook for 1 minute. Working in batches if necessary, add the beef cubes and cook, turning occasionally, until browned on all sides, about 10 minutes. Stir in the chile powder and cumin and cook, stirring frequently, until fragrant, about 2 minutes.

STOVE TOP: Transfer the beef mixture to a Dutch oven. Add the tomatoes, chipotle chiles, jalapeño chile, tomato paste, broth, beer, and beans. Season with salt and pepper and stir well. Bring to a simmer over medium-high heat. Cover, reduce the heat to medium, and cook, stirring frequently, until the beef is tender, about 1 hour. If desired, uncover and simmer the chili, stirring occasionally, for 15 minutes longer to thicken the sauce.

SLOW COOKER: Transfer the beef mixture to a slow cooker. Add the tomatoes, chipotle chiles, jalapeño chile, tomato paste, broth, beer, and beans. Season with salt and pepper and stir well. Cover and cook until the beef is tender, 8 hours on the low-heat setting. If the sauce is too thin, uncover, set the temperature to high, and continue to cook for up to 30 minutes.

Spoon the chili into warmed bowls and serve at once.

Short Ribs with Ancho Chile Sauce

Ancho chiles impart a smoky depth of flavor to this dark and intense sauce. When you pour it over the ribs, you may wonder if there's enough liquid to cook them, but hours later you'll uncover tender meat falling off the bone and an abundance of tempting sauce.

Put the chiles in a small bowl and add enough boiling water to cover. Let soak until softened, about 20 minutes. Drain and coarsely chop, discarding the seeds. Set aside.

Season the ribs all over with salt and pepper. In a large frying pan over medium-high heat, melt the butter with the canola oil. Working in batches if necessary, add the ribs and cook, turning frequently, until browned on all sides, about 10 minutes. Remove from the pan and set aside.

Pour off all but 1 tablespoon of the fat in the pan. Add the reserved ancho chiles, onion, bell pepper, garlic, chipotle chiles, lemon juice, tomato, 1 teaspoon salt, and 1/2 teaspoon pepper. Sauté over medium-high heat until the onions and peppers have softened, 8–10 minutes. Transfer to a food processor or a blender and add 1/2 cup (4 fl oz/125 ml) water. Process or blend until the mixture is nearly smooth and has a thick consistency.

OVEN: Preheat the oven to 350°F (180°C). Transfer the ribs to a roasting pan large enough to hold them in a single layer. Add the chile mixture and turn the ribs several times to coat. Cover the pan tightly with aluminum foil. Cook, removing the foil and turning the ribs several times, until they are very tender, about 3 hours.

SLOW COOKER: Transfer the ribs to a slow cooker. Pour in the chile mixture and turn the ribs several times to coat. Cover and cook until the ribs are very tender, 8 hours on the low-heat setting.

Transfer the ribs to a warmed platter. Use a large, shallow spoon or a ladle to as much fat as possible from the surface of the sauce. Spoon some of the sauce over the ribs and serve at once. Pass the remaining sauce at the table.

2 ancho chiles, stems removed

4 lb (2 kg) beef short ribs, cut into 3-inch (7.5-cm) pieces

Salt and freshly ground pepper

2 tablespoons unsalted butter

2 tablespoons canola oil

1 yellow onion, chopped

1 green bell pepper (capsicum), seeded and chopped

2 cloves garlic, minced

2 chipotle chiles in adobo, chopped

2 tablespoons fresh lemon juice

1 tomato, seeded and chopped

Veal Shoulder with Onions and Thyme

1 boneless veal shoulder roast, 3–4 lb (1.5–2 kg)

Salt and freshly ground pepper

2 tablespoons canola oil

1 lb (500 g)frozen pearl onions, thawed

$\frac{1}{2}$ cup (4 fl oz/125 ml) dry white wine such as chardonnay

$\frac{1}{2}$ cup (4 fl oz/125 ml) chicken broth

Lay the veal flat on a cutting board with the boned side up. Roll up the veal. Securely tie the veal at regular intervals with kitchen string. Season the roll generously with salt and pepper. In a large frying pan over medium-high heat, warm the canola oil. Add the veal and cook, turning frequently, until browned on all sides, about 10 minutes. Remove from the pan and set aside.

Pour off all but 1 tablespoon of the fat in the pan. Add the onions and sauté over medium-high heat until softened and lightly browned, about 5 minutes. Pour in the wine, raise the heat to high, and deglaze the pan, stirring and scraping up the browned bits on the bottom of the pan with a wooden spoon. Stir in the broth and bring to a boil.

OVEN: Preheat the oven to 325°F (165°C). Transfer the veal to a large Dutch oven. Pour in the broth mixture. Cover and cook in the oven until the veal is very tender, about 2$\frac{1}{2}$ hours.

SLOW COOKER: Transfer the veal to a slow cooker. Pour in the broth mixture. Cover and cook until the veal is very tender, 8 hours on the low-heat setting.

Transfer the veal to a cutting board and cover loosely with aluminum foil to keep warm. Using a sharp knife and working against the grain, cut the veal into thin slices. Arrange the slices on a warmed platter or plates, and surround with the onions. Spoon the cooking juices over the top and serve at once.

Be sure you ask the butcher to remove the tough nerve that runs along one side of the roast. Serve with buttery Mashed Potatoes. You can strain the sauce before serving, if desired.

Hearty Beef Stew

Here, rich beef chuck is simmered slowly in a red-wine based liquid and is similar to the classic Bœuf Bourguignon. It's important to brown the meat well so the end product will be a distinctive caramel-colored stew that's visually enticing as well as great-tasting. Sautéed mushrooms, browned bits of smoky bacon and chopped fresh parsley make excellent additions.

On a plate, stir together the 3 tablespoons of the flour, 1 teaspoon salt, and 1 teaspoon pepper. Turn the beef pieces in the seasoned flour, shaking off any excess. In a large Dutch oven over medium heat, melt the butter with the canola oil. Working in batches if necessary, cook the beef, turning frequently, until browned on all sides, about 10 minutes. Remove from the pan and set aside.

Add the carrots, celery, yellow onion, pearl onions, and peppercorns to the pan. Cook over medium-high heat, stirring often, until the onions and carrot begin to brown, about 5 minutes. Pour in the wine and deglaze the pan, stirring and scraping up the browned bits from the bottom of the pan with a wooden spoon. Stir in the tomatoes and broth and bring to a boil. Stir in the remaining flour and the tomato paste and cook, stirring frequently, until the mixture has thickened, about 1 minute. Return the beef to the pan. Season to taste with salt and pepper.

OVEN: Preheat the oven to 350°F (180° C). Cover and cook, stirring occasionally, until the meat is tender, 1 1/2–2 hours.

SLOW COOKER: Transfer the beef and wine mixture to a slow cooker and stir to combine. Cover and cook, stirring ocassionally, until the meat is very tender, 4 hours on the low-heat setting.

Divide the stew among warmed shallow bowls and serve at once.

1/2 cup (2 1/2 oz/75 g) all-purpose (plain) flour

Salt and freshly ground pepper

3–4 lb (1.5–2 kg) beef chuck, cut into 2-inch (5-cm) pieces

2 tablespoons unsalted butter

2 tablespoons canola oil

2 carrots, cut into 1-inch (2.5-cm) pieces

2 ribs celery, sliced

1 yellow onion, thinly sliced

1 lb (500 g) frozen pearl onions, thawed

1 teaspoon peppercorns

1 bottle (24 fl oz/750 ml) hearty red wine such as burgundy

1 can (28 oz/875 g) tomatoes, drained and chopped

1 cup (8 fl oz/250 ml) beef broth

1 tablespoon tomato paste

Beef with Mushrooms and Barley

1 oz (30 g) dried mushrooms such as porcini

2 tablespoons unsalted butter

2 lb (1 kg) beef chuck, cut into 2-inch (5-cm) pieces

2 yellow onions, finely chopped

2 cloves garlic, minced

1 lb (500 g) fresh mushrooms, preferably cremini, brushed clean, stems removed, and caps thinly sliced

2 cups (16 fl oz/500 ml) beef broth

1/2 cup (4 oz/125 g) pearl barley

3 carrots, finely chopped

2 parsnips, peeled and finely chopped

Salt and freshly ground pepper

2 tablespoons chopped fresh dill

Put the dried mushrooms in a bowl and add 2 cups (16 fl oz/500 ml) boiling water. Let soak for 20 minutes. Strain through a fine-mesh sieve lined with a double layer of cheesecloth (muslin) placed over a bowl. Rinse the mushrooms under cold running water and finely chop. Set the mushrooms and soaking liquid aside.

In a large frying pan over medium-high heat, melt the butter. Working in batches if necessary, add the beef and cook, turning frequently, until browned on all sides, about 10 minutes. Remove from the pan and set aside.

Add the onion to the pan and sauté over medium-high heat until softened, 3–5 minutes. Add the garlic and cook for 1 minute. Stir in the rehydrated mushrooms. Add the fresh mushrooms and sauté over medium heat until they start to brown, about 5 minutes. Stir in the mushroom soaking liquid and the broth.

OVEN: Preheat the oven to 300°F (150°C). Transfer the beef to a Dutch oven. Add the mushroom mixture and stir to combine. Cover and cook until the beef is tender, about 2 hours. Uncover and stir in the barley and 1 cup (8 fl oz/250 ml) water. Cover and cook for 1 hour. Uncover and stir in the carrots and parsnips. Cover and cook until the beef and barley are tender, about 30 minutes longer. Season to taste with salt and pepper.

SLOW COOKER: Transfer the beef to a slow cooker. Add the mushroom mixture and stir to combine. Cover and cook for 3 hours on the low-heat setting. Uncover and stir in the barley and 1/2 cup (4 fl oz/125 ml) water. Cover and cook for 2 hour. Uncover and stir in the carrots and parsnips. Cover and cook until the beef and barley are tender, about 1 hour longer. Season to taste with salt and pepper.

Spoon the stew into warmed bowls, garnish with the dill, and serve at once.

Barley, cooked by absorbing the broth in the stew, adds an interesting texture that complements the slow-cooked beef in this recipe. The liquid from the porcini mushrooms becomes part of the sauce, adding a nice depth of flavor. Slow cooking also enhances the hearty flavor of root vegetables for a perfect accent to this hearty stew.

Lamb Tagine with Dates and Almonds

The combination of dried fruits, crunchy nuts, and fragrant hot and sweet spices in this slow-cooked lamb stew typify the special-occasion cooking of North African kitchens. For the most authentic presentation, present the stew atop a mound of the tiny pasta known as Couscous (page 261) on a large platter or individual plates.

Put the lamb in a large bowl. Sprinkle with 1 teaspoon salt and 1 teaspoon black pepper and toss to coat evenly. In a large frying pan over medium-high heat, warm the olive oil. Working in batches if necessary, cook the lamb cubes, turning frequently, until evenly browned on all sides, about 5 minutes. Remove from the pan and set aside.

Add the onions to pan and sauté over medium-high heat until just starting to brown, 5–7 minutes. Add the cinnamon, ginger, cumin, cayenne, and saffron and sauté until the spices are fragrant and evenly coat the onions, about 1 minute. Add the broth and deglaze the pan, stirring and scraping up the browned bits on the bottom of the pan with a wooden spoon. Bring to a boil.

STOVE TOP: Transfer the lamb and any accumulated juices to a large Dutch oven. Add the broth mixture. Cover and cook over very low heat until the lamb is very tender, about 3 hours. Uncover and add the toasted nuts and the dates to the lamb. Drizzle with the honey and stir to combine, making sure that the dates are submerged in the cooking liquid. Cover and continue to cook until the dates have softened, about 10 minutes longer.

SLOW COOKER: Transfer the lamb and any accumulated juices to a slow cooker. Add the broth mixture. Cover and cook until the lamb is very tender, 4 hours on the high-heat setting or 8 hours on the low-heat setting. Uncover and add the toasted nuts and the dates to the lamb. Drizzle with the honey and stir to combine, making sure that the dates are submerged in the cooking liquid. Cover and continue to cook until the dates have softened, about 10 minutes longer.

Taste and adjust the seasonings with salt and pepper if necessary and serve at once.

3 lb (1.5 kg) boneless lamb from leg or shoulder, cut into 1½-inch (4-cm) cubes

Salt and freshly ground black pepper

3 tablespoons olive oil

2 yellow onions, finely chopped

1 teaspoon ground cinnamon

1 teaspoon ground ginger

½ teaspoon ground cumin

¼ teaspoon cayenne pepper

¼ teaspoon saffron threads, crumbled

1½ cups (12 fl oz/375 ml) chicken broth

1 cup (5 oz/150 g) slivered almonds, toasted

1⅔ cups (10 oz/300 g) pitted dates, halved

2 tablespoons honey

½ cup (2½ oz/75 g) slivered almonds, toasted

Italian Pot Roast

¼ cup (2½ oz/75 g) all-purpose (plain flour)

Salt and freshly ground pepper

1 eye of round roast, about 4 lb (2 kg)

2 tablespoons unsalted butter

2 tablespoons canola oil

6 oz (185) pancetta, finely chopped

2 carrots, finely chopped

1 onion, chopped

1 rib celery, thinly slices

1 clove garlic, minced

½ lb (250 g) assorted fresh mushrooms, brushed clean, stems removed, and thinly sliced

2 cups (16 fl oz/500 ml) hearty red wine, such as Chianti

1 cup (8 fl oz/250 ml) beef broth

2 tomatoes, peeled, seeded, and chopped

1 tablespoon chopped fresh rosemary

On a plate, stir together the flour, 1 teaspoon salt, and ½ teaspoon pepper. Turn the roast in the seasoned flour, shaking off any excess. In a large frying pan over medium-high heat, melt the butter with the canola oil. Add the roast and cook, turning occasionally, until evenly browned on all sides, 5–7 minutes. Remove from the pan and set aside.

Add the pancetta to the pan and sauté over medium-high heat, until the fat is rendered, about 5 minutes. Using a slotted spoon, transfer to a paper towel–plate and set aside.

Pour off all but 1 tablespoon of the fat in the pan. Add the carrots, onion, and celery and sauté over medium-high heat until softened, about 5 minutes. Add the garlic and cook for 1 minute. Add the mushrooms, cover, and cook until they begin to release their liquid, about 5 minutes. Reduce the heat to medium, uncover, and cook, stirring frequently, until most of the liquid has evaporated, 10 minutes. Pour in the wine and deglaze the pan, stirring and scraping up the browned bits on the bottom of the pan with a wooden spoon. Stir in the broth, tomatoes, and rosemary and bring to a boil. Stir in the reserved pancetta and season with salt and pepper.

OVEN: Preheat the oven to 325°F (165°C). Transfer the roast to a large Dutch oven. Pour in the wine and vegetable mixture. Cover and cook, turning occasionally, until the roast is tender, about 4 hours.

SLOWCOOKER: Transfer the roast to a slow cooker and pour in the wine and vegetable mixture. Cover and cook, turning occasionally, until the roast is tender, 10 hours on the low-heat setting.

Transfer the roast to a cutting board and cover with aluminum foil to keep warm. If the sauce is too thin, pour the cooking liquid into a saucepan, bring to a boil over high heat, and cook until it thickens slightly to a sauce consistency, about 10 minutes. Taste and adjust the seasonings with salt and pepper if necessary.

Using a sharp knife, cut the roast into thick slices. Arrange the slices on a warmed platter or plates, top with the sauce, and serve at once.

Eye of round becomes tender, moist and melting in this hearty Italian-style roast. The intense sauce, fragrant with pancetta and fresh rosemary, begs to be served over pasta or perhaps buttered egg noodles.

Irish Stew

2 pounds (1 kg) lean leg of lamb

2 tablespoons unsalted butter

2 tablespoons vegetable oil

1 yellow onion, chopped

3 carrots, trimmed and cut into large pieces

2 tablespoons all-purpose flour

1½ cups (12 fl oz/375 ml) beef broth

1 cup stout or ale

3 Yukon Gold potatoes, cut into large pieces

2 tablespoons chopped fresh Italian (flat-leaf) parsley

Salt and freshly ground black pepper to taste

Cut the lamb in to 1½–2 inch pieces and pat dry. Season generously with salt and pepper.

Melt the butter with the oil over medium-high heat in a large Dutch oven. Add the lamb and cook, turning often, until browned on all sides, 5–7 minutes. Remove from the pan and set aside.

pour off all but 1 tablespoon fat and add the onions and carrots to the Dutch oven. Cook, stirring often, until slightly softened, about 3 minutes. Sprinkle with the flour and cook, stirring, for 1–2 minutes. Pour in the broth and ale and bring to a boil, stirring, over medium-high heat to pick up any browned bits on the pan bottom.

OVEN: Preheat the oven to 325°F. Return the lamb to the casserole, cover and cook in the oven until the meat is tender, about 1 hour. Add the potatoes along with 2 cups (16 fl oz/500 ml) of water and cook, covered, in the oven until there is no resistance in the potatoes with pierced with the tip of a knife and the lamb is very tender, about 45 minutes longer

SLOW COOKER: Transfer the vegetable-broth mixture to a slow cooker and add the lamb. Cover and cook on high for 3 hours. Add the potatoes during the last hour of cooking.

Transfer the lamb to a serving platter and surround with the onions, carrots and potatoes. Spoon the sauce over the meat, sprinkle with the parsley, and serve at once.

Irish stew is the ideal slow-cooked meal, and this version, with generous chunks of lamb, balances the meat and vegetables in classic proportions. Use dark stout for a deeper flavored sauce, or ale for a lighter touch.

Braciole

These slowly simmered stuffed beef rolls called *braciole* are a standby in Italian home kitchens and trattorias. Some recipes feature individual-serving rolls. This one uses a single flank steak, pounded thin, spread with a stuffing, and then rolled and tied for cooking in a tomato-based sauce.

In a bowl, combine the sausage, bread crumbs, Parmesan, parsley, basil, and egg. Stir together with a fork until thoroughly combined. Set aside.

Place the steak between 2 sheets of plastic wrap and pound gently with a meat pounder until the steak is roughly rectangular and about 1/4 inch (6 mm) thick.

Arrange the prosciutto slices evenly over the steak. Using the fork, spread the sausage mixture evenly over the prosciutto, leaving a border of about 1/4 inch on all sides. Starting at a short edge, roll up the steak. Securely tie the roll at regular intervals with kitchen string. Season the steak generously with salt and pepper.

In a large frying pan over medium-high heat, warm the olive oil. Add the steak and cook, turning frequently, until browned on all sides, about 10 minutes. Remove from the pan and set aside.

Add the onion and garlic to the pan and sauté over medium-high heat until they start to turn tender, about 3 minutes. Stir in the carrot and celery and sauté until glossy, about 1 minute. Add the tomato paste and sugar and stir until the tomato paste is well blended, about 30 seconds. Pour in the wine and deglaze the pan, stirring and scraping up the browned bits on the bottom of the pan with a wooden spoon. Stir in the tomatoes, oregano, and bay leaves and bring to a boil.

OVEN: Preheat the oven to 350°F (180°C). Transfer the steak to a large Dutch oven. Pour in the tomato mixture. Cover and cook until the beef is very tender, about 2 hours.

SLOW COOKER: Transfer the steak to a slow cooker. Pour in the tomato mixture. Cover and cook until the beef is very tender, 3 hours on the high-heat setting or 6 hours on the low-heat setting.

Transfer the steak to a cutting board and cover loosely with aluminum foil to keep warm. Let rest for about 15 minutes. Meanwhile, taste the cooking liquid and adjust the seasonings with salt and pepper if necessary.

Using a sharp knife, cut the beef crosswise into slices about 1/2 inch (12 mm) thick, removing the strings as you slice. Arrange the slices on a warmed platter, top with the cooking juices, and serve at once.

1 Italian sweet or hot fresh pork sausage, about 1/4 lb (125 g), casing removed

1/3 cup (1 1/2 oz/45 g) dried bread crumbs

1 1/2 tablespoons freshly grated Parmesan cheese

1 tablespoon finely chopped fresh flat-leaf (Italian) parsley

1 tablespoon finely shredded fresh basil

1 egg

1 flank steak, about 1 1/2 lb (750 g)

2 oz (60 g) thinly sliced prosciutto

Salt and freshly ground pepper

3 tablespoons olive oil

1 yellow onion, finely chopped

2 cloves garlic, minced

1 carrot, chopped

1 rib celery, chopped

2 tablespoons tomato paste

1 tablespoon sugar

1/2 cup (4 fl oz/125 ml) dry red wine such as Chianti or Valpolicella

1 can (28 oz/875 g) crushed plum (Roma) tomatoes

1 tablespoon dried oregano

2 bay leaves

Stuffed Leg of Lamb

The simple stuffing in this recipe combines shallots and garlic with a mixture of herbs that you can vary according what is in your garden or found fresh at the market, such as thyme, oregano, tarragon, or marjoram. You can ask your butcher to butterfly the boned lamb for you and pound it to an even thickness.

Using a sharp knife, trim away most of the fat from the surface of the lamb. Lay the lamb flat out on a cutting board with the bone side up and trim away any large pockets of fat. Cut several shallow slashes through the thicker muscles to make the lamb a more even thickness. Using a meat mallet, pound the lamb to an even thickness of 1–1¼ inches (2.5–3 cm).

Preheat the oven to 325°F (165°C).

In a small bowl, stir together the parsley, the mint, the shallots, half of the garlic, ½ teaspoon salt, and ½ teaspoon pepper. Rub the cut side of the lamb with 1 tablespoon of the olive oil and then spread the herb mixture almost to the edges of the lamb. Starting from the short side roll up the lamb tightly around the stuffing, forming a cylinder. Securely tie the roll at 2-inch (5-cm) intervals with kitchen string. Season the lamb all over with ½ teaspoon salt and ½ teaspoon pepper.

In a large Dutch oven over medium-high heat, warm the remaining 2 tablespoons olive oil. Add the lamb and cook, turning occasionally, until browned on all sides, 12–15 minutes. Remove from the pan.

Add the onion and parsnip to the pot, reduce the heat to medium, and sauté, until the vegetables are softened, 4–5 minutes. Add the remaining garlic and cook for 30 seconds. Add the wine and deglaze the pot, stirring and scraping up the browned bits on the bottom of the pot with a wooden spoon. Bring to a boil and cook until the wine is reduced by half, 2–3 minutes. Stir in the broth and bring to a simmer.

Return the lamb and any accumulated juices to the pot and bring the liquid to a very gentle simmer. Cover and cook in the oven, turning once or twice, until the lamb is very tender, about 2 hours. Transfer to a carving board, cover loosely with aluminum foil, and let stand for 10 minutes.

Use a large, shallow spoon or a ladle to skim as much fat as possible from the surface of the cooking liquid. Bring to a boil over medium-high heat and cook until the liquid is reduced to a sauce consistency, 5–6 minutes. Season to taste with salt and pepper.

Remove the strings from the lamb. Using a sharp knife, the lamb crosswise into slices and arrange on a warmed platter. Pour any accumulated juices into the pot and bring to a simmer. Spoon some of the sauce over the lamb and serve at once.

1 boneless leg of lamb, about 4 lb (2 kg)

¼ cup (⅓ oz/10 g) chopped fresh flat-leaf (Italian) parsley

¼ cup (⅓ oz/10 g) chopped fresh mint

4 shallots, chopped

4 cloves garlic, minced

Salt and freshly ground pepper

3 tablespoons olive oil

1 yellow onion, sliced

1 parsnip, peeled and sliced

1 cup (8 fl oz/250 ml) dry white wine such as sauvignon blanc

2 cups (16 fl oz/500 ml) chicken broth

Braised Lamb Shanks

½ cup (2½ oz/75 g) all-purpose (plain) flour

Salt and freshly ground pepper

4 lamb shanks, about 1 lb (500 g) each, trimmed of excess fat

2 tablespoons unsalted butter

2 tablespoons canola oil

2 yellow onions, thinly sliced

1 carrot, chopped

1 rib celery, chopped

2 cloves garlic, minced

2 tomatoes, seeded and chopped

1 cup (8 fl oz/250 ml) dry red wine such as Côtes du Rhone

1 cup (8 fl oz/250 ml) beef broth

On a plate, stir together the flour, 1 teaspoon salt, and ½ teaspoon pepper. turn the shanks in the seasoned flour, shaking off any excess. In a large frying pan over medium-high heat, melt the butter with the canola oil. Add the shanks and cook, turning frequently, until browned on all sides, 5–7 minutes. Remove from the pan and set aside.

Pour off all but 1 tablespoon of the fat in the pan. Add the onions, carrot, and celery and sauté over medium-high heat until softened, about 5 minutes. Add the garlic and cook for 1 minute. Stir in the tomatoes, wine, and broth. Bring to a boil.

OVEN: Preheat the oven to 300°F (150°C). Transfer the shanks to a large Dutch oven. Pour in the broth mixture. Cover and cook until the lamb is very tender, about 3 hours. Uncover and continue to cook until the juices are slightly reduced, about 30 minutes longer.

SLOW COOKER: Transfer the shanks to a slow cooker. Pour in the broth mixture. Cover and cook until the lamb is very tender, 7–8 hours on the low-heat setting. Uncover and continue to cook until the juices are slightly reduced, about 1 hour.

Transfer the shanks to a warmed platter and cover loosely with aluminum foil to keep warm. Use a large, shallow spoon or a ladle to skim as much fat as possible from the surface of the cooking liquid. Strain the liquid into a saucepan, bring to a boil, and cook over medium-high heat until reduced and slightly thickened, about 5 minutes. Spoon the cooking juices over the lamb and serve at once.

There is probably no other cut of lamb that lends itself to slow cooking more than the shank. Its meaty flavor and velvety texture make an excellent braise. Serve with Roasted Potatoes (page 260), Creamy Polenta (page 261), or Orzo Pilaf (page 263).

Indian Lamb Curry with Spinach

Not too spicy hot but full of fragrant flavor, this typical Indian lamb-and-spinach curry is almost a one-dish meal. All you need is Steamed Jasmine Rice (page 262) to soak up the sauce. Parboiling the spinach and then plunging it into an ice-water bath ensures that its color stays bright green, and diligently squeezing all the water from the cooked spinach helps it thicken the sauce toward the end of cooking.

Put the lamb in a large bowl. Sprinkle with 1 teaspoon salt and 1/2 teaspoon pepper and toss to coat evenly. In a large frying pan over medium-high heat, warm the canola oil. Working in batches if necessary, cook the lamb cubes, turning frequently, until evenly browned on all sides, about 5 minutes. Remove from the pan and set aside.

Add the onions to the pan and sauté over medium-high heat until golden brown, 7–10 minutes. Add the garlic, chiles, ginger, mustard seeds, cumin, coriander, cardamom, and turmeric and stir until the spices are fragrant and evenly coat the onions, about 1 minute. Pour in the broth and deglaze the pan, stirring and scraping up the browned bits on the bottom of the pan with a wooden spoon. Bring to a boil.

STOVE TOP: Transfer the lamb and any accumulated juices to a large Dutch oven. Add the broth mixture. Cover and cook over very low heat until the lamb is very tender, about 3 hours.

SLOW COOKER: Transfer the lamb and any accumulated juices to a slow cooker. Add the broth mixture. Cover and cook until the lamb is very tender, 4 hours on the high-heat setting or 8 hours on the low-heat setting.

Meanwhile, bring a large saucepan of water to a boil. Fill a large bowl with ice water. Working in batches, immerse the spinach leaves in the boiling water. As soon as the leaves have wilted completely, after 30–45 seconds, use a slotted spoon to transfer them to the bowl of ice water. Squeeze all the water from the spinach, finely chop, and set aside.

Add the chopped spinach to the lamb. Sprinkle evenly with the garam masala and stir to combine.

Divide the curry among warmed shallow bowls, garnish with the sour cream, and serve at once.

3 lb (1.5 kg) boneless leg of lamb, cut into 1 1/2-inch (4-cm) cubes

Salt and freshly ground pepper

1/2 cup (4 fl oz/125 ml) canola oil

2 yellow onions, finely chopped

4 cloves garlic, minced

3 small fresh hot green chiles, seeded and minced

1-inch (2.5-cm) piece fresh ginger, peeled and grated

1 tablespoon brown mustard seeds

1 tablespoon ground cumin

1 tablespoon ground coriander

1 1/2 teaspoons ground cardamom

1 teaspoon ground turmeric

1 1/2 cups (12 fl oz/375 ml) chicken broth

6 cups (6 oz/185 g) prewashed baby spinach leaves

1 tablespoon garam masala

1 cup (4 oz/125 g) sour cream

Basic Recipes

This collection of classic side dishes, from creamy mashed potatoes to tangy cole slaw to fragrant basmati rice, can be used to round out your meals beyond the recipes in this book. There are also recipes for homemade herbed flat bread and buttermilk biscuits as well as tips for cooking beans.

Mashed Potatoes

1 1/2 lb (750 g) Yukon gold or russet potatoes, peeled and cut into 2-inch (5-cm) chunks

4 tablespoons (2 oz/60 g) unsalted butter, softened

3/4 cup (6 fl oz/180 ml) milk or half-and-half (half cream), warmed

Salt and freshly ground pepper

Bring a large saucepan of water to a boil over high heat. Add the potatoes, reduce the heat to medium-low, cover, and cook until tender when pierced with a knife, 20–25 minutes.

Drain the potatoes, return to the pan, place over low heat, and stir gently for about 1 minute to dry the potatoes. Remove from the heat.

Using a potato masher or an electric mixer on medium speed, mash or mix the potatoes until smooth. Return the pan to low heat and mix in the butter and milk. Season to taste with salt and pepper. Serve at once. To keep the potatoes warm for up to 30 minutes, place the pan in a larger pan partly filled with hot water, stirring the potatoes occasionally.

Makes 4 servings

Roasted Potatoes

1 1/2 lb (750 g) fingerling, Yukon gold, or red potatoes, cut into 1 1/2-inch (4-cm) chunks

3 tablespoons olive oil

Salt and freshly ground pepper

1 tablespoon chopped fresh flat-leaf (Italian) parsley

Preheat the oven to 425°F (220°C). Put the potatoes in a roasting pan or rimmed baking sheet. Drizzle with the olive oil and season with 1/2 teaspoon salt and 1/2 teaspoon pepper. Toss the potatoes to coat evenly and spread out in a single layer.

Roast the potatoes, turning occasionally, until golden and crisp, 25–30 minutes. Season to taste with salt and pepper. Serve at once.

Makes 4 servings

Celery Root and Potato Purée

1 celery root (celeriac), about 1 lb (500 g), peeled and cut into 1 1/2-inch (4-cm) chunks

1 lb (500 g) russet potatoes, peeled and cut into 1 1/2-inch (4-cm) chunks

3 tablespoons unsalted butter, softened

1/3–1/2 cup (3–4 fl oz/80–125 ml) milk or half-and-half (half cream), warmed

Salt and freshly ground pepper

Bring a large saucepan of water to a boil over high heat. Add the celery root and potatoes, reduce the heat to medium-low, and cook until just tender when pierced with a knife, 20–25 minutes.

Drain the celery root and potatoes, return to the pan, place over low heat, and stir gently for about 1 minute to dry the vegetables. Remove from the heat.

Using a potato masher or an electric mixer on medium speed, mash or mix the vegetables until smooth. Return the pan to low heat and mix in the butter and 1/3 cup milk. Season to taste with salt and pepper. Add the remaining milk if the purée seems too dry. Serve at once. To keep the vegetables warm for up to 30 minutes, place the pan in a larger pan partly filled with hot water, stirring the vegetables occasionally.

Makes 4 servings

Root Vegetable Purée

1 1/2 lb (750 g) winter squash such as butternut or acorn, peeled, seeded, and cut into 2-inch (5-cm) chunks

1/2 lb (250 g) carrots, cut into 2-inch (5-cm) chunks

3 tablespoons unsalted butter

2 teaspoons minced fresh ginger

1 tablespoon chopped fresh sage

Salt and freshly ground pepper

Preheat the oven to 375°F (190°C). Lightly oil a roasting pan.

Put the squash and carrots in the prepared pan, spreading them in a single layer. Add enough water to come about 1/4 inch (6 mm) up the sides of the pan. Cover tightly with aluminum foil and cook until the vegetables are nearly tender, 25–30 minutes. Uncover and roast until the vegetables are tender and lightly browned, 15–20 minutes longer.

Meanwhile, in a small frying pan over medium heat, melt the butter. Add the ginger and sage and cook, stirring constantly, for 1 minute.

Working in batches, place the roasted vegetables in a food processor or blender and process until a smooth purée forms. Transfer the purée to a bowl. Stir in the butter mixture and season to taste with salt and pepper. Serve at once. The purée can be prepared 1 day ahead and refrigerated. Reheat in a saucepan over low heat, stirring frequently, or in a covered baking dish in a 300°F (150°C) oven.

Makes 4 servings

Creamy Polenta

3¾ cups (30 fl oz/940 ml) water or chicken broth

Salt and freshly ground pepper

1 cup (5 oz/155 g) medium- or coarse-grind cornmeal

2 tablespoons unsalted butter, at room temperature

3 tablespoons grated Parmesan cheese (optional)

In a saucepan, bring the water and 1 teaspoon salt to a boil over high heat. Whisking constantly, very slowly pour the cornmeal into the boiling water. Bring just to a simmer, reduce the heat to low, and cook, whisking constantly, for 5 minutes.

Cover and continue to cook, stirring frequently with a wooden spoon and taking care to scrape the bottom of the pan, until the polenta is thick and creamy, 20–30 minutes. You will have about 3 cups (24 oz/750 g) polenta.

Stir in the butter and the cheese (if using). Season to taste with salt and pepper. Serve at once.

Makes 4 servings

Grilled Polenta

3¾ cups (30 fl oz/940 ml) water or chicken broth

Salt and freshly ground pepper

1 cup (5 oz/155 g) medium- or coarse-grind cornmeal

2 tablespoons unsalted butter, at room temperature

¼ cup (1 oz/30 g) grated Parmesan cheese

1½ tablespoons olive oil

In a saucepan over high heat, bring the water and 1 teaspoon salt to a boil over high heat. Whisking constantly, very slowly pour the cornmeal into the boiling water. Bring just to a simmer, reduce the heat to low, and cook, whisking constantly, for 5 minutes.

Cover and continue to cook, stirring frequently with a wooden spoon and taking care to scrape the bottom of the pan, until the polenta is very thick, 30–40 minutes.

Stir in the butter and cheese, and season to taste with salt and pepper. Lightly oil a 9-inch (23-cm) square baking pan or a 9-inch pie pan. Transfer the polenta to the prepared pan. Let cool completely and then refrigerate until the polenta is very firm, at least 2 hours or up to 24 hours.

Prepare a charcoal or gas grill for direct grilling over medium-high heat. Oil the grill rack. Cut the polenta into 3-inch (7.5-cm) squares or into wedges. Brush the polenta with the olive oil and grill, turning once, until grill marks appear and the polenta is crispy, about 4–6 minutes. Serve at once.

Makes 4 servings

Couscous

1 cup (8 fl oz/250 ml) water or vegetable broth

1 cup (6 oz/185 g) instant couscous

1 tablespoon unsalted butter (optional)

Salt and freshly ground pepper

In a small saucepan over high heat, bring the water to a boil. Put the couscous in a small, deep, heatproof bowl. Pour the boiling water over the couscous and stir briefly. Cover the bowl and let the couscous stand until the liquid is absorbed and the couscous is fluffy, 5–6 minutes. You will have about 3 cups (18 oz/560 g).

Stir in the butter (if using) and season to taste with salt and pepper. Serve at once.

Makes 4 servings

Couscous with Almonds and Raisins

1 cup (8 fl oz/250 ml) water or chicken broth

2 tablespoons olive oil

1 shallot, finely chopped

½ teaspoon curry powder

¼ cup (1 oz/30 g) sliced (flaked) almonds

¼ cup (1½ oz/45 g) small raisins or currants

1 cup (6 oz/185 g) instant couscous

2 tablespoons chopped fresh cilantro (fresh coriander)

Salt and freshly ground pepper

In a small saucepan over high heat, bring the water to a boil.

Meanwhile, in a saucepan over medium heat, warm the olive oil. Add the shallot and sauté until softened, 1–2 minutes. Stir in the curry powder and almonds and sauté until the almonds are golden, 2–3 minutes. Stir in the raisins and the couscous.

Pour the boiling water over the couscous and stir briefly. Cover and let the couscous stand until the liquid is absorbed and the couscous is fluffy, 5–6 minutes.

Stir in the cilantro and season to taste with salt and pepper. Serve at once.

Makes 4 servings

Israeli Couscous Pilaf

3 tablespoons (2 oz/60 g) unsalted butter

¼ cup (1½ oz/45 g) pine nuts

1 yellow onion, chopped

¼ teaspoon ground cinnamon

1 bay leaf, broken in half

1 teaspoon grated lemon zest

1 teaspoon grated orange zest

1¼ cups (8 oz/250 g) Israeli toasted couscous

1½ cups (12 fl oz/375 ml) water or chicken broth

Salt and freshly ground pepper

¼ cup (⅓ oz/10 g) chopped fresh flat-leaf (Italian) parsley

In a saucepan over medium heat, melt 1 tablespoon of the butter. Add the pine nuts and sauté until golden and fragrant, 2–3 minutes. Transfer to a plate and set aside.

Melt the remaining 2 tablespoons butter in the pan and sauté the onion over medium heat until soft and golden, about 5 minutes. Stir in the cinnamon, bay leaf, lemon and orange zests, and couscous. Stir in the water and bring to a simmer, stirring frequently. Cover, reduce the heat to low, and simmer, stirring occasionally, until the liquid is absorbed and the couscous is tender, 8–10 minutes.

Season to taste with salt and pepper. Remove

and discard the bay leaf. Stir in the parsley and reserved pine nuts. Serve at once.

Makes 4 servings

Warm Farro Pilaf

1 cup (8 oz/250 g) farro

4 tablespoons (2 fl oz/60 ml) olive oil

1 small leek, white and pale green parts only, halved lengthwise and thinly sliced

2 cloves garlic, minced

½ teaspoon grated lemon zest

1½ tablespoons fresh lemon juice

Salt and freshly ground pepper

Bring a large pot of salted water to a boil over high heat. Add the farro and cook for 5 minutes. Reduce the heat to medium-low and cook, stirring occasionally, until the farro is tender, 25–30 minutes. Drain well.

Meanwhile, in a frying pan over medium heat, warm 2 tablespoons of the olive oil. Add the leek and garlic and sauté until beginning to soften, about 2 minutes. Stir in the farro and the remaining 2 tablespoons oil. Add the lemon zest and juice, season to taste with salt and pepper, and toss to combine. Serve at once.

Makes 4 servings

Steamed Jasmine Rice

1 cup (7 oz/220 g) jasmine rice

Place the rice in a sieve and rinse under cold running water. Drain well.

In a saucepan, combine 1 cup (8 fl oz/250 ml) water and the drained rice. Cover and bring to a boil. Reduce the heat to medium-low and cook until the rice is tender, 25–30 minutes. Fluff the rice with a fork and serve at once.

Makes 4 servings

Spiced Basmati Rice

1 cup (7 oz/220 g) basmati rice

1 cinnamon stick, broken in half

2 teaspoons finely chopped fresh ginger

1 teaspoon allspice

½ teaspoon ground turmeric

1¼ cups (10 fl oz/310 ml) chicken broth or water

Salt and freshly ground pepper

2 green (spring) onions, white and pale green parts, thinly sliced

2 tablespoons fresh chopped mint

Place the rice in a sieve and rinse under cold running water. Drain well and set aside.

Place the cinnamon, ginger, allspice, turmeric on a 4-inch (10-cm) square of cheesecloth (muslin). Gather the corners and tie with kitchen string. Place the spice bundle in a saucepan and add the broth and ½ teaspoon salt. Bring to a boil over high heat. Stir in the rice, cover, reduce the heat to low, and simmer gently until the liquid is absorbed and the rice is tender, about 25 minutes. Remove from the heat.

Sprinkle the green onions and mint over the rice. Do not stir. Cover and let stand for 5 minutes. Stir gently to combine the rice, onions, and mint. Remove and discard the spice bundle. Season to taste with salt and pepper. Serve at once.

Makes 4 servings

Herbed Rice Pilaf

2 tablespoons olive oil or unsalted butter

2 shallots, finely chopped

1 cup (7 oz/220 g) long-grain white rice

1¾ cups (14 fl oz/430 ml) chicken or vegetable broth

Salt and freshly ground pepper

¼ cup (⅓ oz/10 g) chopped mixed fresh herbs such as marjoram, thyme, tarragon, basil, oregano, mint, and cilantro (coriander)

In a saucepan over medium heat, warm the olive oil. Add the shallots and sauté, until softened, 1–2 minutes. Stir in the rice and cook, stirring, until the grains are coated, about 1 minute. Add the broth and ¼ teaspoon salt. Bring to a boil over high heat. Cover, reduce the heat to low, and simmer gently until the liquid is absorbed and the rice is tender, about 20 minutes. Remove from the heat.

Sprinkle the herbs over the rice. Do not stir. Cover and let stand for 5 minutes. Stir gently to combine the rice and herbs. Season to taste with salt and pepper. Serve at once.

Makes 4 servings

Creamy Risotto

3½ cups (28 fl oz/875 ml) chicken broth

1 cup (8 fl oz/250 ml) dry white wine such as sauvignon blanc

2 tablespoons unsalted butter

1 yellow onion, finely chopped

1½ cups (10½ oz/330 g) Arborio rice

⅓ cup (1½ oz/45 g) grated Parmesan cheese

Salt and freshly ground pepper

In a saucepan over medium heat, bring the broth and wine to a simmer. Adjust the heat to maintain a gentle simmer.

In heavy-bottomed saucepan over medium heat, melt 1 tablespoon of the butter. Add the onion and sauté until softened, 4–5 minutes. Add the rice and stir until the grains are coated with the butter and turn translucent at the edges, about 1 minute. Stir in 1 cup (8 fl oz/250 ml) of the simmering broth mixture, reduce the heat to low, and cook, stirring almost constantly, until the liquid is absorbed, 3–5 minutes.

Continue adding the broth mixture, ½ cup (4 fl oz/125 ml) at a time, always waiting until the rice is just moist before adding more, and stirring almost constantly. The risotto is done when the rice is tender and very creamy, but still slightly firm in the center, about 20 minutes after the first addition of the broth mixture.

Gently stir in the cheese and remaining 1 tablespoon butter. Season to taste with salt and pepper. Serve at once.

Makes 4 servings

Saffron Risotto

3½ cups (28 fl oz/875 ml) chicken broth

1 cup (8 fl oz/250 ml) dry white wine such as sauvignon blanc

½ teaspoon crushed saffron threads

3 tablespoons unsalted butter

1 yellow onion, finely chopped

1½ cups (10½ oz/330 g) Arborio rice

½ cup (2½ oz/75 g) frozen baby green peas, thawed

⅓ cup (1½ oz/45 g) grated Parmesan cheese

Salt and freshly ground pepper

In a saucepan over medium heat, bring the broth, wine, and saffron to a simmer. Adjust the heat to maintain a gentle simmer.

In heavy-bottomed saucepan over medium heat, melt 1½ tablespoons of the butter. Add the onion and sauté until softened, 4–5 minutes. Add the rice and stir until the grains are coated with the butter and turn translucent at the edges, about 1 minute. Stir in 1 cup (8 fl oz/250 ml) of the simmering broth mixture, reduce the heat to low, and cook, stirring almost constantly, until the liquid is absorbed, 3–5 minutes.

Continue adding the broth mixture, ½ cup (4 fl oz/125 ml) at a time, always waiting until the rice is just moist before adding more, and stirring almost constantly. The risotto is done when the rice is tender and very creamy, but still slightly firm in the center, about 20 minutes after the first addition of the broth mixture. Add the peas about 5 minutes before the end of the cooking time.

Gently stir in the cheese and remaining butter. Season to taste with salt and pepper. Serve at once.

Makes 4 servings

Orzo Pilaf

3 cups (24 fl oz/750 ml) chicken broth, plus more if needed

2 tablespoons olive oil

2 carrots, chopped

2 cloves garlic, minced

1½ cups (10½ oz/330 g) orzo

2 green (spring) onions, white and pale green parts, thinly sliced

2 tablespoons finely shredded mint

1 tablespoon chopped fresh marjoram

Salt and freshly ground pepper

½ cup (2½ oz/75 g) crumbled feta cheese

In a saucepan over medium heat, bring the 3 cups broth to a simmer.

In another saucepan over medium heat, warm the olive oil. Add the carrot and sauté until barely softened, 2–3 minutes. Add the garlic and sauté for 30 seconds. Stir in the orzo. Add the simmering broth and bring to a simmer. Cover, reduce the heat to medium-low, and cook, stirring often, until the liquid is absorbed and the pasta is tender, about 15 minutes. If the pasta seems dry, add more broth, 1 tablespoon at a time.

Stir in the green onions, mint, and marjoram.

Season to taste with salt and pepper. Serve at once, sprinkled with the feta cheese.

Makes 4 servings

Buttered Egg Noodles

Salt and freshly ground pepper

³⁄₄ lb (375 g) dried curly egg noodles

3 tablespoons unsalted butter

2 tablespoons chopped fresh flat-leaf (Italian) parsley

Bring a large pot of water to a boil. Add 2 tablespoons salt and the egg noodles, stir well, and cook, stirring occasionally, until al dente, according to the package directions.

While the pasta is cooking, in a small frying pan over medium heat, melt the butter. Continue to cook, swirling the pan, until the butter turns golden and has a nutty fragrance, 1–2 minutes.

When the pasta is done, drain well and transfer to a serving bowl. Pour the butter over the noodles. Add the parsley and toss to coat the noodles. Season to taste with salt and pepper and toss again. Serve at once.

Makes 4 servings

Rosemary Flatbread

2³⁄₄ cups (14 oz/440 g) bread flour

¹⁄₄ cup (1 oz/30 g) cornmeal, plus more for dusting

1 package (2¹⁄₂ teaspoons) active dry yeast

Salt and freshly ground pepper

1 cup (8 fl oz/250 ml) warm water (110°–120°F/43°–49°C)

2 tablespoons olive oil

1 tablespoon chopped fresh rosemary

Hand: In a bowl, whisk together the flour, ¹⁄₄ cup cornmeal, yeast, and 1 teaspoon salt. Make a well in the center and pour in the water and 1 tablespoon of the olive oil. Using a wooden spoon, mix until a dough forms, about 5 minutes. Turn the dough out onto a lightly oiled work surface and knead until smooth and elastic, about 10 minutes.

Mixer: In the bowl of a stand mixer fitted with the paddle, whisk together the flour, ¹⁄₄ cup cornmeal, yeast, and 1 teaspoon salt. Pour in the water and 1 tablespoon of the olive oil. Beat on medium-low speed until a dough forms. Switch to the dough hook and knead the dough on low speed until smooth and elastic, about 5 minutes.

Lightly oil a bowl. Place the dough in the bowl and turn to coat with the oil. Cover lightly with a kitchen towel and let rise at room temperature until doubled in bulk, about 30 minutes.

Punch down the dough. Lightly oil a baking sheet and sprinkle with cornmeal. Divide the dough into 6 portions. Shape each into a flat round about ¹⁄₂ inch (12 mm) thick. Arrange the rounds on the prepared sheet, spacing them at least 2 inches (5 cm) apart. Brush the rounds generously with the remaining 1 tablespoon oil. Sprinkle generously with salt, pepper, and the rosemary. Let rise for 10 minutes.

Meanwhile, preheat the oven to 450°F (230°C). Bake the flat breads until golden, firm, and well browned at the edges, 9–11 minutes. Serve warm.

Makes 6 servings

Corn Bread

1 cup (5 oz/155 g) yellow cornmeal

1 cup (5 oz/155 g) all-purpose (plain) flour

2 tablespoons sugar

4 teaspoons baking powder

Salt and freshly ground pepper

1 egg

1 cup (8 fl oz/250 ml) milk

4 tablespoons (2 oz/60 g) unsalted butter, melted and cooled

Preheat the oven to 425°F (220°C). Butter a 9-inch (23-cm) square baking pan.

In a large bowl, whisk together the cornmeal, flour, sugar, baking powder, 1 teaspoon salt, and ¹⁄₂ teaspoon pepper. In a small bowl, whisk together the egg, milk, and butter.

Make a well in the center of the dry ingredients and pour in the liquid ingredients. Stir to combine just until no lumps remain. Do not overmix. Spread the batter in the prepared pan.

Bake until the corn bread is golden brown and a toothpick inserted into the center comes out clean, about 20 minutes. Serve warm, cut into squares.

Makes 12–16 squares

Buttermilk Biscuits

2 cups (10 oz/315 g) all-purpose (plain) flour

2 teaspoons baking powder

¹⁄₂ teaspoon baking soda (bicarbonate of soda)

¹⁄₂ teaspoon sugar

Salt

4 tablespoons (2 oz/60 g) chilled unsalted butter, cut into small pieces

¹⁄₄ cup (2 oz/60 g) chilled vegetable shortening, cut into small pieces

³⁄₄ cup (6 fl oz/180 ml) buttermilk

Preheat the oven to 450°F (230°C).

In a bowl, whisk together the flour, baking powder, baking soda, sugar, and 1 teaspoon salt.

Scatter the butter and shortening pieces over the dry ingredients. Using your fingers or a pastry cutter, mix or cut in the butter and shortening until the mixture resembles coarse meal. Make a well in the center and pour in the buttermilk. Stir just until a dough forms. Do not overmix.

Turn the dough out onto a lightly floured work surface. Knead once or twice, and then roll or pat the dough to an even thickness of 1/2 inch (12 mm). Cut out biscuits with a 2-inch (5-cm) biscuit cutter. Arrange the biscuits on a baking sheet, spacing them out 2 inches apart. Gather the scraps of dough, roll out once, and cut additional biscuits.

Bake for 5 minutes. Reduce the oven temperature to 425°F (220°C) and bake until the biscuits are well risen and rich golden brown, 8–10 minutes longer. Serve warm.

Makes about 16 biscuits

Cooking Dried Beans

1 cup (7 oz/220 g) dried beans

Salt and freshly ground pepper

Pick over the beans, removing any misshapen beans or grit. Rinse under cold running water and drain.

Put the beans in a bowl, add enough cold water to cover by at least 2 inches (5 cm), and let stand at room temperture overnight. Alternately, for a quck soak, put the beans in a saucepan, add enough cold water to cover by at least 2 inches, bring to a boil, remove from the heat, cover, and let soak for 1 hour. Drain.

In a saucepan, combine the beans with enough cold water to cover by about 4 inches (10 cm) over high heat, skimming off the foam that rises to the surface. Reduce the heat to low, cover partially, and simmer until the beans are tender, 1 1/2–2 1/2 hours. The timing will depend on the variety and age of the beans. Use at once, or refrigerate in an airtight container for up to 1 week.

Makes 3 cups (21 oz/655 g) beans

Sautéed Green Beans

1 1/2 lb green beans, stem ends trimmed

1 tablespoon olive oil

1 garlic clove, crushed

1 tablespoon fresh lemon juice

Salt and pepper to taste

Have ready a large bowl of ice water. Bring a large saucepan three-fourths full of water to a boil. Add the green beans and 1 teaspoon salt and cook, uncovered, until just crisp-tender, 1–2 minutes. Immediately drain the beans and transfer to the ice water to stop the cooking. When cool, drain the beans, transfer to a kitchen towel, and pat dry.

In a large frying pan over medium-high heat, warm the olive oil. Add the garlic and let cook for 30 seconds. Add the beans and sauté until just tender 2–3 minutes. Transfer to a warmed serving platter, drizzle with the lemon juice, season with salt and pepper to taste, and serve at once.

Makes 8 servings

Steamed Broccoli

1 1/2 lb 1 large bunch broccoli

1 tablespoon extra-virgin olive oil

Salt and pepper to taste

Trim off 1/2 inch (12 mm) from the stem ends of the broccoli stalks, then peel the tough outer layer from the stalks. Cut off the florets and the slender stems from the tops of the stalks, trimming them so that they are 1–2 inches (2.5–5 cm) long. Cut the large stalks into sticks 1/3 inch (9 mm) wide.

Put the broccoli in a steamer rack set over boiling water, cover tightly, and cook until tender 5–6 minutes. Transfer to a warmed serving bowl and toss with the oil. Season with salt and pepper to taste and serve at once.

Makes 4 servings

Cole Slaw

1/2 cup (4 fl oz/125 ml) mayonnaise

1 tablespoon honey

2 teaspoons cider vinegar

1 teaspoon celery seed

1/2 medium green cabbage, thinly sliced (about 2 cups/6 oz/185 g)

1/2 medium red cabbage, thinly sliced (about 2 cups/6 oz/185 g)

1 small red onion, grated

2 carrots, grated

Salt and freshly ground black pepper to taste

In a small bowl, mix together the mayonnaise, honey, cider vinegar, and celery seed.

In a large bowl, toss together the green and red cabbage, red onion, and carrot. Add the dressing and salt and black pepper to taste and toss well.

Makes 8 servings

Pork Cuts

Many U.S. butchers divide the pig into five primal sections, illustrated below. Some also divide the loin into the sirloin and center loin. The cuts range from the small, lean tenderloin and single-serving chops to the large, moist leg enveloped in a layer of fat and the elegant tenderloin.

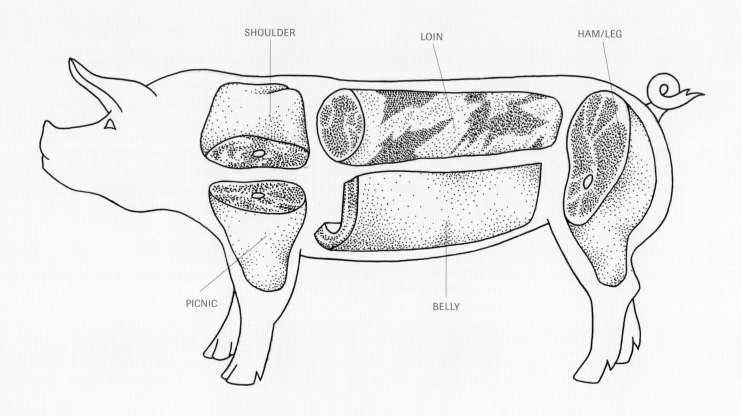

SHOULDER

LOIN

HAM/LEG

PICNIC

BELLY

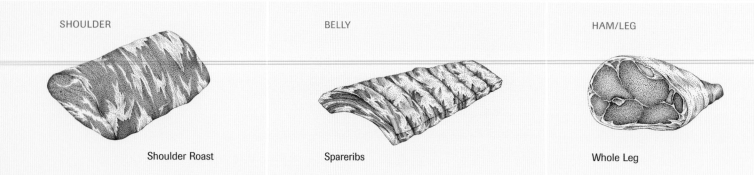

SHOULDER

Shoulder Roast

BELLY

Spareribs

HAM/LEG

Whole Leg

PORK CUTS FOR SLOW COOKING

The cuts described here are those featured in the recipes in this book. For information on purchasing pork, see page 13.

Shoulder Roast

Cut from the top of the shoulder, this roast has an abundant amount of connective tissue and good supply of fat. The meat can be transformed into juicy, falling-apart shreds after long cooking at low temperature (see Pulled Pork, page 178).

Whole Leg

A large cut weighing up to 20 pounds (10 kg), the hind leg usually becomes a cured ham. Smaller roasts from the butt, or top, end and the shank, or bottom, end are also available. The buttis more compact than the shank but the latter is easier to carve.

Tenderloin

The boneless tenderloin, averaging 1 pound (500 g), comes from the lower-middle back. Of all pork cuts, it is the most tender and most lean. A variety of seasonings can be used to flavor the meat.

Boneless Loin Roast

This upper back section is the most tender part of the pig. The front pasrt of the loin, known as the blade and center loin, has rich, tender meat that is cut into large blade roasts or sliced into chops. Toward the center of the loin, the meat becomes juicier and more tender still.

Pork Belly

The pork belly is the underside of the pig, from which bacon is made in the United States.. It also takes very well to brining and then cooking over a very low heat until tender. (see Brined Pork Belly, page 189).

Baby Back Ribs

Loin Roast

Tenderloin

Beef Cuts

Butchers in the United States divide the steer into eight primary sections, illustrated below.
In general, cuts from the top of the steer are more tender than those from the bottom of the steer,
which benefit from the use of flavorings such as rubs and marinades.

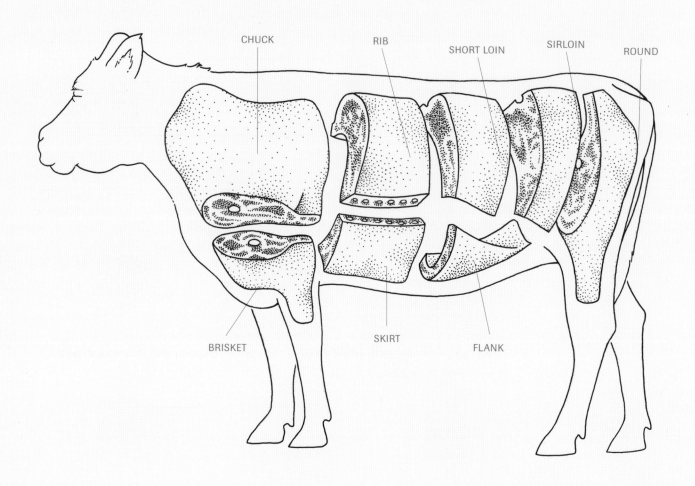

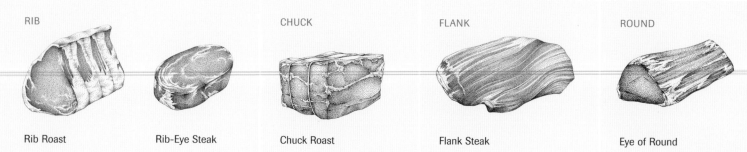

RIB — Rib Roast

— Rib-Eye Steak

CHUCK — Chuck Roast

FLANK — Flank Steak

ROUND — Eye of Round

BEEF CUTS FOR SLOW COOKING

The cuts described here are those featured in the recipes in this book. For information on purchasing beef, see page 13.

Chateaubriand

Many cuts of beef are sold as chateaubriand. All are tender and sized to serve two. The most authentic cut comes from the tenderloin and averages 1–1 1/4 pounds (500–625 g). This boneless steak is appreciated for its tenderness and flavor.

Short Ribs

Short ribs are a popular cut of beef. They are larger and unsually more tender and meatier then their pork counterpart, pork spareribs. Short ribs are best when long-cooked, barbecued, or braised.

Chuck Roast

The chuck roast comes from the muscular shoulder section, also the source of chuck steak and stewing beef. These tougher cuts are best slow cooked by moist methods such as stewing or braising, which allows the meat to soften and become tender (see Hearty Beef Stew, page 245).

Eye of Round

Lacking the internal fat of other cuts, boneless eye of round is lean. Slt is a true source of round (or rump) roasts as well as ground beef. Top round is the most tender part of this section (see Belgium Beef Stew, page 237).

Brisket

Brisket is a beef cut from the breast section of the cow, beneath the first five ribs. Fresh brisket is an inexpenssive cut that requires long, slow cooking to break down the thick muscle tissues and become tender. It is sold in both a flat cut or a point cut (see Barbeque-Style Brisket, page 234).

Flank Steak

Cut from the underbelly, the thin, fibrous flank steak benefits from marinating to enhance the tenderness of the meat. This boneless steak can be butterflied, stuffed, and slow cooked (see, Braciole, page 251).

SHORT LOIN

Chateaubriand

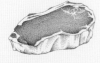

Strip Steak

Porterhouse Steak

Tenderloin

Lamb Cuts

Lamb sold in the United States is divided into six primary cuts, shown below. The rib and loin, the less exercised parts of the animal, yield the most tender cuts, though the leg and shoulder yield moist, flavorful meat when slow cooked.

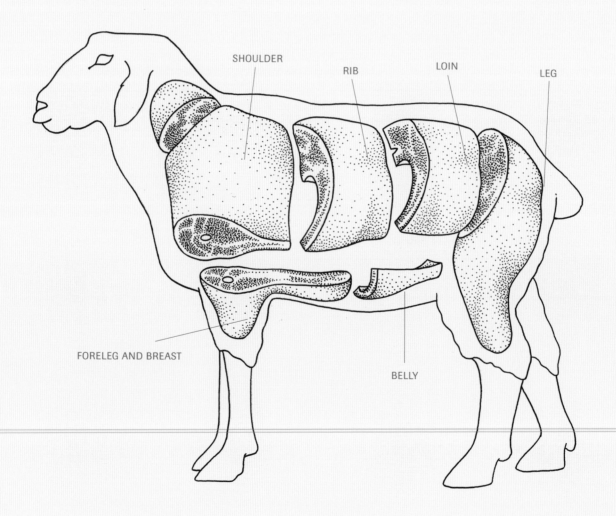

SHOULDER

RIB

LOIN

LEG

FORELEG AND BREAST

BELLY

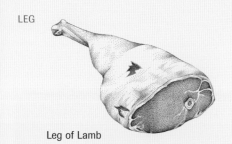

Leg of Lamb

Boneless Leg of Lamb

Loin Chop

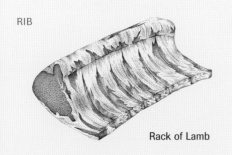

Rack of Lamb

Shoulder Roast

LAMB CUTS FOR SLOW COOKING

The cuts described here are those featured in the recipes in this book. For information on purchasing lamb, see page 14.

Leg of Lamb

A whole bone-in hind leg of lamb is a tender cut that is easy to roast and yields enough flavorful meat to serve crowds. The meat can be seasoned prior to roasting with herbs, spices, and aromatics (see tk, page xx). A half leg of lamb can be taken from the shank (bottom) end or butt (top) end, the latter of which offers more meat. Compared with a whole leg, which weighs 6 to 7 pounds (3 to 3.5 kg), the half leg is 4 to 5 pounds (2 to 2.5 kg) and serves six.

Boneless Leg of Lamb

Not only is a boneless leg of lamb flavorful and tender, but it is very easy to carve. The meat can be flattened and trimmed, then rolled around a stuffing of vegetables or other ingredients to make a compact, cylindrical roast (see Stuffed Leg of Lamb, page 255). A whole leg is easy to bone, but butchers will bone the leg on request. When cubed, a leg of lamb is also good for stewing and braising.

Shoulder Roast

Although not as tender as other cuts of lamb, the shoulder develops a depth of flavor and succulence when slow cooked, which softens the connective tissue and renders the fat. Seasoning the meat in advance and searing it before further cooking—enhance the flavor and texture. Shoulder roasts are available with the bone in and also boneless and tied, ready to roast.

Lamb Shanks

These come from the lower, shin section of the leg. Hearty, economical, and fill flavored, tough shanks require long, gentle braising. A few hours of gentle simmering will result in rich, moist meat. The small, lean foreshank is usually braised as an individual-serving cut (see Braised Lamb Shanks, page 256).

Basic Techniques

CARVING A CHICKEN OR OTHER SMALL BIRD

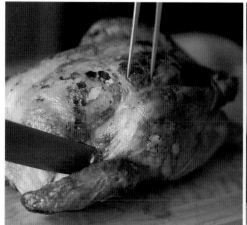 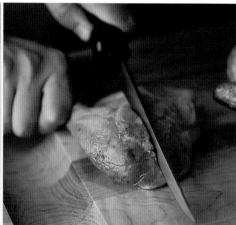 

1 Using a carving knife, cut through the skin between the thigh and breast. Move the leg to locate the thigh joint, then cut through the joint to remove the leg. Use the same procedure to remove the wing from the breast by cutting through the shoulder joint.

2 If the bird is small, the leg, with both the drumstick and the thigh, may be served whole. If it is large, cut through the joint to separate the drumstick and thigh. Larger thighs may be cut into 2 pieces by removing the meat from the bone.

3 Just above the thigh and wing joints, make a deep horizontal cut toward the bone. Starting at the breastbone, carve downward along the bone toward the horizontal cut to remove the breast in a single piece, then thinly slice the breast if desired.

CARVING A BONELESS ROAST

1 Place the roast on a carving board. Leave the strings in place to hold the roast together. Insert a carving fork to secure the roast alongside where you will be slicing.

2 Using a carving knife, carve the meat across the grain into horizontal slices $1/4$–$1/2$ inch (6–12 mm) thick, removing the strings from the roast as you reach them.

CARVING A BONE-IN LEG OF LAMB I

1 Place the leg on a carving board and, with a kitchen towel, hold it firmly by the end of the shank bone. Position the leg so the rounded, meaty side will be carved first.

2 Tilt the leg slightly upward and cut a slice about 1/2 inch (12 mm) thick from the meaty side, cutting away from you and parallel to the bone.

3 Continue carving the meat parallel to the first slice and to the bone. Rotate the leg to expose the flatter side and repeat to cut slices about 1/2 inch thick.

CARVING A BONE-IN LEG OF LAMB II

1 Holding the leg firmly with a kitchen towel, cut 1 or 2 slices from the flat side for stability, then turn the leg meaty side up. About 6 inches (15 cm) up from the shank end, remove a small, wedge-shaped piece of meat.

2 Starting at the wedge, cut slices about 1/2 inch (12 mm) thick, working perpendicular to the bone and cutting through the meat to the bone. Make a cut along the bone, starting at the wedge, to free all of the slices.

3 Cut down along each side of the bone and around the leg to release the remaining meat from the bottom side of the leg. Remove the meat in a single large piece. Cut it across the grain into slices 1/2 inch thick.

Glossary

BALSAMIC VINEGAR A dark brown, syrupy, aged vinegar that is sweet and mellow while still possessing a complex, lightly acidic tang. It adds rich flavor to marinade, glazes, and pan sauces. Select a relatively young balsamic vinegar for these uses; long-aged vinegars should be used sparingly and never cooked.

BEANS, DRIED Practical and economical, dried beans are designed for slow cooking. You;ll need to pick ut any misshappen beans or grit and soak the beans before cooking.

Black Small and uniformly black with a shiny surface. Used widely in Latin American cooking to make pot beans and soups.

Cannellini Ivory-colored bean of moderate size with a fluffy, smooth texture when cooked. White kidney beans or Great Northern beans can be used in their place.

Chickpea Also known as garbanzo bean or ceci bean. They are often large and beige in color with a rich, nutty flavor and a firm texture.

BELL PEPPERS Sweet-fleshed, bell-shaped members of the pepper family, bell peppers are also known as sweet peppers or capsicums. Green bell peppers are usually more sharply flavored than red ones, the latter being simply a sweeter and more mature stage of the former. Orange and yellow peppers are separate varieties.

BREAD CRUMBS Fresh or dried, these are the good cook's secret weapon, bestowing a crisp topping on casseroles and a crunchy coating on pan-fried and roasted meats. When a recipe calls for bread crumbs, it usually means dried crumbs unless otherwise specified. Do not substitute one for the other, as fresh crumbs contain more moisture than dried and the two will behave differently in recipes.

BROCCOLI RABE A relative of turnip greens, broccoli rabe, also known as broccoli raab, *rapini*, and rape, has leafy, dark green stems topped with clusters of broccoli-like florets. Be sure to remove any of the tough stems and wilted leaves before cooking. If the skin on the lower part of the stalks is fibrous, peel it with a vegetable peeler.

CABBAGE Like broccoli or cauliflower, cabbage is a cruciferous vegetable, a group believed by some scientists to safeguard against cancer. Buy firm, heavy heads of cabbage with closely furled leaves.

CAPERS A Mediterranean shrub is the source of these small unopened flower buds. The buds are bitter when raw; once they are dried and packed in brine or salt, they are used to add a pleasantly pungent flavor to a variety of dishes. Capers packed in sea salt retain their intense floral flavor and firm texture better than brined capers, but the latter are more commonly available. Rinse and drain brined capers before using; salted capers should be rinsed, then soaked in several changes of cold water for 30 minutes before using.

CARAWAY SEEDS Caraway is a member of the parsley family. It has a strong, pungent taste that is closely identified with rye bread. It is often added to meat and poultry dishes and casseroles and most often used whole.

CARDAMOM This spice has an exotic, highly aromatic flavor and is used ground in curries, fruit dishes, and baked goods. It may also be added whole. The whole pods may be added to mulled wine, the spicy tea known as chai, and braised dishes, stews, and tagines. Cardamom is sold in small round pod, or as whole or ground black seeds. The seeds are best removed) from the pod and ground, although the whole pod may also be ground.

CELERY ROOT Also called celeriac, celery knob, or turnip-rooted celery, celery root is the root of a celery plant. The gnarled, knobby brown root bulb, once peeled, can be eaten raw or cooked. Celery root tastes similar to the more common celery but has a more pronounced nutty, earthy flavor, and a softer texture.

CHEESE Some types are used in stuffings for slow-cooked meats and poultry, while others are sprinkled on foods just before serving to create a flavorful finish.

Parmesan An aged, hard grating cheese made from partially skimmed cow's milk, with a salty flavor and a rich, assertive fragrance. The most prized version, produced in the Emilia-Romagna region of Italy, is always labeled with the trademark name Parmigiano-Reggiano.

Romano A term that refers to several hard grating cheeses originating in Italy but now also produced outside the country. *Pecorino romano* is one of the better known of the romano cheeses.

CHILE POWDER A pure powder made by grinding a single specific variety of dried chile. Ancho and New Mexico chile powders are the most commonly available. Do not confuse these pure powders with chili powder, typically a blend of powdered dried chile, oregano, cumin, and sometimes other seasonings.

CHILES Fresh chiles range in size from tiny to large, in heat intensity from mild to fiery hot, and in use from seasoning to vegetable. Select firm, bright-colored chiles with blemish-free skins. To reduce the hotness of a chile, remove the membranes and seeds, where the heat-producing compound, called capsaicin, resides. When working with hot chiles, wear gloves to avoid burning your skin, then wash your hands and any utensils thoroughly with hot, soapy water the moment you finish.

Ancho A mild, dark reddish brown or brick red, squat-looking dried poblano chile. About 4 inches (10 cm) long, anchos can pack a bit of heat along with their natural sweetness. Ancho chile powder is available in Latino markets and is generally considered to make the best pure ground chile powder. Use California chiles or mulato chiles when anchos are not available abd they have similar heat levels.

Jalapeño The jalapeño measures from 2 to 4 inches (5 to 10 cm) long, has a generous amount of flesh, and ranges from mildly hot to fiery. Green jalapeños are widely available, but you can sometimes find red ones, the ripened form, which are slightly sweeter. A chipotle chile is a dried and smoked jalapeño chile. They may be bought dried, or in cans or jars in an oniony tomato mixture called adobo sauce.

Pasilla Dark, narrow, and wrinkled, this 6-inch (15-cm) chile is hot and sweet.

Serrano The serrano is similar to the familiar jalapeño in heat intensity and appearance, although it is smaller, usually about 2 inches (5 cm), and more slender. It can be green or red.

Thai Small, thin green or red chiles, usually only about 1 inch (2.5 cm) long. Also knon as bird chiles, they are very hot.

COCONUT MILK With its rich and nutty flavor, coconut milk, made by soaking grated coconut in water, is an essential ingredient in the tropics. It thickens sauces, turns rich dishes creamy, and is the perfect foil for the heat of chiles.

COLLARD GREENS Large, thick, dark green leaves, each branching from a central stem. The flavor is mild, but the tough textire calls for long cooking. A favorite in the American South.

COUSCOUS A staple of North African cooking, couscous are tiny beads made from coarsely milled semolina. Precooked dried couscous, sometimes instant or quick-cooking couscous is available either packaged or in bulk. It requires only rehydrating in boiling water before serving. Isreali couscous is larger than regular couscous, with beads about the size of peppercorns. Couscous is bland enough to accompany any meal as a side dish.

CURRY POWDER Typical ingredients of this ground spice blend from South Asia include turmeric, cumin, coriander, pepper, cardamom, mustard, cloves, and ginger. Curry powders are usually categorized as mild, hot, and very hot. Madras curry powder is considered a well-balanced version with medium heat.

EGGPLANT Native to Africa and Asia, the eggplant, or aubergine, is technically a fruit. The most familiar eggplant is called a globe eggplant and is usually large and egg or pear shaped, with a thin, shiny, deep purple skin that looks almost blackskin. Asian eggplants, also purple skinned, are smaller, longer, and narrower. Other varieties may be slightly smaller and have white, rose, green, or variegated skin.

ESCAROLE A slightly bitter member of the chicory family with broad, ruffled leaves.

FARRO Cultivated by the ancient Romans, *farro* is one of the world's most oldeast grains. *Farro* grains are oval shaped, with a long groove running down their length. The skin is brown, concealing a pale interior that becomes plump and starchy as it absorbs liquid during cooking. *Farro* has a deliciously nutty, wheatlike flavor.

FENNEL BULB This popular Mediterranean vegetable has the flavor of anise and is celery-like in appearance, with stalks and feathery leaves, and a thick, rounded base.

FIGS This soft, pear-shaped "fruit" is, in fact, a flower swollen and turned on itself, while the many tiny "seeds" are the actual fruit of the tree. Dried figs are delicious when served with poultry or game. Dried figs can be chopped and added to couscous or rice pilaf.

FISH SAUCE A clear liquid, ranging from amber to dark brown, fish sauce is famous for its pungent aroma and strong, salty flavor. Look for fish sauce, known as *nam pla* in Thailand and nuoc mam in Vietman, in Asian food stores and the international food aisle of the supermarket.

GARAM MASALA A mixture of toasted, ground spices used in South Asia. The blend may consist of as many as a dozen spices, including black pepper, cumin, cloves, cardamom, coriander, fennel, fenugreek, and mace. Traditionally it is added in a small quantity at the end of cooking or sprinkled over the finished dish just before serving to add a subtle flavor. Garam masala is available in Indian markets and many well-stocked supermarkets.

GINGER A refreshing combination of spicy and sweet in both aroma and flavor, ginger is a standard ingredient in most Asian cuisines and adds a lively note to many dishes, including sauces and marinades for roasted foods. Hard and knobby fresh ginger has thin, pale brown skin. Although called a root, it is actually a rhizome, or underground stem. Select fresh ginger that is firm and heavy with smooth, unbroken skin.

GREMOLATA A mixture of chopped garlic, lemon zest, and parsely traditionally sprinkled over osso buco before serving.

HERBS Using fresh herbs is one of the best things you can do to improve the flavor of your cooking. If necessary, use dry herbs.

Basil A member of the mint family, this iconic Mediterranean herb adds a highly aromatic flavor to foods. It is traditionally paired with tomatoes. Always use fresh basil.

Bay Leaf Strong and spicy, the whole glossy leaves of the bay laurel tree are indispensable in many long-simmered savory preparations. European bay leaves have a milder, more pleasant taste than the California-grown variety. The leaves are almost always sold dried and should be removed from a dish before serving.

Marjoram A close cousin of oregano, marjoram has a delicate floral flavor that complements tomato-based dishes. If possible, always use fresh, rather than dried, marjoram.

Oregano Unlike most herbs, strongly scented oregano gains flavor when dried. Related to mint and thyme, it is often added to sauces, especially those based on tomatoes or other vegetables. Before using dried oregano, or any dried herb, crush the leaves to release the herb's aromatic oils, the source of its flavor.

Parsley, Flat-leaf Also called Italian parsley, this flat-leafed, dark green variety of the popular Mediterranean herb has a more complex, peppery flavor than curly-leaf parsley. It is commonly used as both a seasoning and a garnish. Always use fresh parsley.

Rosemary Taking its name from the Latin for "dew of the sea," reflecting its relationship to oceanside climates, this Mediterranean native contributes a powerful but pleasantly aromatic flavor to lamb, veal, chicken, and other foods. It can be used fresh or dried.

Sage An ancient healing herb that takes its name from the Latin *salvus,* meaning "safe," this strong, heady, slightly musty-tasting herb is used either fresh or dried to season meats, poultry, vegetables, beans, and brown-butter sauces.

Thyme Highly aromatic and yet subtle in flavor, this ancient Mediterranean herb is included in many slow-cooked dishes and is especially useful for the digestive properties it contributes to dishes featuring fat-rich meat or poultry.

HOISIN A thick, sweet, reddish brown sauce made from soybeans, sugar, garlic, and spices. Throughout China, hoisin sauce is used as a glaze or sauce for meats and poultry. Use sparingly, as it has a strong flavor.

HOMINY Dried corn kernels that have been soaked in alkali such as lime or lye, washed to remove their outer skin, and boiled for several hours. Hominy is sold in either whole kernels or cracked intobits that are cooked in liquid.

JUNIPER BERRIES These dark blue berries from the evergreen juniper bush give gin its distinctive taste. They add pungency to a variety of preparations, and are sometimes crushed before using.

LEEKS The mildest member of the onion family, the leek, which resembles a giant green (spring) onion, has a bright white stalk and long, overlapping green leaves. Native to the Mediterranean, leeks bring a hint of both garlic and onion to the dishes they flavor. Choose smaller leeks with dark green leaves that are crisp, firm, and free of blemishes.

To clean: Trim off the roots and the tough, dark green tops of the leaves. If the outer layer is wilted or discolored, peel it away and discard. Quarter or halve the stalk lengthwise. If using the leek whole, leave the root end intact. Rinse well under cold running water, separating the layers and rubbing the leaves to remove any silt between them.

LEMONGRASS An aromatic herb used in much of Southeast Asia, lemongrass resembles a green (spring) onion in shape. The slender, gray-green stalk has a fresh lemony aroma and flavor. Use only the pale bottom part of the stalk for cooking, removing the tough outer leaves before crushing it with a pestle or the side of a knife blade and then chopping.

MADEIRA A fortified wine from Portugal, Madera comes in many versions from nutty and dry to sweet.

MARSALA An amber-colored fortified wine made in the area around the Sicilian city of the same name. Available in sweet and dry forms, it is enjoyed as a dessert wine and is used as a flavoring in savory and sweet dishes.

MIRIN A sweet, syrupy Japanese rice wine used in Asian-style marinades, glazes, and sauces. It is available in Asian markets and well-stocked grocery stores.

MISO A staple food in Japan, this fermented soybean paste is used to flavor robust dishes. Miso comes in two main types: sweet, mild light (or yellow) miso; and strong, salty dark (or red) miso.

MOLASSES This thick syrup, a by-product of sugarcane processing, is used as a sweetener in sauces and glazes for savory foods, as well as in baked goods. Light molasses has pure cane syrup added. Dark molasses is thicker and less sweet than its light counterpart.

MUSHROOMS, DRIED To reconstitute dried mushrooms, cover with boiling water and let soak for 10–30 minutes. Drain, reserving the flavorful soaking liquid for use in the same recipe as the mushrooms or for another use.

Porcini Fresh porcini, also called ceps, are difficult to find and expensive outside the locations where they grow. The dried version is a good alternative. Porcini have a sweet fragrance, meaty texture, and earthy flavor.

Shiitake Dried shiitakes have meaty flesh and a delicate, complex flavor. If you can not find dried shiitakes, you may substitute Chinese mushrooms.

Morel Considered the king of mushrooms, the morel has an intense, musky flavor that makes it highly sought after. The uncultivated mushroom has a dark, elongated, spongelike stem.

MUSHROOMS, FRESH The popularity of all types of mushrooms has resulted in the successful farming of many different varieties, blurring the distinction between cultivated and wild.

A few species have resisted cultivation and are truly still wild, requiring foraging. Wild or farmed, contribute a deep earthiness to many recipes.

Cremini Also known as the common brown mushroom, this everyday mushroom is closely related to the white mushroom, but has a firmer texture and a slightly stronger flavor. Brown-capped cremini may be substituted for white mushrooms in most recipes.

Portobello Portobello mushrooms are actually mature cremini that are allowed to grow until the caps are about 6 inches (15 cm) in diameter. They are dark brown and have a smoky flavor and meaty texture.

White The ubiquitous, versatile, smooth white mushrooms sold in supermarkets. The term button mushrooms is used for the same species, but only when the mushrooms are small, young, and tender, with closed caps.

MUSSELS These saltwater mollusks have a slightly pointed shells ranging in color from blue-green to yellowish brown to inky black. Mussels have cream or orange-colored meat that is sweeter than that of oysters or clams. Mussels are an excellent buy, too, since they generally are less expensive than other shellfish.

Discard any mussels that feel very light, as they are likely dead, or any that feel very heavy, which probably contain sand. Remember that live mussels will close tightly, if a little slowly, when touched. If in doubt, try twisting the shells sideways in opposite directions, as if unscrewing a bottle cap. The shells of dead mussels will bread apart easily, the mussels should open up again after cooking. Check cooked mussels and discard any that failed to open during cooking.

NUTS Nuts provide protein, fat, and texture to a variety of classic dishes, especially sauces and stews.

Almonds The meat found inside the dry fruit related to peaches, the almond is delicate and fragrant in taste. It has, a pointed, oval shape and a a smooth texture.

Cashews A smooth, kidney-shaped nut from a tree native to Africa and India. They are always sold removed from their hard shells and caustic linings. Most commonly eaten whole or roughly chopped.

Chestnuts Known as *marrons* in France, chestnuts are large and wrinkled and have a smooth, shiny, mahogany-colored shell shaped like a turban slightly flattened on one side. You must cook chestnuts by briefly boiling or roasting them to loosen their tough outer shells and thin bitter skins.

Pine Nuts The seeds of pine trees, nestled in the scales of their cones. Pine nuts are small, rich nuts with an elongated, slightly tapered shape and a resinous, sweet flavor. Pine nuts are used in both savory and sweet dishes; they appear salads, stuffings, and sauces (most famously, pesto), as well as in baked goods and desserts.

OILS Before cooking, foods are often brushed, rubbed, or tossed in oil, which helps retain moisture and enhance browning. Oils such as

olive or peanut add a distinctive flavor to recipes, while a neutral oil like canola is preferred when a more assertive variety might conflict with other seasonings called for in a recipe. Still other oils are used to garnish foods at the end of cooking, shortly before serving.

Asian sesame A deep amber-colored oil pressed from toasted sesame seeds with a rich, nutty flavor. It is used sparingly as a seasoning.

Canola A bland oil noted for its healthful monounsaturated fats and recommended for general cooking.

Olive Olive oil contributes a delicate, fruity flavor to dishes. Deeply flavorful extra-virgin olive oil is used to best advantage in dressings or as a seasoning. Virgin and pure olive oils are not as fragrant as extra-virgin, but are good, less-expensive cooking oils that add subtle flavor.

Peanut Pressed from peanuts, this mildly fragrant oil has a nutty flavor and does not smoke at high temperatures.

OLIVES First cultivated in the Mediterranean basin thousands of years ago, the olive is one of the world's oldest and most important crops. The fruit of a hardy, long-lived tree, fresh olives are too bitter to eat, even when completely ripe. After harvest, they are either pressed to make olive oil or coaxed by long curing into table olivescured for eating. The color of olives depends on when they are picked. Green olives are harvested before they ripen, while black olives have been left on the tree until completely ripe.

ONIONS Onions come in many varieties and are used as a staple ingredient in countless recipes.

Green Although often used interchangeably with spring onions, green and spring onions are actually slightly different. The former are slim all the way from their dark green leaves down to their light green and white root, while the latter's white root swells into a small rounded shape.

Pearl Pearl onions are small onions no more that 1 inch (2.5 cm) in diameter. They are traditionally white, although red ones are now available. They have a mild onion flavor and are often used in stews and braises. They are also available pickled and frozen.

Red Also called Bermuda onions or Italian onions, red onions are purplish and sweet.

Shallots A small member of the onion family, shallots look like large garlic cloves covered with papery bronze or reddish skin. They have white flesh lightly streaked with purple, a crisp texture, and a flavor subtler than that of a yellow onion.

Spanish These very large, round onions are a good source of flavor for numerous slow-cooked dishes.

Sweet Fresh onions with mild, sweet, and juicy flesh that results from the soil and climate where the onions are grown. Varieties are named for their place of origin. Maui onions from Hawaii and Vidalia onions from Georgia come into season in the Spring; Walla Walla onions from Washington arrive in late summer. When slowly cooked, they caramelize deeply, becoming rich and tender.

White Although more pungent than a red onion, the all-purpose white onion is milder and less sweet than the yellow onion.

Yellow This all-purpose onion has parchmentlike golden brown skin and pale yellow flesh. Usually too strongly flavored to eat raw, it becomes rich and sweet when cooked. Yellow onions are usually reserved for cooking, while sweeter white or red onions may be eaten raw in salads.

PANCETTA This Italian bacon made by seasoning belly pork with spices, rolling it into a tight cylinder, and then curing, rather than smoking, it for at least 2 months. It is used to flavor soups, sauces, meats, and vegetables.

PAPRIKA This red or orange-red ground spice made from dried peppers, and is used both as a seasoning and as a garnish. The finest paprikas come from Hungary and Spain in three basic grades: sweet, medium-sweet, and hot. The sweet types, which are mild but still pungent, are the most versatile.

PLANTAINS A close relative of the banana, plantains taste a little less sweet but have a higher starch content that allows them to be cooked for much longer. Plantains are available year round. Look for them in major supermarkets or Latin markets. Choose fruits that are firm and have darkened peels.

POLENTA Cornmeal that is cooked in liquid until it thickens and the grains become tender. The Italian term *polenta* is used both for the grain and the finished dish, a specialty of Northern Italy.

POTATOES Thousands of potato varieties grow in the world, although we see only a handful in markets. Increasingly, specialty potatoes are finding their way into produce bins.

Fingerling Small, white potatoes with waxy skins that get their name because of their long, narrow shape. Low in starch, they are good roasted, steamed, or boiled.

Red One of the best choices for roasting, smooth-skinned red potatoes are high in moisture and low in starch, with a waxy flesh that holds its shape well during cooking.

Russet Also called baking or Idaho potatoes, russets are the familiar large, oblong potatoes with dry brown skin. When cooked, they have a dry, fluffy texture.

Yukon gold These all-purpose, thin-skinned potatoes have golden yellow flesh, a dense texture, and a slightly buttery flavor. They hold their shape well when cooked.

PROSCIUTTO This famed Italian ham is cut from the rear leg of the pig, lightly seasoned, cured with salt, and then air-dried. Celebrated for its subtle but intense flavor, prosciutto is eaten raw or cooked as a flavoring agent.

RICE The seed of a species of grass, rice is the most widely eaten of all the grains. Move than 40,000 distinct varieties have been identified, explaining the diverse characteristics of rice dishes around the world, although only a few cultivated commercially.

Arborio A variety of medium-grain rice (although it is considered a short-grain rice in Europe) whose grains have a high surface-starch content. When the rice is simmered and stirred, the starch dissolves and contributes a creamy texture to dishes such as risotto.

Basmati A long-grain rice with a sweet, nutlike taste and perfume. Grown primarily in India, Iran, and the United States, it is ideal for use in pilafs. Brown and white varieties are available.

Brown Any rice that has not been processed by milling or polishing and therefore has its brown hull still intact. As a result, brown rice takes longer to cook than comparable white rice. It also has a chewier texture and more robust taste. Short-, medium-, and long-grain brown rice varieties are available.

Jasmine Cultivated in Thailand and also in the United States, this long-grain rice variety has a sweet floral scent.

White, long-grain Any white rice variety with grains three to five times longer than they are wide. The cooked grains separate and are generally fluffy. Long-grain rice is commonly used in pilafs and as an accompaniment to main dishes.

RICE VINEGAR Vinegars made from fermented rice are widely used in Asian cuisine. They are mild and add a light acidity to cooked foods.

SAFFRON The stigmas of a Mediterranean crocus, saffron lends a pungent and earthy flavor and bright yellow color to foods like stews, risotto, and tagines. When soaked in liquid, it turns the liquid a dark yellow. Because it must be handpicked, and because each crocus has only three stigmas, saffron is the world's most expensive spice. Only a tiny bit, however, is needed to tint and flavor a recipe. It is available as "threads" (the whole stigmas) or powdered. Thread saffron, although more expensive, is preferable, as powdered saffron is sometimes adulterated with other ingredients to extend it, and it loses flavor more rapidly.

SAKE Japanese rice wine typically drunk but also often used as seasoning.

SAUERKRAUT A dish of salted, fermented green cabbage. Although known as a German specialty, sauerkraut likely originated in Asia or ancient Rome, where fermentation was widely used to protect produce. Sauerkraut can be served raw or alongside a braised or slow-cooked dish. If serving raw, rinse before serving.

SESAME SEEDS Tiny flat seeds that range in color from white to tan to black and are added to a recipe or sprinkled over a finished dish to contribute a nutty flavor and subtle texture.

SOY SAUCE Popular Asian seasoning made from fermented soybean meal and wheat.

STAR ANISE Brown, star-shaped pods with an aniselike flavor from a Chinese evergreen tree. They are a main ingredient in Chinese five-

spice powder. Star anise is often used whole or snapped into points, and is also ground.

SQUASH The large, sprawling squash clan, all members of the gourd family and native to the Americas, may be neatly divided into into two branches: winter squash and summer squash. Winter squash are allowed to mature until their flesh is thick and their shells are hard, and they have a long shelf life. They come in many shapes, colors, and sizes. Summer squashes are generally harvested while small and tender, and are best eaten young and fresh. The blossoms of both winter and summer squashes can be eaten.

SQUID Many seafood merchants sell squid (calamari) cleaned and ready to go. If you need to clean the squid yourself, begin by cutting off the tentacles just above the eyes. Grab the tentacles at their base and squeeze to pop out the squid's beak, discarding it. With your fingers, pull out and discard the clear quill from the body, then rinse well, discarding the entrails.

SWEET POTATOES Sweet potatoes have either pale yellow skins and yellow flesh or reddish brown or purple skins and orange flesh. The latter type is often called a yam, although the true yam is actually a different species and is cultivated primarily in the tropics.

TOMATILLOS Literally "little tomatoes," tomatillos are actually not related to the tomato. Firm and green, the tomatillo has a tart, citrusy flavor when raw; cooking tempers the sharpness and sweetens the flesh. Choose firm specimens with tightly clinging husks; remove the sticky, papery husks. Rinse before using.

TOMATO PASTE Dense purée made from slow-cooking tomatoes that have been strained and reduced to a deep red concentrate.

TOMATO SAUCE Thinner purée than tomato paste, with salt and other seasonings added. Tomato sauce is ready to use in recipes, often as a base for sauces. Look for high-quality, low-sodium products.

TOMATOES Like the potato, this fruit (which is generally treated as a vegetable), is a member of the nightshade family and is native to South America. The tomato comes in a wide range of sizes, from tiny currant tomatoes no bigger than blueberries to fat beefsteaks up to 5 inches (13 cm) in diameter. Look for vine-ripened tomatoes during summer months. At other times of the year, fresh plum, or Roma, tomatoes, which are small and have a plump pear shape, offer the best quality. Canned plum tomatoes are also a good choice year-round.

TURMERIC The root of a plant belonging to the ginger family, turmeric, like saffron, is valued for both its taste and its bright color, although it is much less expensive. Ground turmeric is often added to powdered saffron or substituted for it in recipes. It is also one of the primary ingredients in Indian curry owder.

Index

OXMOOR HOUSE INC.

Oxmoor House books are distributed by Sunset Books
80 Willow Road, Menlo Park, CA 94025
Telephone: 650-321-3600 Fax: 650-324-1532
VP and Associate Publisher: Jim Childs
Director of Sales: Brad Moses

Oxmoor House and Sunset Books are divisions of
Southern Progress Corporation

WILLIAMS-SONOMA, INC.
Founder & Vice-Chairman: Chuck Williams

WELDON OWEN INC.
CEO, Weldon Owen Group John Owen
CEO and President Terry Newell
Chief Financial Officer Simon Fraser
VP Sales and New Business Development Amy Kaneko
VP and Creative Director Gaye Allen
VP and Publisher Hannah Rahill
Senior Designer Andrea Stephany
Designer Rachel Lopez Metzger
Editor Lauren Hancock
Production Director Chris Hemesath
Color Manager Teri Bell
Production Manager Michelle Duggan
Photographer Bill Bettencourt
Photographer Assistants Angelica Cao, Ana Borquez
Food Stylist Kevin Crafts
Food Stylist's Assistant Alexa Hyman
Text Writer Denis Kelly

ACKNOWLEDGMENTS
Weldon Owen would like to thank the following people
for their generous support in producing this book: Heather Belt,
Ken DellaPenta, Judith Dunham, Peggy Fallon, Norman Kolpas,
Jeff Larsen, Erin Quon, Sara Remington.

THE ESSENTIALS SERIES
Conceived and produced by
WELDON OWEN INC.
415 Jackson Street, San Francisco, CA 94111
Telephone: 415-291-0100 Fax: 415-291-8841

In Collaboration with Williams-Sonoma, Inc.
3250 Van Ness Avenue, San Francisco, CA 94109

A WELDON OWEN PRODUCTION
Copyright © 2008 Weldon Owen Inc.
and Williams-Sonoma, Inc.

First printed in 2008
10 9 8 7 6 5 4 3 2 1

ISBN 13: 978-0-8487-3259-2
ISBN 10: 0-8487-3259-6

Printed by Midas Printing Limited
Printed in China